KNOWN UNTO GOD
SEARCHING FOR THE MISSING

KNOWN UNTO GOD
SEARCHING FOR THE MISSING

SIMON FOWLER

First published 2025

Amberley Publishing
The Hill, Stroud
Gloucestershire, GL5 4EP

www.amberley-books.com

Copyright © Simon Fowler, 2025

The right of Simon Fowler to be identified as the Author of this work has been asserted in accordance with the Copyright, Designs and Patents Act 1988.

ISBN 978 1 3981 0366 5 (hardback)
ISBN 978 1 3981 0367 2 (ebook)

All rights reserved. No part of this book may be reprinted or reproduced or utilised in any form or by any electronic, mechanical or other means, now known or hereafter invented, including photocopying and recording, or in any information storage or retrieval system, without the permission in writing from the Publishers.

British Library Cataloguing in Publication Data.
A catalogue record for this book is available from the British Library.

1 2 3 4 5 6 7 8 9 10

Typesetting by SJmagic DESIGN SERVICES, India.
Printed in the UK.

Appointed GPSR EU Representative: Easy Access System Europe Oü, 16879218
Address: Mustamäe tee 50, 10621, Tallinn, Estonia
Contact Details: gpsr.requests@easproject.com, +358 40 500 3575

CONTENTS

Preface		7
Acknowledgements		9
1	Introduction	10
2	Before the First World War	31
3	The Missing and their Disappearance	53
4	Grief	74
5	Informing the Relatives	96
6	The Search for the Missing	118
7	The Imperial War Graves Commission	140
8	Memorialising the Missing	162
9	Chasing Ghosts	183
10	Recording the Missing of the Second World War	207
11	The Search for the Missing of the Second World War	225
12	After the War	240
Conclusion		249
Appendices		252
Endnotes		260
Bibliography		305

PREFACE

Every night at 8pm, rain or shine, an immaculately dressed fireman raises his bugle to play *The Last Post* under the echoing arches of the Menin Gate in the small Belgian city of Ypres. Traffic stops for a few seconds. The crowds of visitors to the battlefields and members of British Legion groups stand to attention and hold their breath. Even noisy groups of schoolchildren fall silent: awed by something they perhaps barely understand. Duty done, the bugler nods and then marches briskly away and the crowds shuffle off in search of frites or a beer. This simple ceremony has taken place every evening for nearly a century, with the exception of the years when Ypres was occupied by the Nazis.[1] It began almost immediately after the memorial was unveiled by Field Marshal Lord Plumer in July 1927.

On the walls are the names of 54,395 British and Commonwealth soldiers who died in the Salient but whose bodies have never been identified: the population of a market town like Canterbury or Keighley.[2] The Australian writer Scott Bennett found it hard to identify any single name: 'Perhaps that's way that Sir Reginald Blomfield, the architect ... intended it: no individual name should be distinguished from the masses: a visitor's gaze should never penetrate the endless lists.'[3]

There are a dozen other memorials to the missing on the battlefields of France and Flanders, most notably at Thiepval which commemorates the missing of the Somme. But it is Blomfield's memorial at the eastern side of this otherwise undistinguished market town that brings home in no other way, to tourist, schoolchild and military historian alike, the tragedy of the Great War. Sir Fabian Ware, the first director of the Imperial War Graves Commission, thought that the minds of the visitors to Menin Gate would 'after a few poignant hours ... move from bewilderment to reflection under the force of mere numbers which bring a new revelation or perhaps the sting of a forgotten remembrance that should never be absent from their thoughts.'[4]

How and why these young men were commemorated on such memorials is truly disturbing, as was the impact on their families. Their pain was equal, if not greater, to that felt by the widows and mothers of the identifiable men who had been killed in action or subsequently died of wounds. For these families at least there was a grave which they could hope one day to visit. But for the relatives of the missing there was nothing but huge impersonal memorials, like the ones along the Western Front or the Tomb of the Unknown Warrior in Westminster Abbey, which their creators hoped would provide some sort of closure. Field Marshal Plumer attempted to lessen the agony for tens of thousands of families in his address when opening the Menin Gate: 'He is not missing. He is here.'

The British monuments to the missing on the Western Front are now largely regarded as being memorials to the futility of the Great War. Their original intention has been lost as memories of the men they commemorated has faded. And what is worse, the story of the missing themselves has all but been forgotten.

Who were the missing and why were they missing? How were they commemorated? And are there parallels to other wars? This book attempts to provide some answers

ACKNOWLEDGEMENTS

No author of non-fiction writes on their own. I am grateful to Colin Chapman, Paul Cowan, Marion Mollett, Philip Richardson and Phil Tomaselli for sharing their research and to Rosalyn Vickers for providing details of her uncle David Lesser.

John Boaler, Nigel Venus and Dan Weinbren and the Surrey Branch of the Western Front Association offered perceptive comments and useful sources.

Staff at NAM, Sarah Paterson and colleagues at IWM were always helpful despite an insane booking system. Andrew Fetherstone, the archivist at the CWGC, pointed me in several new directions.

Thanks to Shaun Barrington and his colleagues at Amberley for their help seeing the book through to press.

Perhaps the greatest thanks are for my wife Sylvia who accepted my being 'missing in action' for too many months. As always, errors and omissions are mine.

1

INTRODUCTION

> We count those who are saved
> but the unknown remainder
> neither alive
> nor definitely dead
> is described by a strange term
> the missing.
> They still have the chance
> to return to us
> from fire
> from water
> the interior of the earth.
> If they return – that's fine
> if they don't – too bad.
>
> Zbigniew Herbert, 'Mr Cogito On the Need for Precision' in
> *Report from The Besieged City and Other Poems* (1983)

This book is about the men who went 'missing' during the First World War. It is easy to understand that on a battlefield, a man can be killed or be wounded badly enough so that he no longer plays any part in the fighting. There is a third category of soldier,

Introduction

those who disappear during the action. One minute he is present and correct, the next minute he has gone. It was purely the luck of the draw whether a soldier was killed in action or became missing in action. The writer Max Pemberton described the mystery in an article on the missing published in 1917:

> If, in an hour of calm, you look from a height over No Man's Land, you realise chiefly that it is a scene of mystery. The dead lie there whom no human hands have buried. The black earth has hidden the bodies of many for whom perchance British homes are waiting. Men have crossed that wilderness with the fire of life in their eyes, have been seen for an instant in the whirlwind of the fight, and then have been no more heard of. 'Carry on' may have been the last words they were heard to speak. The loom of the smoke enveloped them. The crash of the guns forbade question or answer. And so they were lost to our knowledge.[1]

Families back home had to face the fact that their boy had no burial place and there was no body to grieve over. They wondered whether indeed he was actually dead. Max Pemberton considered that 'There is, perhaps, no penalty of the war quite so heavy as this, its burdens are the same for rich and poor. Alike in the cottage and the castle, the daily thought is of the son whose fate is unknown. Every item of news is scanned eagerly for those tidings which shall enlighten.'[2]

The term 'Missing in Action' is American in origin and has a subtly different meaning to 'Missing'. It only seems to have come into usage in Britain during the Korean War.[3] Put simply, the 'Missing' of the First World War were men who had died in action but had no identifiable resting place. Their bodies were either torn apart during the fighting itself or their graves subsequently destroyed. Sometimes it proved impossible to identify corpses recovered from the battlefield. As such they have no known place of burial. In the case of the British missing, they are commemorated on memorials at the Menin Gate and elsewhere, or when a body lies in a particular cemetery but cannot be positively identified, there is a headstone with a simple phrase: 'A Soldier of the Great War/Known only unto God'.[4]

That a man was in fact missing was not always clear cut and this frustrated many mothers and wives and gave unfeasible hope to some. Some men who had initially been thought to be missing had become prisoners of war. Others eventually rejoined their units days or weeks after having been lost on the battlefield. They may well have initially been reported missing and their families informed.[5]

The United States used the ugly although useful term, 'Killed in Action: Body Not Recovered' (KIA-BNR). The American writer Michael Sledge defines such a person as not being 'present at his or her duty due to apparent involuntary reasons and whose location is unknown.' The term indicates a high level of confidence that the individual was killed, but no remains could be found, no recovery effort could be mounted, 'or even if it could, the likelihood of recovering remains would be small.'[6] As well as unidentified bodies, the definition includes those Prisoners of War whose whereabouts were unknown.

There were other ways of categorising the Missing. Major William Chettle, Head of the Records Branch at the Imperial War Graves Commission (later the Commonwealth War Graves Commission), wrote in December 1918 that there were three such types:

1. those killed in action for whom there is no burial place;
2. those reported killed in action, for whom no burial report was received and whose grave has not been found;
3. those reported 'missing' for whom no graves were found.[7]

In some cases, men are known to have been buried but their burial places were destroyed in subsequent fighting. Private George Dent, Durham Light Infantry, for example, was killed in action on 13 August 1915 at Armentières. His burial place is, most unusually, described in the battalion war diary but his name is now one of 11,000 found on the Plogsteert Memorial to the Missing.[8] Or Private Patrick Sullivan, Royal Irish Rifles, who died of wounds on 14 July 1916 and was buried near the casualty clearing station or hospital where he died, is now only recorded on the Thiepval memorial.[9]

In many cases there was never a body to bury. An eyewitness to the death of Second Lieutenant H F Allanson, Suffolk Regiment on 21 July 1916, for example, reported that the officer was seen '100 yards in front before [a] shell burst, no trace of body was seen after. A large shell hole existing on the spot where the officer had stood.' Another eyewitness said 'He was struck on the head by shrapnel and killed outright. He was left lying there when we retired.'[10] Another officer, Second Lieutenant James Matheson, Argyll and Sutherland Highlanders, went missing during a bombing attack on enemy trenches on 26 March 1916. His bombing sergeant, Sergeant Wilson, reported that:

> He went to him [Matheson] when he was taking someone in more severely wounded, put his coat over him, and said he would come back for him. Mr Matheson told him to take the other man in first. Sgt Wilson went back to find him and searched till nearly daylight, but could not do so. He was last seen by one of the bombers ... going into German lines, presumably in mistake for ours.

Another man reported that Lieutenant Matheson had 'lost an arm ... Sgt Simpson put him in a shell hole, and a search party sent went out to fetch him in, but he was gone.'[11]

There are far fewer men who fit Chettle's second category: most were erroneously reported as being killed and actually became prisoners of war. Between a quarter and a third of those initially thought as missing eventually returned home. Some 170,000 British prisoners of war survived capture by the Germans and their allies. However, it might take weeks, even months, for the news of a soldier's survival to filter back to the authorities, let alone his anxious family. Until then nobody had any idea what had happened to these men except that they had disappeared on the battlefield. One such example was Private John Wilkinson, East Yorkshires, who was reported missing on 27 May 1918. In early August 1918 the *Hexham Herald* reported that his family had received a postcard via the Red Cross stating that he was uninjured, although his parents were subsequently informed that he had died of his wounds in a prisoner of war camp on 12 August.[12]

The First World War was the first major conflict in which large numbers of men went missing on the battlefield. The same heartrending tragedy was experienced by families of all the combatant nations. No lover of the Germans, Max Pemberton admitted that 'in Germany, no less than here, are the doubts and the prayers and the unceasing questions.'[13]

This book is largely about the British Army on the Western Front, because this is where much of the fighting took place and where eventually the missing were commemorated in a unique way. However, the terrain and the nature of the fighting in Gallipoli also meant that many British, ANZAC and French soldiers were also buried without a grave. And most men who died in Mesopotamia (now Iraq) are commemorated on memorials rather than in war cemeteries. The names of sailors – naval and merchant navy – who were lost at sea are listed on memorials near the Tower of London and overlooking the naval ports of Chatham, Portsmouth and Plymouth.[14]

During the Great War the vast majority of deaths occurred in the infantry in France and Flanders as infantrymen were swallowed in the mud or their corpses blown into a thousand pieces by shellfire. The Second World War was much more mobile, and it was relatively rare for soldiers to find themselves bogged down in trench warfare. Instead, the war increasingly took place in the air or at sea, so losses were proportionately higher in the

Royal Navy and, especially, in the RAF's Bomber Command, where over a third of men who died on active operations have no known grave. This was a far greater rate of loss than experienced by any British infantry formation in either world war.

Total War

The first time that there was a large number of fallen soldiers whose bodies were never found occurred during the American Civil War. It is no coincidence that this was the first modern industrial war in which both sides used the machines created by the Industrial Revolution, the railway, cannon and the rifle, to kill the enemy more effectively than had ever been thought possible. The historian Drew Gilpin Faust suggests that this conflict 'presaged the butchery of World War I's Western Front and the global carnage of the twentieth century'.[15]

This industrial capacity was developed yet further in the years before and during the Great War: the machine gun, aircraft and, above all, the artillery shell led to mass deaths on a scale which would have been unthinkable even a generation before. Very roughly 16,400 officers, non-commissioned officers and other ranks in the British Army were killed or died of disease during the French and Peninsular wars between 1794 and the Battle of Waterloo on 18 June 1815.[16] 101 years later, almost to the very day, 19,240 British and colonial officers, non-commissioned officers and other ranks were killed on the First Day of the Somme. Many of those who fell on 1 July 1916 have no known grave, like eighteen-year-old Private Henry William Simpson of the Royal Fusiliers, who is commemorated on the Thiepval Memorial to 'The Missing of the Somme'.

Slightly under one-third of the British and colonial soldiers who died during the Great War have no known grave and are thus commemorated on one of the memorials to the missing at Menin Gate, Thiepval and elsewhere on the Western Front. Rather fewer French and Americans suffered this fate, even though conditions on the frontline and the tactics employed by their commanders were roughly similar to that of the British, perhaps because they put rather more effort into recovering and identifying the dead after the Armistice than the British did. The numbers of Germans, Russians and other nationalities who went missing, particularly on the Eastern Front, cannot easily be determined: the sheer scale of the deaths overwhelmed the record keepers.

There may be a number of contributory factors. Firstly, the poor standard of British trenches and dug-outs compared with those of the enemy, which made them easy to destroy. Paul Fussell described them as being 'Amateur, vague, ad hoc, and temporary'. In comparison the German ones were 'efficient, clean, pedantic and permanent'. George Coppard, a British veteran, remembered that:

> The whole conduct of our trench warfare seemed to be based on the concept that we, the British, were not stopping in the trenches for long, but were tarrying awhile on the way to Berlin and that very soon we would be chasing Jerry across country. The result in the long term, meant that we lived a mean and impoverished sort of existence, in lousy scratchy holes.[17]

Second Lieutenant Edward Underhill described the conditions in trenches near Ploegsteert, south of Ypres, in November 1915: 'The conditions here are appalling… We have had about three days continuous rain, and the result is the trenches are flooded and the country around is a sea of mud ankle deep, and in some places today I have been over my knees in it.'[18] In the same area a few months previously, Lieutenant Robert Fieldsend, Lincolnshire Regiment, took over an exposed trench 'where bullets came from all directions' near Messines in April 1915: 'The smell in the trench is terrible. I shall never forget it. We were surrounded with partly buried dead Englishmen and altogether it was a most unsavoury trench.'[19] Communications between the rear and the

Introduction

frontlines often ran over the ground, an easy target for German artillery and snipers. Lieutenant Fieldsend noted in his diary for 10 April 1915: 'Fell in at 7.30pm & went up to the fire trenches. We went across the open all the way. Pte Noriss walking two yards in front of me was shot through the chest.'[20]

Secondly, the British high command insisted on continuous aggression through raids across No Man's Land to the enemy's trenches. The intention was usually to take prisoners or gain other intelligence about the enemy troops in front. Raids could lead to relatively large numbers of casualties as men were strafed as they crossed between the trenches or were shot by their own sentries. When they weren't engaged in raiding, parties of men would be expected to go out most nights replacing barbed wire and looking out for enemy activity. After these activities the inevitable casualties lay in shell holes, were trapped by one of the multiple rolls of barbed wire that separated the two sides, or in the open air, where they would either be rescued by their comrades or eventually die and their bodies slowly absorbed into the mud. As the old song went: 'If you want to find the old battalion, I know where they are/They're hanging on the old barbed wire...'

But perhaps the major factor was that, as we will see, the British Army and the Imperial War Graves Commission made only a half-hearted attempt to recover and identify bodies from the Western Front in the years after the Armistice. It was cheaper and considerably easier to build memorials to their memory than to find and identify their bodies.[21]

The Missing in Action are a phenomenon of modern industrialised warfare. The American writer Michael Sledge notes that you need a level of bureaucracy to record military deaths and where the casualties were buried. Of course, it is not easy work keeping such records in the heat of battle:

> The actions of large numbers of people trying to capture and/or destroy one another do not result in complete and tidy record

keeping or organised and efficient movement of bodies. How do you provide a ... complete account of the missing when the circumstances surrounding their loss are so chaotic and violent?[22]

Describing the lack of detailed records of German losses, Robert Weldon Whalen suggests that:

> Part of the problem, no doubt was that harried company clerks, armed with pencil stubs and typewriters, were hard-pressed to complete the army's multitude of standard forms, and their colleagues at each higher headquarters were just as swamped by waves upon waves of reports. However, a greater reason for the confusion was that German soldiers were killed, wounded or went missing in such enormous numbers, and whole units were destroyed so quickly, that no one could hope to tally the losses.[23]

Burying the dead

In the pre-industrial world the burial of the fallen was perhaps less of a problem. The poet Edmund Blunden pointed out that at the Battle of Waterloo, which had taken place on just one day and in a fairly concise area there had been: 'no insuperable difficulty in finding the men who had fallen, and in giving them just burial'.[24] What was not recorded however were the names of the dead and where exactly they were buried. Most bodies ended up piled on funeral pyres or tossed higgledy-piggledy into burial pits.

Matters were of course very different during the First World War. By January 1915 the old peacetime Army had all but disappeared as the pre-war soldiers and their officers were killed or wounded. A new wartime Army emerged, which reflected to a greater or lesser extent British society in uniform. The men who made up the New Armies were civilians in arms who enlisted for the War with families at home who were keenly interested in what they were doing. The pre-war Regular might have accepted burial in a pit on the Veldt or in an Indian cantonment, but his wartime successor and, particularly his family, expected more if the worse happened.

This reflected a changing attitude to death during the nineteenth century, particularly among the working and middle classes. A pauper burial – where the body was laid to rest in an unmarked grave unmourned by the family – was regarded as abhorrent. Thomas Hood's poem 'The Pauper's Funeral' captures the grimness:

> Rattle his bones, his bones, his bones,
> Over the stones, the stones, the stones,
> He's only a pauper, who nobody owns,
> Nobody owns, nobody owns.

In discussing the American Civil War, Drew Gilpin Faust argued that:

> There have been many revolutions in warfare in the past two centuries and the emerging recognition of an obligation to dead and missing soldiers and their families is one of the least visible. Yet changing attitudes and policies concerning the dead and missing may have had a more significant impact than any other transformation affecting home as well as battle front, civilians as well as soldiers.[25]

Another American historian Thomas Laqueur has observed how death had become democratised in British society:

> The army of the first world war could no longer be treated as the 'scum of the earth', which is how Wellington characterised his soldiers, but the reason was not so much a change in attitude as a change in the emotional infrastructure of a society that went far beyond how someone might have viewed the military. Every life now demanded a denouement in a way not true in earlier ages.[26]

This reflected changes in wider society in Victorian Europe and America where people increasingly expected a decent funeral within their means for themselves and their families. Professor Jay Winter suggests that: 'Twentieth century warfare democratized bereavement. Previously armies were composed of mercenaries, volunteers and professionals. After 1914, Everyman went to war. The social incidence of war losses was thereby transformed. In Britain, France, and Germany, virtually every household had lost someone – a father, a son, a brother, a cousin, a friend.'[27]

Where possible during the First World War the fallen were buried close to where they had died with an appropriate funeral service, although a full service was rarely possible when a burial took place close to the front line. A pamphlet, *The Care of the Dead*, was published in 1916 with official approval, stressing how well the deceased were treated after their death:

> If killed in action, he may still be buried in the old way, somewhere near the trench. If so the chaplain or officer who buries him reports the position of the grave, and one of the officers of the Grave Registration Unit visits, verifies it, verifies the record, affixes if necessary, a durable cross with the date, regimental number upon it, clearly stamped on aluminium tape, and enters these particulars and the exact site of the grave into the register.

The author stressed that more and more burials were taking place in purpose-built cemeteries, where 'Everything is done as tenderly and reverently as if the dead man were in an English churchyard.'[28]

Individual soldiers of course thought that death wouldn't happen to them. Lord Moran, a medical officer, observed: 'War is the business of youth, and no young man thinks he can die.' Arthur Gibbs noted on seeing a pile of weapons recovered from the dead: 'The idea of my being killed was absurd, fantastic.'

But infantry troops in particular were soon surrounded by death – and dead bodies – and most inevitably began to fatalistically think the next bullet 'might have their name on it'. John McCauley was one of the few soldiers who wrote about the sudden descent into a sense of vulnerability: 'Today, Death snatches the life of my chum. Tomorrow, who? Me?'[29] Memoirs often talk about men, officers in particular, who had premonitions of their deaths. Once soldiers lost confidence in their ability to survive, all too often it became a self-fulfilling prophecy.

The War Office often struggled to meet the expectations of the families of the fallen and the missing during the First World War. It was not uncommon, for example, for families to hear from the comrades before the official notification was received. Yet every family was eventually informed whether their boy had been wounded, killed or had gone missing. Mistakes were inevitably made, but considering the difficulties faced by the general headquarters in France and Flanders and by under-resourced clerks in the War Office, their work was as accurate as could reasonably expected.

Any notification – official or unofficial – posed additional problems for the families of those who had been reported missing. Here there was no certainty as to his death, although his comrades and officers would have known that, in all likelihood, the man had been killed. Perhaps understandably, eyewitnesses when questioned later merely reported that a man was missing and hoped that he might have been captured by the enemy, leaving the most likely option hanging in the air. Several of those who described Lieutenant Matheson's last hours suggested that 'the general belief is that Mr Matheson was picked up by a German patrol or else he walked into their lines.'[30]

In the early months of the War the War Office Casualty Branch did not have the resources required to cope with large numbers of deaths – the assumption being that any European conflict would be short and thus would result in relatively few deaths.

Indeed, initially rather oddly to modern eyes, the work of locating the dead was largely left to a charity, the British Red Cross, and interested individuals, most importantly Fabian Ware. Ware had volunteered to run a motor ambulance unit, but he was soon struck by the lack of an official mechanism for marking and recording the graves of those killed. As early as September 1914, six weeks after war was declared, Wade reported back to the Red Cross that his men had been searching behind the lines for information about the dead and the missing:

> The experience gained ... has helped the Unit in taking up another more useful piece of work viz: the identification of places in which British killed have been hastily buried and the placing of crosses on the spots thus identified, with inscriptions designed to preserve the rough records which in many cases are already in danger of becoming obliterated.[31]

General Sir Douglas Haig, then commander of I Corps, reminded the War Office in March 1915, that '...it should be borne in mind that on the termination of hostilities the nation will demand an account from the government as to the steps taken to mark and classify the burial places of the dead, steps which can only be effectively taken at, or soon after, burial.'[32]

Encouraged by the British Army's Adjutant General Sir Nevil Macready, Fabian Ware founded an organisation to do this, and in 1915 Ware and his organisation were transferred from the Red Cross to the Army, as the Directorate of Grave Registration and Enquiries. Macready later recalled he had his interview with Ware in 'an old-fashioned bedroom' in a chateau which served as an office. Ware reminded Macready that they had first met when they were small boys at a religious service; 'Before he left my room, I had booked him to create an organisation to [find] and record the names of our soldiers.'[33] This was the origin of the Imperial War Graves Commission.

Introduction

Each nation chose to honour its dead differently. The British and the dominions, through the Imperial War Graves Commission, buried their dead together in cemeteries regardless of rank with the intention of showing the equality of sacrifice made by the fallen. They remain today a silent and dignified reminder of the cost of war. Despite a vociferous campaign no bodies were allowed to be repatriated for reburial by their families at home and no personalisation of headstones allowed except a short epitaph that could be added by the next of kin to the headstone.[34] During a debate in the House of Commons on the Commission's plans, William Burdett-Coutts told the House:

> I cannot help reading one sentence from a letter I received a day or two ago, the letter is marked 'private', but I do not think he will object to my quoting this sentence... The words are these: 'You see we shall never have any grave to go to. Our boy was missing at Loos. The ground is of course battered and mined beyond all hope of any trace being recovered. I wish some of the people who making this trouble realise how more than fortunate they have to have a name on a headstone in a known place.'[35]

The British response to this question was to build a series of memorials along the Western Front, on which the names of the missing were engraved. As Jay Winter noted, for the missing, 'The names of the dead were all that remained of them, and chiselled in stone or etched on plaques, these names were the foci of public commemoration both on the local and the national scale.'[36] In Britain itself there are two memorials on which no names appear at all: the Cenotaph, which marks the sacrifice of all the fallen, and further down Whitehall in Westminster Abbey the Tomb of the Unknown Warrior, where the inscription on the tomb, reads:

> Beneath this stone rests the body of a British warrior known by name or rank brought from France to lie among the most

illustrious of the land... Thus are commemorated the many multitudes who during the Great War of 1914-1918 gave the most that man can give, life itself for God, for King and Country, for loved ones, home and Empire, for sacred cause of justice and the freedom of the world.[37]

The French experience was defined by the fact that it had been the country over which most of the fighting had taken place. The initial plan was to bury the dead where they had fallen, following the lead of the British: 'Don't separate those whom death had united,' wrote one advocate.[38] But the families of the dead had other ideas. 'Our sons, no, no, we don't want to leave them there' wrote one father. 'They did their duty. Now we must do ours for them, to let them rest in peace in the cemetery of their ancestors. To abandon them there is to condemn them to eternal torment.'[39] Although the exhumation and reburial of their sons and husbands was forbidden, it was easy enough to bribe officials to allow bodies to be removed. In September 1920 the French government caved in to the inevitable and promulgated a decree establishing the right of families to claim the bodies of their loved ones and to take them home at state expense. About forty per cent of the families of men who had been killed or who had died of wounds repatriated their bodies for reburial at home.

The French war cemeteries are vast and curiously impersonal. At their heart often are to be found ossuaries: vast collections of the remains of the fallen who have not been identified, all mixed up together. To British eyes the effect is rather ghoulish. The largest at Douaumont contains the remains of 130,000 soldiers who were killed during the Battle of Verdun in 1916. Henry de Montherlant, the man behind it, wrote approvingly that: 'Thousands of people have gone away from this incomprehensible charnel house, some grieving, others without grief. They only know of some obscure name on a map. Everything which was

Introduction

found out there is in this tomb, they were told... There they kneel confronting the possible. An astonishing source of comfort.'⁴⁰

Geography, too, determined the American response. In effect the United States adopted the British solution of burying the dead in mass cemeteries, but instead of separate memorials to the missing, each of the dozen cemeteries contained a memorial stone listing the missing. In the years after the war Congress was lobbied by mothers (as well as by funeral directors) to have bodies of their sons returned home. Instead, the Coolidge Administration agreed in 1928 to pay for a pilgrimage to the Western Front by 'Gold Star Mothers', a government programme that paid the travel expenses to the grave sites for mothers and widows whose sons and husbands had died overseas as members of the American Expeditionary Forces. Over the next few years almost seven thousand women availed themselves of the opportunity to visit France.⁴¹

German losses on the Western Front were as heavy as those of the French and the British. But geopolitical realities of course meant there were relatively fewer cemeteries in France and Belgium. They are very sombre, forbidding places. The missing are rarely marked in any special way. In many cemeteries there are markers recording the numbers of unnamed men found in a particular grave. The care of German cemeteries was left to a charity – the *Volksbund Deutsche Kriegsgräberfürsorge* – which was established in December 1919.⁴²

As with the Allies, during the War the Germans constructed cemeteries behind the front line, such as one at Roeselare which one journalist described as a 'field of seeds of the German future' while conjuring up images of a mythical past filled with Valkyries carrying the fallen soldiers to the hall of the slain, Valhalla, in the afterlife.⁴³ In the 1920s those cemeteries which had not been destroyed or badly damaged during the fighting of 1918 were allowed to decay. The Versailles Treaty placed the care of war graves on the country in which they lay. Neither

Belgium nor France was prepared to help the former enemy. Visiting in 1920, Stephen Graham found 'decaying monuments of the German dead – *Hier ruht* Friedrich Blohm, Paul Vogel, August Dill and the rest, till Germany comes and takes back again or in time they are forgotten and lost.'[44] Other travellers, however, remark on a number of small, neat cemeteries, 'often well cared for and planted with cypress trees – or the usual crosses marking isolated graves.'[45] The Star of David punctuates the field of crosses.

Few German burial parties were allowed onto the former battlefields, so the remains of their soldiers were subject to the tender mercies of the Allied exhumation parties, Graham asked one man in a British burial unit what they did with the remains of Germans: 'Leave them where they are. We notifies the authorities, that's all. Of course, Jerry buried most of his own, and I'll give him credit for that, he gave every man his eight foot. You don't so easy come across a man the Germans buried, but some of ours...'[46]

It was not until after the Second World War that the position was regularised. In 1954, the Volksbund took over responsibility for German cemeteries on Belgian soil, with a similar agreement with France concluded in the 1960s. The bodies of the 25,000 men who could not be identified were moved to the Langemark cemetery a few miles from Ypres, with the epitaph from Isaiah 43:1: 'I have called you by name, you are mine.'[47]

The reason just why there were so many soldiers whose bodies were never found lies in how the First World War was conducted. It was not a war of movement, as the Boer War had been or the Second World War would be. Between October 1914 and August 1918 two equally matched foes hunkered down in 440 miles of trenches along the Western Front. The British sector of the front was initially only around twenty miles long around Ypres and, although it gradually grew to more than eighty miles, combat was largely concentrated along only a few miles of the line in two places: the Ypres salient in Flanders and the Somme valley in Picardy. In trenches, millions of British troops lived, raided the German lines and were raided in turn, rarely advancing or retreating more than a few miles. Only in the first few and last few months of the war was there much movement. The exception was the huge German push, the *Kaiserschlacht*, between March and May 1918 through weakened British lines, which came close to winning the war for the Central Powers. The chaotic fighting led to the deaths of tens of thousands of British soldiers, many of whose bodies were lost in the confusion, with thousands of other men falling into enemy hands as prisoners. The Allies in turn defeated ever weaker German armies in a series of battles from August 1918 until the Armistice on 11am on 11 November 1918.

Strategic thinkers soon realised that the side who killed more of the enemy would achieve final victory. As early as October 1914, the War Secretary Lord Kitchener argued that 'before Germany relinquishes the struggle, she will have exhausted every possible supply of men.' Sir Henry Rawlinson's draft plan for the Battle of the Somme was 'to kill as many Germans as possible with the least loss to ourselves' by seizing points of tactical importance and waiting for the Germans to counter-attack.[48]

If horror is reduced to the dry statistics of the daily loss rate for dead or missing and wounded men in the British Expeditionary Force (BEF) then the dubious honour belonged to the almost forgotten Battle of Arras, which was fought in April and May 1917, and had the heaviest casualties per day (4076). This was followed by the Hundred Days offensive in the summer and autumn of 1918 (3645) and the Somme in 1916 (2943). The Third Battle of Ypres (Passchendaele), with a daily loss rate of 2323, rated as the fourth most deadly experience endured by the BEF, although perhaps first in popular memory. In absolute terms, the Somme (141 days, 420,000 losses), followed by the 'Hundred Days' campaign of the autumn of 1918 (which actually lasted 96 days, and resulted in 350,000 casualties) were the bloodiest battles. Third Ypres, at 105 days (244,000 casualties) is the third. Arras, which lasted for 39 days, was the fourth most lethal battle (159,000 casualties), but had it continued for the same length of time and at the same intensity as the Somme, losses at Arras might have reached 575,000.[49]

The Battle of the Somme brought home the nature of this new warfare. The staff of Field Marshal Sir Douglas Haig, commander in chief of the British Expeditionary Force, initially estimated the total number of casualties (wounded as well the dead) would be over 40,000, just on the first day of the offensive, 'Which cannot be considered severe,' Haig said, 'in view of the numbers engaged.' The commanders in the field, and some historians, believed that the losses had been worthwhile. The Battle, which lasted four months to mid-November, bled the German army dry. The British and French losses, killed, wounded and missing, were calculated as being about 533,000. It was estimated that the Germans had suffered about 600,000 casualties – about fifty thousand more;[50] the horrible reality of a war of attrition.

The same strategy was largely repeated at Arras and Passchendaele in 1917. The Chief of General Staff in London Sir William Robertson admitted that he stuck to the strategy 'because I see nothing better, and because my instinct prompts me to stick to it' rather than because he had 'any convincing argument by which I can support it.' By the end of 1917 the politicians, notably the British Prime Minister Lloyd George, were becoming sceptical and dismayed about Field Marshal Haig's ever-increasing demands for manpower, for men who inevitable ended up as fodder for the shells. 'Haig does not care how many men he loses,' Lloyd George once wrote 'He just squanders the lives of these boys.'[51]

The problem was that there really was no obvious alternative. To open up other fronts in southern and eastern Europe, in what Winston Churchill called the 'soft underbelly', was just an expensive distraction, as the Gallipoli disaster in 1915 showed. Both sides also tentatively put out feelers towards a negotiated peace treaty, although it was clear that this would have resolved nothing, it would simply allow time for recuperation and rearmament for another war.[52]

The way to victory was not just on the battlefields. It was an industrial war where the adversaries pitted not just armies but their economies against each other. The nation which produced most submarines, aircraft and horses, but especially munitions, would win. This was not lost on the troops. In his memoirs Private Alfred Burrage, who went to the front line for the first time in the spring of 1917, wrote:

> ...we are slowly realising that the job of the infantry isn't to kill. It is the artillery and the machine gun corps who do the killing. We are merely there to be killed. We are the little flags which the General sticks on the war-map to show the position of the front line.[53]

At the end of 1915, Edmund Blunden noted a subtle yet important change in the conduct of the war: 'The dethroning of the cloth cap [in favour of steel helmets] clearly symbolised the change that was coming over the war, the induration from a personal crusade into a vast machinery of violence.'[54]

During 1916, Britain rapidly introduced a command economy designed for total war. It saw the introduction of conscription in the British Army in March, the battles of Verdun and the Somme and at the end of the year the arrival of David Lloyd George as the British Prime Minister with a clear mandate to win the war.

Each side hurled huge numbers of shells at each other and fired endless belts of machine guns and rifle bullets across No Man's Land.[55] It has been calculated that the Royal Artillery fired 170 million rounds on the Western Front alone.[56] Nearly one and a half million shells were thrown by British guns into the German lines during the week before the opening of the Battle of the Somme in, as it turned out, the vain hope of killing or disorientating the enemy. Veterans would always remember the constant noise of explosions and the particular sound that each type of shell or mortar bomb had.[57]

It was the artillery that caused the most wounds and the greatest number of deaths. Post-war analysis found that 58 per cent of wounds to British soldiers were caused by shellfire and 39 per cent by gunshot wounds.[58] Frederic Manning thought that it was 'infinitely more horrible and revolting to see a man shattered and eviscerated than to see him shot'.[59] And because an explosion could kill a number of men at one time, leading to the mixing up of bodies, it was sometimes subsequently impossible to identify them. Inevitably, many men were killed by British shells falling short of their targets. Some bombardments were horribly accurate though. Frank Richards remembered trenches near High Wood during the Battle of the Somme:

> Down in the valley below us a company of Argyles were occupying some shell holes and shallow trenches: they seemed to be just outside the barrage. I had to pass by them when I was taking back a message to Brigade Headquarters, about a hundred yards beyond. I had just reached the Brigade when it seemed that every German artillery gun had lengthened its range and was firing directly on the Argyles. This lasted about fifteen minutes, and then the shelling slackened. I waited awhile before making my way back and when I did pass the Argyles' position I could only see heads, arms, legs and mangled bodies.[60]
>
> ... I have often wondered since then, if all the leading statesmen and generals of the warring countries had been threatened to be put under that barrage during the day of 20th July 1916, and were told that if they survived it they would be forced to be under a similar one in a week's time, whether they would have all met together and signed a peace treaty before the week was up.

But it was not to be.

2

BEFORE THE FIRST WORLD WAR

> The ancients regarded the soldier in the mass and felt no difficulty in consigning him accordingly without name or details into some come sepulchre. He was called Legion, or nothing; he was merely the means by which someone else pursued the glory of a name.
>
> Edmund Blunden, Introduction to *The Immortal Heritage*[1]

With one key exception, battle fatalities in the wars and battles of the nineteenth century were relatively small compared to the industrialised warfare of the two world wars. The Battle of Waterloo, the greatest British military victory of the nineteenth century, saw between 3000 and 3,500 British deaths.[2] Only the American Civil War saw death rates that came close and perhaps on occasion even exceeded those of the two world wars.[3]

Before the First World War very few soldiers in the British Army were posted as being missing. Indeed, the concept did not really exist. Men were either killed in action or more often died of wounds or sickness. Those who lost contact with their units during battle generally found their way back to their regiments within a few days or were taken as prisoners of war. One exception was Private William Clemenger, 24th Foot, who apparently wandered into the South African bush after the Battle of Blaauwberg in January 1806 and was reported as 'missing believed killed in action'. His body was never found.[4]

Most missing men were generally deserters. By the end of the day's fighting at Waterloo the British army had suffered 16,084 casualties (3024 killed, 10,222 wounded and 2838 missing) a combined loss of about a quarter of the British troops present at the battle. The missing made up about eighteen per cent of the total number of casualties.[5] The *London Gazette* published a rough summary of those killed and wounded in the British and Hanoverian forces between 16 and 18 June 1815. It suggested that one lieutenant colonel, a major, four captains, six lieutenants, five staff sergeants, 29 sergeants, 32 drummers or trumpeters, and 1542 'rank and file' were missing. The Victorian historian of Waterloo William Siborne commented: 'The men returned missing had gone to the rear with wounded officers and soldiers and the greatest numbers have since rejoined. The officers are supposed killed.'[6]

Examination of the casualty returns and muster rolls show that the genuinely missing can be counted on the fingers of one hand. Take the 33rd Foot, for example; Siborne suggests that 48 rank and file soldiers went missing. However, the casualty returns record just one man: Assistant Surgeon Donald Finlayson. The returns for November 1815 noted that he had been 'Missing since 24 June 1815 and unaccounted for, supposed to be dead – effects paid to his brother'.[7] The casualty returns for the 63rd Foot record four missing privates (Siborne suggests 41), but three of them are accounted for in the muster roll. Only one – Laurence Flanagan – is shown as being missing. A subsequent muster reveals that he had become a prisoner of war and returned to the regimental strength in early September. Unfortunately, Flanagan must have been severely wounded for the muster recorded that he was still in hospital. In any case, he had died before the award of the Waterloo Medal the following year.[8]

American Civil War

The reaction to the large number of men posted as missing in action and the response by the authorities, by other organisations and by the families of soldiers proved remarkably similar to what happened in Britain during the First World War. It is proof that similar events lead to remarkably similar responses. Yet nobody during the First World War, either at the War Office or the Red Cross, thought to look across the Atlantic to see what could be learnt from what had happened fifty years previously.

The American Civil War was the first modern industrial war where both sides mobilised their populations and their economies in an attempt to comprehensively defeat each other. The numbers of men killed in action or who subsequently died of wounds and sickness was enormous. Because of poor record keeping the exact numbers of deaths is not known, but it is generally accepted that about 620,000 men died, about two per cent of the American population at the time.[9]

The response to the casualties – particularly to the large numbers of men whose fate was not known – was remarkably similar to that which occurred during the First World War. Drew Gilpin Faust argues that the American Civil War – just like the Great War – was:

> ...a war of mass citizen's armies, not of professional, regular forces: it was a war in which the obligation of the citizen to the nation was expressed as a willingness to risk life itself. [It] fundamentally redefined the relationship between the individual and the nation. The affirmation of the right to selfhood and identity reflected beliefs about human worth that bore other implications for the dead as well as the living.[10]

Huge numbers of men and women sought information about their loved ones. Parents flocked to the battlefields trying to find what remained of their sons. They wrote to those who had survived seeking information about their son's whereabouts and some recollection of their boy's last deeds and words, for any scrap to hold and cherish.[11] But all too often – as became common on the Western Front – there was no physical body found or to be found. In the words of one Union soldier, comrades were 'literally blown to atoms'.[12] Any mortal remains had been destroyed in the fighting. Fanny Scott, the mother of Benjamin, a Virginian infantry soldier, wrote a number of times to Robert E Lee as well as Union commanders seeking information about Benjamin's fate. Eventually she was told by General E. A. Hitchcock, responsible for the transfer of prisoners after the end of the war:

> From the length of time since the Battle of Antietam and you not hearing from your son during all this time I am very sorry to say that the presumption is that he fell a victim to that battle. If he were still living I cannot understand why he should not have found means of making that fact known to you.[13]

War Office clerks in 1917 might have written to enquirers in similar if less elegant terms.

The authorities were unable and often unwilling to supply the answers. Despite prodding from politicians on both sides, the commanders in the field were much more interested in the living than supplying details of the fallen, either to the government or to distraught families at home. Much of this work was taken on in a piecemeal fashion by charities, notably the Sanitary and Christian commissions in the Union armies. On the Western Front, detailed records were kept of casualties and there was communication with the families of those killed or missing, even if it was often erratic and less informative then the next of kin would have liked.

Inevitably, people turned to other organisations in order to receive the news about the fate of their loved ones. In the North the non-official Sanitary and Christian commissions did what they could to inform dead and wounded soldiers' families. In the South there were much smaller and less effective city or regional bodies. Clerks at the British Red Cross's Wounded and Missing Enquiry Bureau in the First World War would have recognised letters such as this one sent by Susannah Hampton from New York to the Philadelphia office of the Sanitary Commission:

> Will you please to inform me at your earliest convenience whether my son Joseph H Hampton...is alive or dead if alive and wounded please be so kind as to state what his wounds are where he lies and if cared for and if Dead Oh pray let me know it and relieve my anxiety...I have heard all kinds of rumours about him and his miseries until they have left me in a state boarding on phrensy.[14]

After the war the Sanitary Commission concluded that such work was 'the most gratifying of any undertaken by the Commission'.[15]

In the years after the Confederate surrender the Union government invested millions of dollars in establishing fourteen national war cemeteries at battlefields and other sites across the South. Graves registration units – composed largely of African-American soldiers – swept the battlefields for bodies. Meanwhile expeditions from Washington armed with lists of the missing combed the countryside looking for cadavers. They suffered just as the British units did fifty years later, dealing with decomposing corpses, dreadful weather (heat here rather than cold), and the difficulties of identifying the bodies. This last was not helped by the fact that men were not issued with official identification necklaces, dog tags, as became common in later wars. The South meanwhile was left to its own devices as the Germans were in 1919.[16]

With the arrival of peace, more than ever families wanted to know what had happened to their sons and husbands.

In Washington DC a patent clerk and former volunteer nurse Clara Barton set up the Office of Correspondence with the Friends of the Missing Men of the United States Army in the spring of 1865, which acted as a clearing house for information about the missing. She published lists of missing men and contacted returning soldiers asking for information about their fallen comrades:

> I appeal to you to give such facts relative to the fate of these men as you can recollect or can ascertain. They have been your comrades on march, picket or raid, or in battle, hospital or prison; and failing there, the fact and manner of their death may only be known to you.[17]

Miss Barton's work helped many families come to the terms with the deaths of loved ones. As the result of one such appeal Sergeant W. H. McCowan of the New York Cavalry wrote to the widow of Thomas J Paynter, a private in the same unit:

> The Regt was ordered to fight (on foot) and every fourth man hold his own horse and three others and it fell to him to hold the horses. I was riding by his side and gave him my horse to hold. That was the last time I seen him. We were overpowered and forced to fall back on our Horses and when we found them they were all scattered through others. I could see nothing of mine although I sucseeded in gettin one and made my escape. His horse was found in the Regt the next day.
>
> Thos. J. was returned as missing in action. I thought he was taken Prisnor, but if he has not been heard of yet it is likely he was killed. Alass did I say killed? It makes my heart bleed when I think of the noble dead that has fallen by the hands of tratars in Rebellion.
>
> I think I have written all that will be of interest to you and hope you will excuse the liberty I have taken.[18]

In the four years her Office for Missing Soldiers was in operation, Miss Barton answered 68,182 letters and secured information about 22,000 men who had previously been posted as missing. Some 58,000 appeals for information were circulated and she received 7,500 replies, of which 5,000 led to a successful identification of a fallen soldier. Yet she thought that the fate of about 40,000 men had still yet to be determined.[19] Many of the techniques Clara pioneered would be adopted by the Red Cross and other bodies during the First World War.

Casualty lists

Matters were little better in Britain. Until well after Crimea, little attention was paid by the War Office in Whitehall to the recording of casualties, let alone informing the next of kin. Sir Nevil Macready, who was Adjutant General in France between 1914 and 1916 and thus formally responsible for the burial of the dead and recording their graves, wrote in his autobiography: 'In former wars, when casualties were comparatively insignificant and time not pressing, the matter was simple, regiments as a rule undertaking the erection of monuments for their comrades.'[20]

The Registrar General suggested in December 1854 that details of the fallen be incorporated in the registers of deaths for England and Wales that his department maintained:

> The Act has made no provision for the registration of the officers and soldiers of the whole army out of England; so that while the name, age, rank or profession, place, time, and cause of the death of every man, woman, or child that dies at home are in the preserved registers, men who uphold in arms the cause and the fame of their country abroad find no place in these records. Otherwise every family that has sent forth its sons, and has lost them in the war, would have the satisfaction of knowing that

their names were inscribed in a perpetual record, whether they died at Varna, perished at Scutari, sank under the waves of the inhospitable sea, or slumbered beneath the earth of the Crimea Alma, Balaklava, Inkerman, consecrated only by their bravery.[21]

The offer was not taken up.[22]

Until the late nineteenth century, the keeping of records of casualties seems to have been fairly minimal and, as a result, it is now almost impossible to follow the paper trail. The work, as Macready, suggests was split between the War Office and the regimental depots. A note recording a man's death would be entered in regimental musters and casualty rolls completed by regiments and submitted to Whitehall for accounting purposes.[23] It was rare for any information to be recorded here other than the date and, perhaps, place where a man had died.

In addition, details of the deaths of officers in battle might be given in the official despatches written by the commanders and subsequently published in the British government's official journal the *London Gazette*.[24]

Occasionally the *Gazette* would also include separate lists of casualties. Generally, they only listed officers by name. The publication of lists depended on the zeal of the clerks at Army Headquarters and at the War Office itself. In a despatch written after Waterloo, the Duke of Wellington: 'Being aware of the anxiety existing in England to receive the returns of killed and wounded in the late actions I now send lists of officers and expect to be able to send this evening returns of the non-commissioned officers and soldiers.'[25] No list for NCOs or ordinary soldiers appears to have been published.

The official and comprehensive casualty lists which filled the papers during the First World War seem to have begun in early 1858, when newspapers started to print lists of the British soldiers of all ranks, other ranks as well as officers, who had died during the Indian Mutiny. Brief details of each man's death were given 'killed in action', 'died of wounds in hospital' and so on. The lists had been sent to the Honourable East India Company in London and referred to actions that had occurred the previous June and July. The lists were first published in the *London Gazette* and then picked up by the press.[26]

Publication of subsequent lists depended on the public interest in a particular campaign. Almost all newspapers, for example, published the list giving the casualties at Isandlwana and Rorke's Drift, when it was received by the War Office in mid-March 1879; the disastrous British action with the Zulus had gripped the public's imagination as few actions before or since have done.

Contacting the families

Record-keeping in the British Army had considerably improved by the South African War (1899-1902) so we know exactly how many men were killed in action, died of wounds or sickness or, indeed, who went missing. During the War just 105 men (and no officers) were reported as 'Missing, presumed dead'. This was only 0.2 per cent of the total number of casualties.[27]

Regimental courts of inquiry were established to investigate the case of each man who was posted missing 'for a period of 6 months and not subsequently accounted for as prisoners of war or otherwise' and to establish whether it was 'reasonable to suppose the man is dead'.[28] In a largely English-speaking country, with plenty of well-paid opportunities either in the mines or elsewhere, it is likely that many men just slipped away for more congenial work and the military authorities were unable to track them down.

Considerable efforts were made to identify casualties, both the dead and the wounded, and to inform their people at home. A Casualty Branch was set up in Cape Town, with a branch in Pretoria, who issued instructions about reporting casualties which were circulated to hospitals and other units across the country. They sought to be as accurate as possible in maintaining records of casualties and in contacting relatives, but clearly many orders were widely ignored. The failure to request repeat telegrams either to Cape Town or Pretoria caused 'much unnecessary telegraphing in response'. Many instructions sought to confirm a death, or the correct details of a man reported dead: 'It is a somewhat common occurrence for men to be still reported "dangerously ill" after they have been reported dead.' Details of the deceased were telegraphed to the War Office to be passed to relatives. The system must have been slow: 'A number of cases occur in England of relatives of soldiers receiving by post notification of deaths in South Africa which have not been reported by telegram.' In the case of both officers and men, if it was necessary to inform relatives at home 'at public expense' such telegrams would be transmitted by the branch. In turn, the branch grumbled that 'Considerable difficulties have been experienced in obtaining information in answer [to] queries from home about casualties. All officers from whom such information is requested will, if they are unable to give themselves, use their utmost endeavours to obtain it as quickly as possible.'[29]

In England the information was doubled-checked so far as was possible before a man's details were passed to the regimental depot responsible for contacting the next of kin of other ranks. In addition, details were published in the daily casualty lists. The Effects Branch was responsible for dealing with grieving relatives and arranging for financial support to be provided to widows and orphans through one of the several charities that were formed during the war for this purpose. In addition: 'Personal enquiries were very numerous from all classes of society and a waiting room was provided for the interviews near to the Effects sub-division.'[30]

Some compassion was long been shown to officers' families by the authorities, but very little was offered to the families of ordinary soldiers. In September 1812, Lord Bathurst, then Secretary at War, wrote to the Duke of Wellington about the need to quickly inform relatives of officers killed in the Peninsula:

> The very desirable object of instantly relieving the distressing state of anxiety and suspense in which those persons who have relations or friends in the Army engaged are naturally left, till they can ascertain the fare of those for whom they are interested.
>
> With the view of lessoning this difficulty I have caused a small printing press to put up in my office. By this means we are enabled to circulate lists of the names of those that have suffered, long before the Gazette can be published.[31]

He asked Wellington to send lists of officers killed and wounded: 'If these returns are written in a large hand they can be printed immediately and the public will be in possession of all the names in an hour.'[32] However, it is not clear how much actual use was made of the printing press.

It was the responsibility of the regiment, or the man's commanding officer, to inform the next of kin of his fate. We do not know how a man's death was communicated to his family or, if indeed, it always was. The colonel of the regiment is likely to have written to the families of his officers. An early example was sent to Major General Gordon Forbes, the father of Lieutenant Richard Gordon Forbes of 1st Foot Guards, by Major General Francis D'Oyly, who was Lieutenant Forbes' commanding officer on 21 September 1799:

> I have great satisfaction in informing you that your son has conducted himself in such a manner, upon every occasion, since he has been under my command, as to do himself the greatest credit. He is, I am sorry to say, taken prisoner, and from the report of a soldier who was carrying him off, he himself said, 'He was not badly wounded', as the enemy were very near he directed the

soldier to lay him down and save himself. The soldier on being questioned, said he had one wound in his arm and another that disabled him from walking.

I shall take care to use my interest with the Commander-in-Chief to get him exchanged as soon as possible, and to send him, when an opportunity offers, every comfort his situation demands.[33]

Forbes had been killed near Alkmaar in the Netherlands two days previously.

Few letters of commiseration, however, were as polished as the one sent by Lieutenant C. G. Mundy, a comrade of Lieutenant Richard Forbes, 1st Foot Guards, to Forbes' father:

> The night before the unfortunate action of the nineteenth of September, my poor friend, your son, gave me his pocket book, desiring that if any misfortune befell him, I would, if I lived to return to England, convey it to you together with his sword. I likewise send such letters as have arrived since that fatal day. Your son and myself lived on the most intimate footing in Holland, and I can venture to say no man ever was more universal or deservedly beloved, a braver or a better young man could not exist. I hope, Sir, you will not consider this as an impertinent intrusion in one who is a real partaker in your affliction, and who begs so to remain, with the greatest respect.[34]

It is less clear who contacted the families of NCOs and ordinary soldiers. The regimental depot at home may have written to the deceased soldier's family, although until the 1880s relatively few family members would have been literate, and in Ireland and the Highlands they would have been more familiar with Erse or Gaelic than with English. In some cases, it is likely that comrades of the fallen man wrote to the deceased's family, or a notice would be placed by the regiment on the door of the parish door notifying villagers – including the next of kin – of a man's death.[35]

Matters began to improve in the mid-century. During the Crimean War relatives seem to have contacted the Army Chaplain's Department for advice about locating their loved ones. The Revd H. P. Wright, the 'Principal Chaplain in the East', advised readers of *The Times* 'seeking information about soldiers who were killed in action or died in hospital' that 'direct communication with Lieutenant Colonels commanding regiments, or chaplains of brigades, will secure in the speediest way all particulars that can be supplied.'[36] But few families of ordinary working class soldiers would have had the literacy, let alone the confidence, to write to the regiment for information about their sons.

In 1872, the case of a death of Private George Woodcroft, 16th Foot, was taken up by his local rector, who wrote to *The Times* about it. Woodcroft drowned at Landguard Fort near Harwich on 7 July 1872. The deceased's father had not been informed by his son's commanding officer of the death and subsequent burial until six days later.[37] Private James Holland, 24th Foot, was supposedly killed at Isandlwana on 22 January 1879. His mother, having read her son's name in the published casualty lists, contacted the War Office seeking further information. A clerk, Ralph Thompson, replied on 20 March: 'In reply to your application, I regret to have to inform you that from the list of casualties received at this office it appears that Private James Holland was killed in an engagement which occurred on the 22nd of January last.'[38]

In fact, James Holland was not dead: it was a clerical error. The battalion muster for January 1879 initially indicates that he had been 'killed in action', but he is recorded as being present as normal the following month. Nor does Holland appear on the medal roll, which suggests that perhaps he had gone missing after these traumatic events.[39] However, he managed to write to his mother describing the events of the day, 'a letter in pencil countersigned in the usual way by the commanding officer' on 3 February: 'There can be no mistake about it – the handwriting is his.' The story appeared in a number of other papers. The *Dover Express* added: 'One can imagine the joy of the mother on the receipt of the letter, but one may also imagine from this what the life of a British soldier is thought of at headquarters.'[40]

There was no separate branch at the War Office dealing with casualties until the 1890s. Indeed, it is unclear who was responsible for dealing with these matters even after the great reorganisation of the War Office following the abolition of the Board of Ordnance in 1856. Just four paragraphs are devoted to dealing with casualties in the *King's Regulations and Orders for the Army* prepared in 1912. The assumption made by the War Office was that in wartime a new organisation would quickly be established to deal with casualties, as had happened in the Boer War.[41] King's Regulations, however, required that a telegram should be sent to the next of kin in the case of a soldier's death or his being wounded, which would be followed up by a letter from an officer containing 'any other matters likely to be of [interest]', which might include the circumstance of a man's death.[42]

Cemeteries and memorials

Until well into the first half of the nineteenth century the concept of burying, let alone commemorating, individual soldiers did not exist except for a few exceptional officers. Little thought was given to providing individual burials, let alone gravestones for the fallen. 'Shovelled into a hole and so forgotten', William Makepeace Thackeray wrote after a visit to the battlefield at Waterloo in 1844. 'English glory', he thought 'is too genteel to meddle with those humble fellows. She does not condescend to ask the names of the poor devils whom she kills in her service.'[43]

Men were buried more or less where they fell on the battlefield, or their bodies put into communal pits to prevent the spread of disease. Their bodies were sometimes plundered by sightseers or grave-robbers. For some years 'Waterloo Teeth' torn from the mouths of dead soldiers were popular dentures for those who could afford them.[44] A sergeant in the Royal Artillery wrote to his father in Edinburgh after he had visited Waterloo a day or two after the battle:

> Death had reaped a plentiful harvest and displayed his ravages in their ugliest forms. Poor mutilated wretches still lay in the agonies of death, calling or making signs for a drop of water. There was none to be had... Here a dead man served for a pillow to his dying companion – others lay, as it were, holding each other in a last embrace... I saw several men and women from the adjacent villages stripping the dead; and I am told that these wretches plundered many of the wounded.[45]

The cadavers of the fallen soon became the targets of souvenir hunters. Revd Rudge of Windsor visiting Waterloo soon after the battle picked up a piece of skull as a souvenir, together with a letter from a soldier to a 'female friend', which he sent to her on his return home 'giving an account of the situation in which I found it'.[46]

Treatment of the dead hardly improved in the decades after Waterloo. After the Battle of Alma in the Crimea in 1855, William Howard Russell wrote: 'The British soldiers were buried in pits. Their firelocks, and the useful portions of their military equipment, were alone preserved.'[47]

Sergeant Major Richard Ellis, 3rd Foot, remembered that after the Battle of Balaclava:

> When the sun rose next morning, we were allowed to wander for a short time about the battlefield but the strongest heart was soon affected by the awful scene. Our own men were lying mingled with the enemy one on top of another, many of them clutching at each other in their death agony...We saw such sights that several of the

men in my company fainted with sheer horror and repulsion. One friend of mine in particular suffered terribly.

The pioneers of all the regiments were set to work to dig long trenches about seven foot wider for the internment of the dead. Men were sent out in all directions to collect the bodies which were brought up on stretchers and laid like sardines in a box, in about three layers, as near as I can remember and then the earth was filled in and a large mound made over them. Our dead were buried by themselves, but no volleys were fired over them, and I saw no chaplain in the Crimea till near the close of the war...

The burying of the dead, and collecting the arms, occupied two days. Every man who was not wanted for another duty was ordered to assist; and they made a good collection of money from dead for it did no good to bury it.[48]

New attitudes towards the dead in Victorian society slowly filtered through to the British Army. It helped that after the Crimean War there were no large-scale wars until the Boer War, by which time it had become customary, where possible, to provide each deceased man with his own grave. The change can be first seen during the colonial wars when it became increasingly common to bury the fallen in individual graves. The *Illustrated London News* in 1852, for example, included a drawing of graves at Post Retief in the Eastern Cape for fourteen men and officers who died 'during a desperate fight with the Kaffirs' in October and November 1851.[49] Sixty years later, during the First World War, the only theatre of operations where mass burials took place to any extent was at Gallipoli as conditions on the peninsula rarely permitted the burial of the fallen in individual graves. They were fairly rare on the Western Front. And where this happened men were normally reverently laid side by side, rather than bodies and body parts all mixed up together.

Until well into the nineteenth century, it was unusual to commemorate the memory of the fallen either on the battlefield or at home. Officers, especially senior officers, who died during the wars of the eighteenth and nineteenth centuries might be accorded a grave or a memorial. Few are as old as that to John Hawkwood (c1323-1395), 'British knight, esteemed the most cautious and expert general of his age' in the Duomo at Florence.[50] Most can be found in the Anglican cathedrals and country churches of England. Across Europe and the Empire, there is a thin scattering of graves and memorials for British servicemen, which David Crane suggests were 'almost all products of family or regimental piety and closer in their air of melancholy to forgotten pet cemeteries than to national monuments.'[51]

The exception was at Waterloo, where 135 commemorative monuments can be found on or near the battlefield. Of course, Waterloo was a great and decisive British victory and many memorials commemorate particular actions of regiments or individual officers. Others were built by families in memory of valiant soldiers, like the two funeral monuments to the memory of Alexander Gordon, Wellington's aide-de-camp. Only in 1889 were the dead of Waterloo formally honoured, when seventeen bodies of officers and men were reinterred at Evere Cemetery in the northern suburbs of Brussels, some way from the battlefield. The architectural critic Gavin Stamp suggests that 'This was probably the first British national memorial to the dead, as opposed to a monument to a victory.'[52]

A list of cemeteries and the individual memorials erected in the Crimea was published in 1857 by two Army officers, John Colborne and Frederic Brine. *Memorials of the Brave: or resting places of our fallen heroes in the Crimea and at Scutari*. It is a beautifully illustrated volume clearly aimed at the affluent families of the fallen, who could never hope to visit the battlefields for themselves.[53] The authors hoped that the volume would 'excite an interest relative to the last earthly tenements of those gallant ones who, while they lived, were the country's noblest pride and now they can fight her victories no more, assert a just claim to have undying remembrance.'⁵⁴ They commented that few traces of the British presence on the peninsula now remained except the cemeteries and monuments described in their book, and they stressed their quality and design. The most imposing memorial at Cathcart's Hill was deemed 'an humble imitation of Kensal Green [containing] some handsome monuments in design and execution far from inferior to many in England.'⁵⁵ Captured by the contemporary photographer Roger Fenton, however, the memorial looks more like a moonscape than a neat Commonwealth War Graves Commission cemetery. In complete contrast to Waterloo forty years before, many of the memorials and marked graves were now for ordinary soldiers, such as for Bugler W. R. Murray, Rifle Brigade, who died of wounds received during the assault on the Sedan on 8 September 1855, aged 21 years: 'The stone is erected by his comrades as a mark of respect.'⁵⁶

Despite Colborne and Brine's assertions, little consideration was given to the maintenance of either the graves or the cemeteries. Because of the harsh weather conditions locally, most soon needed attention. Waterloo was again an exception because there were individuals and regimental funds willing to keep the battlefield memorials in good order. Otherwise, HM Treasury, the War Office or the Foreign Office might reluctantly make small grants to employ a caretaker (often a former British NCO) or to pay the local authority to maintain a British cemetery. But smaller ones, such as the one at Marmaris in Turkey that contained the bodies of a dozen or so soldiers and sailors who died there in 1801 and 1841, fell into neglect and have long been forgotten.

An inter-departmental committee investigated the care of British war graves in 1889. They identified 1408 graves and cemeteries, both military and civilian, scattered around the world which held deceased British citizens. They suggested that the scattered burial places be reduced and the bodies removed to large and better maintained cemeteries. The committee also hoped that the host countries would contribute to the maintenance of the cemeteries. Little action was taken as the result of the report.⁵⁷

The Crimean memorials soon fell into neglect, ignored by the host nation and the British Office of Works alike. Throughout the late nineteenth century, British graves here were frequently vandalised and a mixture of apathy on the part of the British government and diplomatic wrangling over land ownership ensured that the repair and upkeep of the sites was never resolved. When Brigadier General J. M. Adye and Colonel C. J. Gordon visited the Crimea in 1872 to inspect the 130 British memorials and cemeteries they found that:

> Tablets and crosses have gradually loosened in their foundations, many have fallen and have become broken, and the weather-worn inscriptions are hardly distinguishable. Stray cattle have in some instances contributed to the destruction. The walls which enclose the Cemeteries were in the first instance roughly built, without mortar or foundations, and of the loose uncut stones in the neighbourhood. Time and weather have led to the rapid decay of these also, and the shepherds have occasionally hastened the destruction, by making entrances for their flocks and herds.⁵⁸

Adye and Gordon did not think that the memorials, cemeteries and individual graves should be brought into one central cemetery as the French had done. Echoing the policy of the Imperial War Graves Commission fifty years later, they commented that: 'Our officers and men were buried by their comrades on the ground where they fell, the whole scene is sacred and historical, and the remains of the dead should not be disturbed.' However, they proposed that a 'large obelisk or memorial' be erected at Cathcart's Hill in memory of all the officers and men who had fallen in the war. They estimated that this could done for less than £5000 and noted that the Russian military authorities were happy to transfer the land to Britain for this purpose.⁵⁹ No action was taken to implement the report. In the 1880s, vital consolidation work was carried out, but full maintenance of the main site, Cathcart's Hill, eluded British interest throughout the twentieth century.⁶⁰

The Boer War

The South African War between 1899 and 1902 has come to be seen as a transitional war between those of the nineteenth century when men fought hand-to-hand and died and were buried together on the battlefield and the industrial wars of the twentieth century, where men rarely saw the enemy and were most often buried in formal cemeteries. Some 7,091 officers and men were killed or died of wounds, and another 13,682 died of disease or non-battle related injury.⁶¹ The fallen are buried in over two hundred cemeteries across South Africa. In the opening weeks of the War Thomas Hardy imagined the fate of 'Drummer Hodge':

> They throw in Drummer Hodge, to rest
> Uncoffined – just as found:
> His landmark is a kopje-crest
> That breaks the veldt around:
> And foreign constellations west
> Each night above his mound.⁶²

Men were, however, almost always buried in large cemeteries or their bodies subsequently removed from smaller burial grounds to gardens of remembrance in municipal cemeteries. The largest cemetery is the President Bland Cemetery in Bloemfontein, where 1730 British and colonial soldiers are to be found.

Many of the cemeteries and individual graves were soon neglected. Initially. they were cared for by a charity, the Guild of Loyal Women of South Africa. The Guild was founded in 1900 in order to boost British influence in southern Africa and soon took it upon itself to locate and maintain British war graves. It was not always easy. At Magersfontein near Kimberley in Cape Colony, the graves in 1903 were being 'disturbed by jackals and other animals burrowing', which was 'causing great grief to those concerned'.[63]

In November 1906, the *Pall Mall Gazette* reported:

> In the course of six years' work every grave has been located which in all human probability will ever be found. Of these only a very few are not identified, and over very many of them some permanent memorial has already been erected. To conclude the heavier part of its task, the Guild wishes to set up over the yet unmarked graves, of which there remain at least 4,000, some simple but permanent memorial, and towards this final outlay an appeal is made for contributions to a permanent fund.[64]

A year earlier, the newspaper had interviewed the Guild's secretary Miss Tillard:

> 'We are ... the link between the grave in South Africa and the relatives at home. It is most satisfactory to know that hardly a single grave remains unidentified.' 'How has it been possible to do this?' 'The Guild of Loyal Women in South Africa have done much, but of course the military authorities have rendered invaluable assistance, and the soldiers themselves have done the rest. There is nothing the soldier will not do to trace the grave of a dead comrade. In our books we have the name of every soldier who fell and all necessary particulars. Their graves are scattered throughout the four Colonies, and it is amazing how they have been located.'[65]

Unfortunately, the Guild was unable to secure permanent government funding – either in South Africa or in Great Britain –

to continue the work. Without this support the task proved too great and by the end of the decade the Guild had collapsed.[66] Subsequently, neither the Afrikaner nor English-speaking white populations wished to remember a deeply divisive war, so the cemeteries were largely neglected. In 2004, responsibility for the maintenance and renovation of the cemeteries was passed to the South African Agency of the Commonwealth War Graves Commission.[67]

The sheer number of casualties that occurred during the First World War meant that the solutions previously adopted for the burial of soldiers and the care of their graves no longer applied. Society too had changed demanding proper respect for the fallen. In addition, there was a new category of the war dead – those men whose bodies had been destroyed in the fighting or whose last whereabouts were not known. It was soon very clear that a new way of burying and commemorating the war dead was required: the Imperial War Grave Commission (IWGC), an autonomous agency of the British Government tasked with the care of the war dead. In part, the Commission was a reaction to the benign neglect of the graves of British soldiers and sailors that had occurred after previous wars. In his memorandum proposing the Commission's creation, Brigadier General Sir Fabian Ware wrote that the Empire must be 'spared the reflections which weighed on the conscience of the British nation when, nearly twenty years after the conclusion of the Crimean War, it became known that the last resting place of those who had fallen in that war had, except in individual instances, remained uncared for and neglected.'[68]

The IWGC ensured this would not be the case again. Nowhere was the difference clearer than in the way the Commission commemorated the missing. But who actually were the missing and how did they vanish from the battlefield?

3

THE MISSING AND THEIR DISAPPEARANCE

Let the reader imagine any narrow strip of twenty-five miles known of him ... suddenly rushed by many thousands of men, many of them falling dead or maimed upon the way. For the look of the charge let him remember some gust of wind on a road in Autumn when the leaves are lying. The gust sweeps some array of leaves into the road and flings them forward in a rush, strangely like the rush of men as seen from a distance. As in the rush of men many leaves drop out, crawl forward again, cease, quiver and lie still.

John Masefield, The Battle of the Somme (William Heinemann, 1919)

During the First World War, death was anonymous, random, unpredictable, and brutal. Often the body disappeared completely, atomised in a second by a shell or torn into pieces by subsequent fighting. In the words of John Masefield there was 'no piece of dust without a man in it'.[1]

Each of the combatants of course lost large numbers of men whose bodies were never recovered. This was the case for about a third of British and Dominion casualties. Of the 1,400,000 men who died for France, 252,900 were declared 'lost or unidentified' (22 per cent) and 2896 Americans of the 116,000 Doughboys who lost their lives, just 2.5 per cent.[2] The German Army lost just over two million men on both the Western and Eastern fronts. It is not known how many have no burial place. During the Battle for Passchendaele, Paul Ham found that the Germans had suffered about 266,000 losses, of whom 49,000 were never found (18 per cent). Robert Foley estimated that of the German losses, 134,000 had been wounded, of whom 35,000 had been killed in action and a further 48,000 were 'missing'.[3] Perhaps only in the early days of the German offensive in late-March 1918 were more men as a whole recorded as being missing by the British rather than having been killed in action.

Rather oddly, despite detailed and sometimes obsessive record keeping by the War Office, there is no complete number of the men who went missing during the First World War.[4] Richard van Emden in his recent book on the missing, for example, suggests that: 'over half the dead were missing: men with no known graves.'[5] If by 'dead' he means Killed in Action, then this seems to be about right. A very rough rule of thumb might be that about a third of British casualties were killed in action, another third went missing and the final third died of wounds or sickness.

There is even no agreed figure for the total number of deaths – do you count just men killed in action or include those who died of wounds, or those who died of sickness, particularly the Spanish Flu which killed many soldiers in late 1918 and early 1919? The British Government told the International Labour Organisation in 1924 that total deaths, including men from all three services who had been killed in action or died of wounds or sickness amounted to 743,702. This did not include deaths from the Dominions, India or the Empire.[6]

One set of official 'final and corrected' casualty figures for the British Army were issued in a parliamentary report in March 1921.[7] The losses covered the period between 4 August 1914 until 30 September 1919 and excluded the losses incurred by other Imperial forces. They indicated 573,507 'killed in action, died from wounds and died of other causes'; 254,176 missing and prisoners, less 154,308 released prisoners (that is almost exactly 100,000 missing men); a net total of 673,375 dead and missing. There had also been 1,643,469 wounded, mainly from gunshot wounds or shrapnel from artillery shells. Of the 254,176 who were identified as being missing or taken prisoner, the overwhelming majority were on the sixty or so miles of the British sector on the Western Front.[8]

The reasons for the discrepancies often revolve around who exactly has been included – the Royal Naval Division that fought bravely in Gallipoli and on the Western Front was technically part of the Navy, for example, so is often omitted – and what exactly were the dates included in the statistics? And it is also not always certain whether the figures include men from the dominions, India or the colonies. Some 210,000 Canadians, Australians and members of other Imperial forces were also killed in action, disappeared, or died of wounds.[9] The fighting stopped, of course, on 11 November 1918, but the war in Europe itself did not formally end until the signing of the Treaty of Versailles on 28 June 1919, so the figures might well include soldiers who died in the first half of 1919, generally as the result of Spanish Flu.

In January 1922, the Imperial War Grave Commission's Committee on Memorials to the Missing estimated that there were 213,000 men whose bodies had not been found, of which 18 per cent came from the Dominions.[10] This turned out to be on the low side, as figures produced by Sir Fabian Ware in 1937 show. He said that the Commission had responsibility for:

Total graves (including 180,861 unidentified)	767,978
Total identified graves	587,117
Total missing commemorated	517,773
Total death casualties	1,104,890[11]

Sir Fabian divided the missing into 180,861 'Unidentifiable dead bodies' who rested in separate graves marked 'Known unto God' and 336,912 men known to have died on the battlefields, or at sea, but who have no recognisable burial place.[12] Although men were posted missing in the other theatres of operations around the world, more than two-thirds of the total were on the Western Front.

In addition, around 26,000 officers and ratings in the Royal Navy and 14,000 seamen in the Merchant Navy also have no known grave. But in almost every case it is because they died at sea. And although many pilots and navigators were posted missing when their aircraft crashed behind enemy lines their fates – whether as German prisoners or fatalities – were almost always quickly established.

The Commonwealth War Graves Commission's memorials to the missing in France and Belgium contain the names of 314,000 men – almost exactly the population of Nottingham today – who have no final resting place. In addition, there are memorials to another 146,000 men who have no known grave because they lost their lives at sea or in other campaigns, notably at Gallipoli and in Mesopotamia, where because of the terrain it was customary for soldiers to be buried in communal graves[13]

Who were the missing of the First World War?

With hindsight, it seems purely arbitrary who went missing and has no identifiably last resting place and those who whose bodies were laid in a grave. This was something that the relations of the missing often found hard to accept. And there seems to be no difference in the survival rate between experienced trench fighters – who might be thought to have developed a better sense of survival – and those soldiers newly arrived at the front. The fates of individual men were outside their control. A man could survive a seemingly dangerous raid only to be killed by a stray bullet in the apparent safety of his trench.

Overwhelmingly, however, the missing were infantrymen in the front line. It thus comes as no surprise that 83 per cent of casualties occurred to foot soldiers. Of the 189 missing men with the surname Fowler who lost their lives in France and Flanders, all but nineteen served in infantry units. Similarly, of the 90 missing men called Wyatt only seven were not infantry.[14]

The Missing and their Disappearance

Relatively few men from the Royal Artillery, Royal Engineers or the other arms and corps of the Army lost their lives in this way, because they were rarely to be found in the trenches.

Did any particular activity – trench raids, for example – produce a greater proportion of missing men than, say, a set-piece action during a battle or a tour of duty in a trench? Surviving records, either operational or medical, do not allow an analysis. Logic says that the trench was safer – which is why of course they were dug all the way along the Western Front in the late Autumn of 1914. But they were not that safe. Private Bernard Livermore mused on 'Death from a sniper's bullet, death from a rifle grenade, death from a Minnie or toffee apple [types of grenade], death from shrapnel (possibly from our own guns) or from gas if the wind were in the right direction. Death might also come from bayonet or nail-studded cosh if the Bosche raided our lines.'[15]

Private Roy Ashford, London Regiment was with his friend Private Hearn in a trench on the Somme when Hearn was killed outright by a shell, blown backwards into the trench as he stood on the firestep on sentry duty:

> First, I went through his pockets and put his treasures into his gas helmet satchel, to be returned to his relatives. Then...we heaved the body over the paradox. I decided the best case would be to scrape at the nearest shell hole, which I did with a spade the Germans had left behind...As reverently as possible we laid the body in the bottom and scraped the earth over it...I stuck his bayonet at the head of the grave and his steel helmet thereon...Then. Having done our best for our lost pal, we climbed back into the trench.[16]

Jimmy Smith of the Northern Cyclist Battalion remembered burying his best friend Ernie Gays:

> I took him by the ankles, the other two took him by the arms, and we laid him in and covered him up. I remember feeling a bit upset,

for the grave was only about four feet deep. I knew for sure he probably wouldn't be there for very long because of the shellfire.[17]

Private Smith was right. Gays is now commemorated on the memorial at Tyne Cot.

Officers were not spared this fate either. About five per cent of officers in total have no known grave, which is roughly the same proportion as for those who died in action or subsequently of wounds.[18] Of the missing 189 Fowlers, for example, just twelve were officers (six per cent), and 29 non-commissioned officers (fifteen per cent). Only the 90 Wyatts only two were officers (both second lieutenants) and fourteen were NCOs; the other missing men were privates. It has been suggested that there slightly fewer missing officers than might be expected. This was because greater efforts were made to retrieve officers' bodies from No Man's Land.

Lieutenant Morris Bickersteth, West Yorkshires, was killed on 1 July 1916 leading his company towards German lines at Serre when he was struck by German machine gun fire. He was initially posted missing because his body could not be retrieved. His brother Julian, a padre also serving on the Somme, tried to reassure their parents: 'You will see then, dear ones, that it is quite impossible to get the body back... But I don't worry about that so much and you mustn't either, dearest ones... His grave is all the world.'[19] Julian Bickersteth subsequently made several trips into the battlefield in unsuccessful searches for the body. He concluded that it had been blown to pieces. However, a fellow officer wrote to Morris's father the Revd Samuel Bickersteth enclosing a handkerchief 'picked up on the battlefield by his Sergeant-Major' and implying that the Sergeant Major had seen 'my son's body, together with other men of the 15th [battalion] buried'.[20] Happily, the information was correct. The Revd Bickersteth heard from the Directorate of Graves Registration in May 1917 that their son was buried just behind the frontline at 'Matthew Copse, 40 yards from the railway going to Puisieux. The grave ... is marked by a durable wooden cross with an inscription bearing full particulars.'[21]

As the war progressed, the number of missing as a proportion of the number of casualties increased. It might be expected that the highest numbers of missing occurred during the great battles of the Somme and Passchendaele in 1916 and 1917, but in fact just over half disappeared in 1918.[22] The chaotic nature of the fighting then also meant that all too often it was impossible to recover the dead. In addition, the bodies of many of those who had already been killed were disturbed in the fighting. Alan Grint suggests that out of the 7500 Tommies who died on the first day of the German offensive (21 March) there are known graves only for 1000 of them.[23] Alfred Burrage described how the Germans the shelling of his retreating company:

> One [shell] smashed on to the hard road right into the middle of the first platoon of the company in my rear. God knows how many limbs and heads went up in the black geyser of flying earth, but even at a distance of a hundred yards, the thinning of the cloud revealed a nasty sight.[24]

There seems to be no particular area or region where the missing came from. There is no reason why this should have been the case, as men from across the United Kingdom and, indeed, the Empire fought together and died together.

The highest proportion of missing to those who died by other means discovered by the author is in Twickenham: 55 of the 129 men (42 per cent) who appear on the St Mary Parish memorial have no grave, eight of whom are officers.[25] In the Grandpoint district of South Oxford, 66 men lost their lives of whom 23 (or 35 per cent) are commemorated on memorials to the missing.[26] In Hexham, 240 men are named on memorials across the town, of whom 67 men (or 28 per cent) appear on memorials to the missing in France and Flanders; another six are commemorated on the Helles or Lone Pine memorials on Gallipoli. The majority of the missing were privates: 44 out of a total of 67. Twelve were officers, seven of whom were Second Lieutenants no doubt killed while leading their platoons across No Man's Land. With few exceptions, the town's missing men were members of infantry regiments, notably the Northumberland Fusiliers, which traditionally recruited men from the area.[27]

Prisoners of war

Prisoners of war are important to our story in several ways. In some sense they were perceived as an almost paranormal link to the missing: they had returned from the dead. They were men who went missing but who survived, something that gave hope to families that their dear ones had perhaps not perished in the Flanders mud. Max Pemberton offered this encouragement:

> Men have been seen to fall apparently stark dead and in a few months' time they have been heard of in German prison camps. In the early days of the war fugitives roved from village to village, slept in hayricks, and in barns, had as many escapes as one of Marryat's romancers, and finally succeeded in crossing the Dutch frontier long after all hope of them had been abandoned. That sort of thing can hardly occur now—yet it is indisputable that the miracles do happen.[28]

During the War, about 190,000 British and Commonwealth soldiers were taken prisoner by the Germans. Some two-thirds were captured during the great German offensive of March 1918 and the months that followed. Men were fell into enemy hands either because they were surrounded by superior forces and thus had no choice, or they crossed by error into enemy territory. Capture was first a surprise, which soon turned to shock. Many were also more likely to surrender when they became demoralised, as happened in many British units in the aftermath of the German assault.[29]

But there is also a darker side. We will never know how many men fell into enemy hands and were subsequently killed. Both sides on occasion operated a practice of 'taking no prisoners' and there is evidence that in some cases the British shot recently captured Germans rather than take them back to their lines.[30] The machine gunner Dick Wills wrote in his memoirs:

> Enemy in full retreat, after him lads, we enter a large village and proceed to mop up any who have not fled, and may be hiding in cellars, the mode of procedure in which case being, to stand at the head of the cellar steps, to one side of course, and shout down instructions to anyone down there to come up, if no one comes up, and the slightest noise is heard below, down goes a Mills bomb with instructions to 'Share this among you.'[31]

On the German side, in March 1918 Ernst Jünger described how an orderly in another officer's company 'shot a good dozen or more' English prisoners who were 'hasten[ing] with upstretched arms through the first wave of storm troops to the rear'. Jünger's feelings were mixed: 'To kill a defenceless man is a baseness,' yet he could not 'blame the men for their bloodthirsty conduct'.[32] Robert Graves reflected that: 'We had every reason to believe that the same thing [killing of captured men] happened on the German side, where prisoners [were regarded] as useless mouths to feed in a country already short of rations.'[33]

Sometimes men were of course taken prisoner as a result of their wounds. In his memoirs Second Lieutenant Ernest Warburton described leading a raid into the enemy's trenches in October 1916:

> ...I was 'dropped' in the wire by a bomb [hand grenade] which was quickly followed by three others. I got them all! According to orders my men carried on without me, hoping to pick me up on

their return. I heard – long afterwards – they tried very hard to find me when they came back, but they missed me in the darkness.

He told the War Office, after his repatriation, that because of his wounds one of his men had dragged him into a shell hole and

> ...then went to fetch help. He never returned & again I lost consciousness but later recovered on in the night & tried to crawl, but I only managed to get up one side of the shell hole, the whole of my right side being useless & I was caught hopelessly in the German wire. I lay the remainder of the night and the whole of the following day & at dusk that evening the Germans came out and carried me into their trenches...I received altogether 36 wounds and was in hospital about 16 weeks.[34]

Other men were overwhelmed by the enemy. Cecil Thomas and his comrades were surrounded by German troops as they escaped from a badly damaged dug-out:

> As for myself my first feeling is one of relief at the end of the terrible suspense of the last sixteen hours... Still to know that the worst has happened, to get into the fresh air after the nightmare in the dug-out is a relief. Being a prisoner is a shameful thing, but having actually been taken, death has lost its terror; and we stand up in all the din of the bombardment no longer fearful and caring not a jot now whatever happens. They will probably question us, and then shoot us. They rarely take prisoners I know. But that is future, the dug-out is past, for the present let me breathe the open air deeply. Nothing else matters.[35]

Thomas had been captured without having ever fired a shot in anger. Inevitably, he felt remorse that he had not done more to fight, but reflected that there was probably nothing he could have done: 'We ought to have made a better show ourselves perhaps, and if we could we should have tried, but yet I think the result would have been the same.'[36]

The Missing and their Disappearance

Although naturally worried about their fate, the new prisoners of war were reassured that the Germans seemed much like themselves and although there were differences in the areas behind the enemy frontline, they was surprisingly similar to the ones they had left, if somewhat neater. It was almost as if the men had died and found themselves, not quite in heaven, but in a parallel universe. The new prisoners would plod ever further eastwards to camps that would be home until the end of the war. Officers lived in relative comfort, the other ranks less so. And some unfortunates were kept behind the German lines engaged in manual labour in ever-worsening conditions.

For their families it was a worrying time. It might take weeks, even months, for the news of their loved one's fate to reach them. In 1917, Max Pemberton explained:

> Generally speaking, despite all our care, it is usually from Germany that we get the first tidings of our missing. They appear to be encouraged to write to us, and although letters come very slowly from prisoners in the occupied territories, we commonly have tidings from their base prisons or hospitals within three months of the capture of any particular man. And these tidings are written by the man himself—a concession which has been wrung from the fact of numbers—so many more Germans are now held by us than British prisoners by Germans.[37]

Pemberton seems to have little idea of how the system worked: the passing of information about individual prisoners was regulated by the Geneva Convention of 1907, to which both Britain and Germany were signatories. Even so, it was a triumph of military bureaucracy on both sides for such information to be made available. Often enough it was a field postcard that arrived home, reassuring a man's family that he was safe, long before they received any official communication from the War Office confirming that the man was in captivity. The hope that a man might in fact be a prisoner but somehow forgotten by the enemy sustained many wives and mothers, even when it had been made abundantly clear that their loved one was dead. Unfortunately, as both the Germans and the Red Cross were meticulous in their recordkeeping, this was a forlorn hope.

Prisoners of war were thought of as being a good source of information about their missing comrades. The International Committee of the Red Cross and other charities regularly circulated lists of men to camps in the hope that prisoners might be able to help. One such charity was the Queen Victoria Jubilee Fund Association, based in Geneva, which promised enquirers to circulate details of missing men with their photographs to 'all camps and hospitals in Germany, Belgium and by special permission to the Chief Medical Officers in the war zone in German occupation'.[38] But there is little evidence that circulating such lists produced very many results.

Conditions on the Western Front

As previously noted, the greatest threat to life and limb was the shell. A shell explosion could kill dozens of men and scramble their bodies in their aftershock. During the week of 25 July 1917 alone, at the opening of the Battle of Passchendaele, the British army fired off 4,285,550 shells (or 107,000 tons of metal) along a front twelve miles wide. Field Marshal Haig and his commanders then expected the infantry to try to wade across the soupy morass of No Man's Land into the German lines in the face of sustained machine gun fire, during one of the wettest summers of the twentieth century. It is hard not to agree with the Canadian journalist Stephen O'Shea who called Passchendaele an act of 'criminal stupidity'.[39]

A man might almost equally be killed by a British shell as a German one. Robert Graves remembered that during the preliminary bombardment prior to the Battle of the Somme in June 1916, 'We had more casualties from our own shorts and from blow-backs than from German shells.'[40] A year earlier at Loos, Frank Richards witnessed the enemy trenches being shelled: 'a lot of [our] shells were falling short again and exploding amongst the men who were lying out in the open. Some of these men were not hit, but if either they or the wounded attempted to return they were immediately fired upon.'[41]

Scattered across No Man's Land were shell craters, which sheltered both the living and the dead. Once when leading a raid, Cecil Summers came across one such crater:

> It was not a nice sensation, going up to that crater, something like walking in your own funeral procession. When we reached it, after passing through a deadly sort of barrage with amazing luck, the crater was an awful sight. By the light of the moon you could see it all, the great yawning hole, a good. fifty feet deep, with dead bodies stretched in ghastly attitudes down its steep sides. Every now and then one of the bodies, stirred by some explosion, would turn over and roll to the bottom, sliding down into a perfect shambles, where it would soon lose its identity among the jumbled heap of corpses and shattered limbs. Around the lip of the crater our men were trying to dig themselves in, but the earth was no firmer than sand, and in a second the crumbling foundations of an hour's desperate work would slide to the bottom, where at least they helped to cover up the awfulness which the first light of dawn was beginning to show up still more clearly.[42]

For others it was the mud that claimed them. Conditions were made by worse by the destruction of the centuries-old drainage system of creeks and canals, which had emptied the former marshes between Ypres and Passchendaele. Lyn Macdonald suggests that 90,000 men were reported missing during the five-month-long battle for Passchendaele: 'Rather more than half must be buried as "unknown soldiers", 42,000 bodies were never recovered at all. Many still lie where they sank into the mud.'[43] On 2 August, the day after the heavens opened, Captain Harry Yoxall wrote to his mother that 'liquid mud filled the craters.' He had heard that four men had drowned: 'They must have been stuck in the mud, become exhausted and fallen face forward.'[44] Private Charlie Miles, Royal Fusiliers, found the sucking of mud underfoot terrible enough, but it was even worse if you did not hear it, since then you knew you had trodden on a corpse: 'It was terrifying. You'd tread on one on the stomach, perhaps, and it would grunt all the air out of its body. It made your hair stand on end. The smell could make you vomit.'[45]

Any soldier who slipped on the duckboards which were laid across the battlefield to help the troops move forward and fell into a shell hole risked drowning, borne down by the total weight of his pack and uniform (which weighed between sixty and seventy pounds).[46] And once in the mud it was extremely difficult to be extracted. Lieutenant Colonel Edgar Mobbs, Northamptonshire Regiment, was one such man who suffered this fate. As he lay sinking in a shell hole, he sent a runner back with details of his position. The runner failed to reach his destination, and Mobbs's body was never recovered.[47]

In his poem *Memorial Tablet (Great War)* Siegfried Sassoon bitterly imagined one nameless victim of the mud:

Squire nagged and bullied till I went to fight,
(Under Lord Derby's Scheme). I died in hell—
(They called it Passchendaele). My wound was slight,
And I was hobbling back; and then a shell
Burst slick upon the duck-boards: so I fell
Into the bottomless mud, and lost the light.[48]

As well as the noise, veterans remembered the smell which intensified as they approached the front line. Charles Carrington recalled:

The smell of burnt and poisoned mud – acrid is I think the right epithet – was with us for months on end, and through it one could distinguish a more biotic flavour – the stink of corrupting human flesh. In the thirty square miles around us [on the Somme] the best part of 200,000 men had been killed in the last few months and had lain unburied, or been buried hastily in shallow graves, or buried and blown out of their graves again. I think 7000 corpses to the square mile is not much of an exaggeration, ten to the acre shall we say, and your nose told you where they lay thickest.[49]

Decomposing bodies and body parts were found scattered across No Man's Land and in the trenches themselves. The presence of the dead initially shocked many men. Ernst Jünger admitted that he had never imagined that 'in this war, the dead would be left month after month to the mercy of wind and weather as once the bodies on the gallows were.'[50]

But eventually, most soldiers hardly thought about the corpses. Even the memory of friends who had 'bought it' soon faded. They were part of the landscape. Frederick Manning remembered the dead in Trones Wood on the Somme:

...the unburied dead with whom one lived ... cheek by jowl, Briton and Hun impartially confounded, festering, fly-blown, corruption, the pasture of rats, blackening in the heat, swollen with distended bellies, or shrivelling away within their mouldering rags; and even when night covered them, one vented in the wind the stench of death.[51]

Lieutenant Robert Fieldsend was asked to find a position for a listening post in No Man's Land: 'I found a good position, but the smell was not very good, as there were a lot of dead Worcesters lying about who had made a charge early in March.'[52]

The poet Wilfred Owen wrote to his mother in February 1917 describing the 'universal pervasion of ugliness' of the frontline:

Everything unnaturally broke, blasted, the distortion of the dead whose un-buriable bodies sit outside dug-outs all day, all night, the most execrable sights on earth. In poetry we call them the most glorious. But to sit with them all day all night ... and a week later to come back and find them sitting there in a motionless group. THAT is what saps the soldierly spirit.[53]

Despite the numbers of cadavers and body parts all around, remarkably there were few outbreaks of cholera, dysentery or other fevers in the trenches on either side. However, basic preventative health measures were instituted and enforced by the military authorities, such as the provision of latrines in the front line, and where possible bodies were covered in lime.

Inevitably, soldiers reacted differently to the carnage they saw all around them. Some never recovered from what they had experienced, still waking up with nightmares decades after the war. After an initial shock, others accepted what they found around them. Private Alfred Burrage thought that 'The only way to live out there was to turn one's face against sentiment and regard human flesh merely as flesh.'[54]

A German solder, Ernst Toller, observed: 'All these dead are men, all these corpses have breathed as I do... I could never pass a dead man again without stopping to contemplate his face and wonder "Who were you?... Where did you come from? Who is mourning for you?"'[55]

On occasion it was possible to restore a cadaver's humanity by identifying who they were. In his diary for 9 April 1917, the Revd Victor Tanner wrote that during a walk he had found a body in a stream near Gommecourt on the Somme:

[It] was a gruesome sight. The skull was in the middle of the water. The trunk was a mass of soft clay and bones. The legs still in top boots were also in the stream a few yards away. Closer investigation resulted in the production of the man's knife and pocket-book and also his Identity Disc tied to a Mill's Bomb. It bore the name B Kendrick, 6th South Staffords... The Pioneers put the remains in a grave and I read the burial service. I am glad to have obtained identification as it will relieve the anxiety of some anxious relatives who may still be clinging to the hope that the 'Missing' one may still be alive.[56]

In November 1918, Driver M Mahon, Royal Field Artillery, wrote to the family of Private Ellis Dean in Formby. He had found the body of a Lancashire Fusilier in a shell hole:

> I made a search to see who he was and found this address in a wallet he had with him. I dug a hole and put him in it and also made a little cross and put it on his grave... I thought it kind to let you know as I dare say he is only reported missing. Every other thing he had him was rotted away, so I did nothing more than bury him.[57]

Despite the graphic description Mahon's letter must have provided much relief to the family, particularly as a subsequent letter enclosed 'a label bearing the name and address of the deceased soldier' which was in his mother's handwriting 'probably taken from one of the parcels sent from home'. Private Mahon also promised to call upon the family on his next leave.

The bodies of the dead became part of the natural order of things as weeds might be in a garden. When fresh the corpse might be looted for anything that could be useful, particularly tobacco and souvenirs. Edmund Blunden ordered his men to plunder a group of 'greying haversacked British dead' near Thiepval in order to replenish the battalion stores: 'My explorers did their work with vigour and the limbers were soon more than brimful.'[58] After all, what need would the deceased have for this kit?

The possessions of the deceased were supposed to be returned to their next of kin. This might take months if not years, and it was common for items to disappear in the process.[59] For most men their few possessions were quickly divided up among comrades. Alfred Burrage felt guilty that 'one was eating cake which a mother had made for her son who was now lying disembowelled in the mud, but one ate it all the same.'[60]

As rigor mortis set in, the occasional corpse might, for a while at least, become a landmark for the troops as they passed. On the Somme, Edmund Blunden remembered that:

> Of the dead, one was conspicuous. He was a Scotch soldier, and was kneeling, facing east ... he was seen at some distance from the tracks, and no one had much time in Thiepval just then for sightseeing or burying. Death should not kneel so I thought, and approaching I ascertained with a sudden shrivelling of spirit that Death could and did.[61]

Frank Richards found a similar figure at Arras in 1917,

> ... down on one knee with his rifle at his shoulder as if he was about to fire. He must have died at that moment and stiffened in that position. One side of his face had been cut away by a piece of falling shell leaving his teeth showing. He looked like a man who doing a fiendish grin as he was taking aim with his rifle.[62]

Battalions rotating in and out of the trenches naturally had no knowledge of who these bodies had once been, except perhaps their nationality, which was usually obvious from the tattered remnants of their uniforms. Because they had no names or were of no further use to the living, the corpses became as much part of the scenery as blasted tree trunks. On his arrival in trenches opposite High Wood on the Somme in the late summer of 1916, Second Lieutenant Max Plowman tripped over a lump on the floor of a foul-smelling trench. It was a corpse. 'Literally we are living among the dead.'[63]

These were the men who could not be rescued by stretcher parties and had died where they had fallen in shell craters, in the mud and entangled in the barbed wire. Cecil Summers' bombing sergeant on the raid into No Man's Land described above was killed on the lip of a crater: 'We buried him that evening, but by next morning all signs of his grave had disappeared as the result of the bombardment to which we were subjected all that night.'[64]

On his first trip to the front line as a very junior officer in early 1916 Edmund Blunden's guide 'L'

> ... pointed out the skulls, jagged bones and wooden crosses with their weather-worn 'TO AN UNKNOWN BRITISH SOLDIER' and RIP on the side of the trench. Of these there was no lack, and out in the open 'L' said that there were still unburied skeletons in rotted uniforms.[65]

John Masefield described the temporary graves and grave markers found on the Somme battlefield:

> One need only look at the ground to know that the fighting here was very grim, and to the death. Near the road and up the slope to the enemy the ground is littered with relics of our charges, mouldy packs, old shattered scabbards, rifles, bayonets, helmets curled, torn, rolled, and starred, clips of cartridges, and very many graves. Many of the graves are marked with strips of wood torn from packing cases, with pencilled inscriptions, 'An unknown British Hero'; 'In loving memory of Pte. ___'; 'Two unknown British heroes'; 'An unknown British soldier'; 'A dead Fritz'. That gentle slope to the Schwaben [Redoubt] is covered with such things.[66]

Although these provided comforting words to the families of the dead, the bitter truth was that many of these makeshift cemeteries would eventually disappear in subsequent fighting. Vera Brittain's friend Geoffrey Thurlow was killed by a sniper near Arras: 'Shot through the chest he died speechless, gazing intently at his orderly. The place where he lay was carefully marked, but when the action was over, his body had disappeared and was never afterwards found.'[67] A few months earlier Lance Corporal Ken Lowell buried a comrade somewhere on the Somme, '... a few yards behind our position in the wood, with a rifle plunged into the earth to mark the grave and his tin hat on top of it. But by the next morning it had disappeared.'[68]

The war in the air

There were very few men missing in the Royal Flying Corps, Royal Naval Air Service and their successor the Royal Air Force. Pilots and observers shot down over enemy lines either died in the crash or shortly afterwards of wounds, or were taken prisoner by the Germans. The RFC took great trouble to find out what happened to these men. In this they were helped by an extraordinary and completely unofficial system of dropping messages over each other's airfields containing the names of men who crashed over enemy lines.

At an early stage in the war German pilots began to drop messages over Allied airfields with details of the aircrew who had either been captured or had been killed when their machines crashed or subsequently died of wounds. In return, British pilots performed a similar service. In late September 1917, attached to a list of British airmen who had crashed during the month which had been dropped on an airfield there was a request: 'Can you give us any news about the fate of our pilots Lt Dostler missed since 21.8.1917 and Lt Voss missed since 23.9.1917. Both officers are possessors of the German order "Pour le merite."'[69]

The British, too, dropped requests for information on particular individuals. Permission was sought at the end of February 1918 for a note to be sent concerning four officers from 50 Squadron who had recently gone missing and for whom no information had been received.[70] After the British Ace Albert Ball VC was lost, his squadron decided to drop message bags 'containing requests

The Missing and their Disappearance

written in German for news of his fate' over Douai, Charles Carrington remembered:

> We crossed the lines at thirteen thousand feet. Douai was renowned for its anti-aircraft. They were not to know the Squadron was in mourning, and made it hot for us. The flying splinters ripped the planes. Over the town the message bags were dropped and the formation returned without encountering a single enemy machine.[71]

The system seems to have become very well developed for mutual benefit, although it is hard to imagine that the authorities on either side approved of it. However, it is clear that the British, at least, turned a blind eye. These messages were regarded as being official enough for them to be used as evidence of a man's death. In the War Office casualty summaries for missing officers the entry for Second Lieutenant W. W. Hutton, RFC, posted missing on 28 October 1917, reads: 'A German message has been dropped into our lines in which it is stated that 2/Lt Hutton is dead.' This, along with the lapse of time since the man went missing, was adduced to be evidence enough of his death.[72]

In addition, German newspapers published lists of aircraft which had been shot down. This was meant to reassure their readers of the superiority of their air force, and the information they contained proved invaluable as evidence of the fate of Allied airmen.[73] Captain J. S. Campbell, RFC was reported missing on 28 September 1917; the War Office eventually concluded that: 'In a list of British air losses in September 1917 published in a German newspaper an entry appears to the effect that Capt. Campbell is dead.'[74]

Fighting along the Western Front was an experience that of course traumatised many men who were there and certainly deeply affected many others. But as deeply affected, in a few cases even traumatised, were the families of the missing. For them was the added uncertainty that the loved one had perhaps not been consumed by the mud, and might, just might, return home.

4

GRIEF

I laugh I laugh – for you will come again
This heart would never beat if you were dead.
    Anna Gordon Keown, 'Reported Missing'[1]

Writing in 1916 the English writer and physician Havelock Ellis realised that:

> All these bald estimates of the number of the direct victims to war give no clue to the moral and material damage done by the sudden destruction of so large a proportion of the young manhood of the world, the ever widening circles of anguish and misery and destitution which every fatal bullet imposes on humanity, for it is probably true that for every ten million soldiers who fall on the field, fifty million other persons at home are plunged into grief and poverty or some form of life-diminishing trouble.[2]

Havelock Ellis was right: three million people in Great Britain and Ireland (out of a population of less than 42 million) lost a close relative, a son or a brother. Indeed, almost the entire population, either directly or indirectly, knew somebody who died during the War or the family of somebody who had fallen.[3] The myth grew up of the slaughter of a 'Lost Generation' of immensely able public-school-educated intellectuals who would have transformed Britain had they only lived. But it was not just gilded youth who were mourned: hundreds of thousands of other men were also among the war dead. Whatever their backgrounds, men were grieved for in the same way with the same questions being asked about their deaths and the same sense of loss. The mourners from the upper and middle classes were more articulate, had connections, and were certainly better able to deal with the bureaucracy, but their emotional responses were naturally the same as their poorer cousins.

Psychologists have long been interested in grief and the process of grieving. In his 1917 essay 'Mourning and Melancholia', Sigmund Freud suggested that there were several stages of recovery and resolution in the grieving process: initial responses of shock, disbelief and denial are following by an intermediate period of acute mourning typified by severe emotional discomfort and social withdrawal, which eventually leads to restitution.[4] More recently, the Swiss psychologist Elisabeth Kübler-Ross in *On Death and Dying*, published in 1969, suggested that are five stages of grief, before the full acceptance of loss is achieved:

1. denial, that is avoidance, confusion, elation, shock, and fear;
2. anger – frustration, irritation, anxiety;
3. bargaining – struggling to find meaning, reaching out to others, telling one's story;
4. depression – feeling overwhelmed, hostility, and flight;
5. acceptance.[5]

The stages do not necessarily occur sequentially and the bereaved can revert to an earlier phase, skip a stage or never reach closure. Pain, guilt, loss of faith and loneliness are common features of the process of bereavement. All of these were certainly experienced by those grieving the loss of the missing during and after the two world wars. The experiences of the families of the missing suggest that there were certain common steps, which largely accord with the stages of grief outlined by Dr Kübler-Ross:

1. An initial assumption on receiving the news that your boy would eventually be found;
2. This would be followed by despair and uncertainty about the future;
3. Establishment of an unofficial support network, either from within the family or from friends and others who had lost relatives in similar circumstances;
4. Determination to discover what really happened;
5. Gradual acceptance that he would not return home.

Of course, the stages of grief are to an extent universal. Every family who has suddenly lost a loved one must experience them in some form. Some, like the parents of Lieutenant Hugh Williamson, Coldstream Guards, become stuck in the early stages of the cycle. Their correspondence with the War Office over the fate of their son demonstrates a continued oscillation between anger and denial. And perhaps as a result, they were never able to accept his death.[6]

It is axiomatic that the bereaved – man or woman, young or old – must come to terms with their loss in their own way. According to Juliet Nicolson: 'Grief is an iceberg of a word concealing beneath its innocent simplicity a dangerous mass of confusion and rage.'[7] Helena Tym, whose nineteen-year-old son was killed in Afghanistan in 2009, wrote that such grief is like: '... a gaping hole, deep and dark, filled with burning pains that reach up from your toes, strangling everything as they creep upwards to turn around and start back down again, never stopping or pausing to rest.'[8] Ruth Holland described in her novel *The Lost Generation*, published in 1932, her experience of grieving over her boy, 'an experience which would have been recognised by many of her readers:

> Something had snapped. Instead of a life that was like a splendid tune in her ears, with ordered sound and movement, a definite form ... she was surrounded by a mocking terrifying jumble of discord, in which she could find no sense at all. It was as if she had lost the key and could no longer read the signs around her.[9]

Even after sixty years Margaret Jones remembered what she felt when her fiancé Philip was killed. She wrote in an unpublished memoir: 'Then everything was shattered: a letter came from the War Office to say he had been killed in action. The shock and loss was terrible, I felt that I had lost half of myself. Or it was my twin. I knew then that I should die an old maid.' Miss Jones re-read what she had written and added the next words in pencil: 'I was only twenty years old.'[10] Then she put down her pen and wrote no more.

Ellen Sanders committed suicide in West Hartlepool a few weeks after hearing of the probable death of her son Michael Ferguson. A neighbour, Sarah Winspear, told the coroner that she had conversed with the deceased after receiving the news and found her constantly crying, and said 'This will be the finish of me; he was a good son to me.' Her husband, William Sanders stoically said 'She had been put about a lot because of the lad.'[11] At the other extreme the death of their man might actually be a relief. After the initial shock of her husband's disappearance Mary Morton's mother had quickly found a new partner – a gentle loving man, according to her daughter – to replace the brutal man that she had married and who had been posted missing in France.[12]

The artist Tirza Garwood remembered one of her teachers:

> Miss Larner became engaged to be married... He was like most young men, a soldier, and he went to France and very soon was

reported missing: she went on with her teaching as though nothing had happened. I was walking past by the school one day and saw her face as she was looking out of the window, thinking no one was by, and realised just how much she minded.[13]

Another fiancée, Emily Chitticks, a farm servant in Essex, never really recovered from the news that her 'young man' Private William J Martin, Devonshire Regiment, had been posted missing at Arras. Her life, she said, ended with his.[14]

It was expected that parents and spouses of those who had died at the front should maintain 'a stiff upper lip', that is to carry on as if nothing had happened. This was especially the case for men, who were expected to act as if their lives had been unaffected by tragedy. Rudyard Kipling wrote to R. D. Blumenfeld, shortly after his son's disappearance: '…one is only one atom in the ten-million man power welter, and so sticks it accordingly', although it is clear from the forced, upbeat tone of the letter and others sent to friends that he was very shaken by events.[15] Carrie, Kipling's wife, wrote to Lady Violet Cecil that she would like to 'bolt into a car and tear off and out and down all the carefully built up commitments and just be a broken-hearted mother for a little bit'. But she never did.[16]

The politician Jack Lawson came from a working-class mining family in the North East. In his autobiography he wrote that his mother: 'never fondled or kissed any of us that I remember, for she clearly regarded these things as weakness, but the death of my brother at the front clearly shook her.' One day when Jack visited with his young daughter, she gave the child a small toy:

'Take that home for your babby, hinny. My babby's gone.' Gone! The words came like the dullness of the first clay on a coffin. There was no sign of emotion, but there was a faraway look in her eyes and a tensing of the mouth as she repeated 'Gone.'[17]

During and after the world wars and other conflicts the grieving process for the families of servicemen most often occurred when there was no body to bury, let alone the chance to say farewell to the deceased through a funeral service. The corpse lay instead in a war cemetery or was eventually commemorated on a memorial to the missing, hundreds or thousands of miles away. In either case, because of the cost and other difficulties, it was unlikely that families would ever be able to visit. In 1916, the British government tried to reassure bereaved families that 'in no great war has so much been done as in this, to prevent the addition of that special torment to the pains of anxiety and bereavement... An eye-witness can assure the friends of soldiers at home that there is nothing perfunctory about these funerals.'[18]

The Imperial War Graves Commission and its predecessors were happy to send photographs of individual graves to the bereaved. A small team of photographers was employed in this work, with a considerable demand for their services. By February 1917 there was a backlog of 11,000 pictures waiting to be taken.[19]

But for about a third of British casualties of the Great War there was no body at all to grieve over, even at a distance. Finding her son's grave became an obsession for Mrs Williamson. 'I shall never believe,' she wrote, 'that my son is dead until his grave is found and it adds greatly to the sorrow of his father and me that we should be left in this awful state of uncertainty.'[20] Despite exhaustive searching of the battlefield after the battle and after the war's end no body was ever found and eyewitnesses could not agree how Lieutenant Williamson died.[21]

There was no obvious way to understand how a man had died or confirm with absolute certainty that he was dead. Carrie Kipling wrote to Lady Violet Cecil in September 1916, a year after her son John's disappearance: 'All day and every day I cry for some confirmation, some real proof that John is dead and there are thousands of mothers who feel as I do.'[22]

A tiny handful of men did indeed appear to rise from the dead by returning home from prisoner of war camps. The psychologist Ludwig Spolyar, who studied widows of men posted Missing in Action (MIA) during the Vietnam War noted that: 'wives ... find themselves emotionally involved in a unique situation... They are in a double bind for they do not know for sure whether their loved one is dead or alive. Unfortunately, this emotional state continues for an indefinite and unknown period, creating greater anxiety.'[23] This was equally true for the widows, mothers and, indeed, fathers of the two world wars.

Receiving the news

Ludwig Spolyar suggests that shock is naturally the first phase of the grief cycle: 'There is commonly a slight sense of unreality, a feeling of increased emotional distance from other people and an intense pre-occupation with the image of the missing person.'[24] There was naturally often a sense of disbelief. The Revd Peter Miller wrote in his diary after receiving the news of his son's death at High Wood on the Somme:

> Our hearts are broken today. Received a letter from one of Peter's friends, telling us that he was killed on the 9th shot by a sniper. I can hardly believe it. There must be a mistake somewhere! It is over a fortnight since we heard from him. It is terrible I cannot write about it.[25]

On New Year's Eve 1915, Vera Brittain learnt of the death of her fiancé Roland Leighton in a Casualty Clearing Station: 'Whenever I think of the weeks that followed the news of Roland's death, a series of pictures, disconnected but crystal clear, unroll themselves like a kaleidoscope though my mind.'[26] And after receiving the telegram of the death of her beloved brother Edward in Italy in June 1918, Vera Brittain went to be alone with her thoughts in the drawing room where there was a portrait of Edward:

And suddenly as I remembered all the dear afternoons and evenings when I had followed him on the piano as he played his violin, the sad, searching eyes of the portrait were more than I could bear, and falling on my knees before it I began to cry 'Edward! Oh Edward!' in dazed repetition as though my persistent crying and calling would somehow call him back.[27]

Donald Overall remembered the day that his mother had received the letter about her husband:

Mother and I were downstairs in the main hall when the doorbell rang. I was hiding behind her as she was handed an envelope. I remembered she opened the letter immediately. I don't know what it said, but she screamed and collapsed on the floor in a dead faint. I tried to wake her up; I didn't know what was wrong. I was holding on to her skirts and called out for help and an elderly couple who lived in a lower flat came out and comforted both of us. Mother came round slowly and they eventually got her upstairs into the bedroom. She was there for about ten days, and it was while she was getting better, that she turned onto her side and said to me. 'Your father's dead, he won't come back. Now you are the man of the house, you must do things as best you can.'[28]

In many cases, however, the initial information about a man's fate came in the form of a letter from a comrade or the commanding officer of the unit in which he served. The widow of Private Samuel Currier, East Surreys, who died of wounds during the Battle of the Somme, received this brief note from a comrade:

I think it best that I should let you know that unfortunately Pte S. C. Currier no 2289 9th East Surreys died of wounds on August 16th. He gave me the address and asked me to let you know. We did our best for him under the conditions. H. Marvin no 16248 A Coy 8th Queens Regt. B.E.F. France.[29]

Currier's family did not receive official notification for another three weeks.

On occasion a relative would pick up the name of a loved one in the published casualty lists. These were supposed to be issued to the press only after the next of kin had been informed, but this was not always the case. In November 1914, Herbert Vacher wrote to the War Office after having spotted the name of his son George in the lists published by *The Times*: 'Sir, amongst the names of killed published in the papers yesterday, I find the name of my son G M Vacher, 2nd Lt Royal Warwickshire Regiment. As that is the first intimation of his fatality, may I ask for an official notification as confirmation thereof.'[30] As Richard van Emden remarks: 'The letter is remarkably controlled, considering the shock of his seeing his son's name must have been severe.'[31]

The news could be received during a visit by a comrade of the deceased. When young 'Pozzie' Gibson was killed, his sergeant visited Gibson's mother in the poorest part of Hunslet to break the news to her: '"I've lost my only boy," was all she had the power to say, and spoke no more, mute with grief.'[32]

Spolyar called weeping 'normal and necessary'. Juliet Nicolson describes how 'On the calmest days, most settled sort of day, there is no predicting when a rogue wave in the shape of a snatch of music, a familiar phrase, even a shared joke, might suddenly roll in and threaten to topple you.'[33] Vera Brittain had a flashback of Roland who had recently died of wounds in late 1915: 'suddenly to the perturbation of the shop assistants, I burst into tears, and find myself helpless and humiliated, unable to stop crying in the tram all the way back to the hospital.'[34] On occasion the widow or mother might become anxious or depressed. As these states were normally only observable by other members of the family, there is little evidence in the archives.[35]

It was not uncommon to feel anger; and for widows to direct this feeling towards the War Office and its bureaucracy, claiming, unfairly, that the Office was unhelpful and hiding information from them.[36] Miss Britain however seems to have borne no malice toward the authorities, although she developed a deep hostility to war itself as the result of her experiences. The novelist Irene Rathbone raged against the supporters of the war, asking a very good question: 'What was the purpose of winning the war ... if none of the men who won it were to live?'[37]

Social networks

Families and friends gathered round after the telegram arrived. Naturally they tried to be supportive and positive, encouraging the next of kin to be optimistic about their 'boy's' fate. This was a natural desire, but on occasion it gave a sense of false optimism to the bereaved. For many of the bereaved there grew up an informal support network offering support and advice. Lady Violet Cecil's son George went missing during the first few weeks of the war. Like the slightly less grand Hazel Macnaghten, whose husband died at about the same time, she used a network of relations, friends, neighbours and contacts with social equals in Britain and, indeed, across Europe in her attempts to trace her son.[38] Mrs Macnaghten wrote to people in Germany, Sweden and the Netherlands. One contact in Germany, General von Viebahn, expressed his sympathy, was pessimistic, and then wrote a long tirade against England, followed by a eulogy of the Kaiser.[39]

Most relatives of the missing did not have such august contacts. Private Ernest Blackburn's lower-middle class family from Bradford relied on the tenacity of Ernest's brother to gather news. By the middle of the war, there were rather fewer contacts available, although that information which was available was more readily accessible.[40]

Like Mrs Macnaghten, Lady Violet's family and friends encouraged her to leave no stone unturned in the search for her son, despite the advice given by George's commanding officer that 'there was no longer any doubt that he was dead.' Her family and friends urged her to follow up all rumours and not assume the worst: he might yet be a prisoner. George's body was soon found in a mass grave near the French village of Villers Cotterets. He was identified by his buttons with the regimental crest, his large boots and body, and the initials GEC on his vest.[41] There followed a dignified funeral for him and his fellow officers, and there was a grave which she could visit once peace returned. Unfortunately, the body of Lieutenant Angus Macnaghten was never found. This tragedy led his widow on an increasingly fruitless search for information which lasted several decades.

In the months after George was buried, Lady Violet became very close to Lady Constance Manners, whose own son, John, had also been killed. They found it invaluable to share their grief with each other in letters and by meeting. Each understood what the other was feeling.[42]

Unusually Lady Violet sought to help the widows and mothers of the other ranks who had died along with her son. She wrote to them explaining what she thought had happened to them. Because the War Office had either not informed them that their 'boy' had been killed, or provided very little information, the relatives were always very grateful for the news. And the personal tragedies that their replies reveal show how badly the wives and families of ordinary soldiers were treated. Elizabeth Wallace, for example, wrote from the Liverpool Royal Infirmary: 'My trouble was twofold as I lost my eldest girl and the father inside ten months, and my baby was only nine months the day he [her husband] was killed so it quite broke my health up.' And Eveline Meadows was overwhelmed by relief: 'I could not get to know whether my husband died from disease or wounds. I have sent to the [War] Office twice.' Above each of the bereaved families were thankful to learn that their sons and husbands had been identified and given a dignified burial. They were no longer missing[43]

It wasn't always the nearest and dearest complete strangers might get in touch offering or seeking reassurance. Hazel Macnaghten was contacted by Lettice Foster, the daughter of the Vicar of Groombridge in Sussex, who offered advice about how she traced her brother who was killed at the same time as Angus. Miss Foster apologised that 'this letter is rather involved, but I do hope it will help you find something. We well know the awful anxiety and suspense and can sympathise with you most truly.'[44] Mrs Blackburn, whose husband Ernest had been posted missing in September 1916, was contacted by a Mrs Lilly Dawes of Scarborough, whose husband had also gone missing at the same time. Mrs Dawes was reaching out to somebody whom she thought was in the same position she was: 'I haven't heard any more [from the War Office] and the suspense is becoming more than I can bear. You will quite understand as you are fixed the same. I have been hoping against hope that my husband might be a prisoner of war.'[45]

Families would contact the comrades of the missing man in the hope of finding additional information. For some this correspondence was a way of maintaining a link with the disappeared: to get to know somebody who lived and worked with their son or husband in their last minutes.

Most men when approached were happy to try to help, although often they had little idea of what happened to the missing man. They empathised with the anguish that the writer was suffering. Miss L. C. Hodges, the sister of Captain Harold Hodges, Monmouthshire Regiment, wrote to Corporal John Davies VC in January 1919 seeking information about her brother who had been in the same action in which Davies had been taken prisoner in March 1918: 'It will be a great relief to my father and mother and the rest of the family.'[46]

Hodges' disappearance was unusual because the circumstances of his death remained a mystery for a number of months. Matters became clearer in an official list sent to the War Office by the

German authorities through the Red Cross in Geneva in October 1918: 'Rodges H A Capt2/Monmouths. Forwarded by Reserve Field Hospital. The disc forwarded by the S I (Central Office for effects) without further details 5.7.18.'

In writing to Hodges' family, the War Office noted that: 'Although the first letter of the surname is different, there is no doubt that the report refers to the officer.'[47]

This did not stop the family from trying to find out more about his last hours. Corporal Davies seems to have known the Captain and perhaps saw him fall during the desperate rearguard action on 23 and 24 March 1918. another member of the family wrote:

> Your letter has been an <u>unspeakable</u> comfort and will be one of my greatest treasures. To hear anything of our dear one is such a comfort. Knowing him, you will understand how we miss him, can't you?.I know you have been a <u>great</u> help and comfort to me. I hope we shall be able to thank you in person some day.[48]

The urge to find out more

After receiving the news there would have been 'a deep-set craving for details of the situation. Any information about the circumstances is anxiously desired, received and considered.'[49] From their friends and colleagues Vera Brittain received a great deal of information about Roland and Edward. With the help of the local vicar, Eliza Booth, whose husband Norman was posted missing in November 1916. contacted the Red Cross. Through their Wounded and Missing Enquiries Bureau she eventually received a letter from a former policeman from Huddersfield who had been serving in the same regiment. He said that he had seen Norman being loaded onto an ambulance which had never reached the hospital. It was assumed that it had been blown up en route. Despite the lack of absolute clarity, the explanation seems to have satisfied Mrs Booth and presumably gave her some closure.⁵⁰ And when Frances Rothe received eyewitness accounts of the death of her husband Lieutenant Sidney Orme Rothe via the War Office it provided enough information for her to accept his death.⁵¹

As we will see, the British Red Cross and smaller charities aimed to provide this information with greater or lesser success.

Acceptance, or refusal

The fact that there no body had been found let alone a funeral service meant that there could never be full closure. The Cenotaph and other memorials, built after the War ended, could only be surrogates. Peace of a kind had to be found in other ways. Families might have to accept the evidence from eyewitness accounts, however contradictory, of a man's death. Or more often the War Office wrote to the family indicating that for 'official purposes' their boy had died on such and such a date. For a few, the fact that their boy did not return from a Prisoner of War Camp must have been a final bitter blow.

Despite the telegram from the War Office, letters from comrades, and the evidence of witnesses gathered by the Red Cross's Wounded and Missing Enquiry Unit, a small number of women were unable to accept their husband's or son's death. It drove them almost mad. After receiving the third of four Red Cross notifications in October 1918, Mrs Joan Harbour still denied that her husband Corporal Ernest Harbour, Australian Imperial Force, had been killed: 'I have such a feeling that my husband is not dead. No one saw him buried, they did not get his body.'⁵² The Red Cross tried to explain, without success: 'Although there is no direct evidence of your husband's burial [a witness] wrote that he died before a stretcher bearer reached him… Attempts later made to recover his body were unsuccessful as the enemy opened fire with machine guns.'⁵³

Hazel Macnaghten never really accepted her husband's death in October 1914. Her son later wrote: 'For many years after the end of the war, whenever there was a newspaper report of a missing soldier turning up having suffered from loss of memory her hopes would be raised.'[54] In June 1931, a friend called Enid mentioned in a letter that in 1922, while working for the Graves Commission: 'at an unknown station in Serbia, or one of those countries between Bulgaria and Trieste I thought I had a fleeting glance of dear old Angus.' Although Enid admitted that she had been in a 'dazed condition' as the result of her work and it was very unlikely that she had actually seen the missing man, her admission according to Macnaghten's son revealed 'the agony of mind that my mother suffered at the time'. There followed a flurry of letters to sympathetic officials at the Foreign Office and the authorities across Europe, although no new information came to light.[55]

In 1923, Mrs A. M. Tennant of Heston corresponded with the Foreign Office about the possibility that her son Private Alan John Tennant, London Scottish, was among a group of very unfortunate prisoners of war who were being returned to Germany from Siberia. Her reasoning was that his unit had subsequently served there after his death. The Russian authorities reassured Whitehall that this was not the case. She had long refused to accept her son's death, circulating posters about him to YMCA huts and elsewhere offering £50 reward for finding him (and £5 for any information about his fate). The authorities were quite clear that Private Tennant had been killed during the Battle of Cambrai and he is commemorated on the memorial to the missing at Louverval.[56] In 1926 she again wrote to the Foreign Office following a press story about British deserters from the French Foreign Legion. A German private detective had assured her that 'many British soldiers who escaped into France, shell-shocked and confused, were induced to join the French Foreign Legion.'[57]

Like a number of other well-to-do families, the parents of Lieutenant Henry Isaacs, Suffolk Regiment, spent a considerable amount of time and money trying to find where he was buried, although the grave seems to have been destroyed in subsequent fighting. Failing to identify him, they bought three-quarters of the acre where Henry had fallen and moved permanently to Arras 'so they could visit their son as often as they wished'. Only the arrival of the German Army in May 1940 forced them to return to Britain.[58]

A number of widows regularly placed memorial notices in the classified advertisement of *The Times* on the death of their husbands. Every 29 September for 42 years after the death of her husband Major William Claude Ash, Middlesex Regiment, from wounds, his widow Edith placed a few lines of verse in the newspaper, which reflected her glacially slow acceptance of William's passing.[59]

Some widows suffered a sense of guilt that for some reason they did not do right by their husband. 'She may accuse herself of negligence and exaggerate minor situations which can increase the guilty feelings.' Rudyard Kipling never forgave himself for the encouragement he gave, and the strings he pulled to get his short-sighted son sent to the battle that saw John's death within days of his arrival.[60]

When he received the news of his son's death the Reverend Miller and his family was about to leave for a new parish. On 30 September, he confided to his diary: 'Left Hornchurch with a sad heart, today I don't seem to care for anything, if only I knew my boy was alive how different it would be! I don't know how I shall manage to get through tomorrow.'[61]

Support in grief
Bereaved families across Britain received no support at all from the state in their time of need, which often made things worse for widows and parents. This was not the case in other countries. In France, for example, the bad news was often delivered by the village mayor or his deputy. Indeed, in

Paris special employees of the municipality, dressed in black, or widows chosen for their tactfulness were sent to grieving households to express patriotic condolences. They were asked to make enquires of concierges and neighbours before visiting the families concerned.[62] In Australia the news was delivered by a local clergyman.[63] Both mayors and ministers could offer condolences on behalf of the state and provide practical advice about what to do next.

In Britain, unfortunately, the next of kin formally only received a telegram (normally sent to officers' families) or letter (other ranks) curtly informing the recipient of their man's fate. It gave no more than the barest of details. Information about Second Lieutenant Sydney Rothe, Middlesex Regiment, was telegraphed to his wife on 18 November 1916, informing her husband 'is reportedly wounded and missing Nov 13. Any further news if received sent immediately'.[64] The message could not have been more calculated to raise questions in the mind of the recipient; questions that could not easily be answered: Has he survived? Or has he died or been captured by the enemy? How was he killed, and where is he buried? What were the wounds and how serious are they? Only the last sentence offered any form of hope.

It was the responsibility of the regimental record office to contact the relatives of NCOs and soldiers who were missing, wounded or killed in action. In the case of Rifleman Ernest Blackburn, the assistant regimental paymaster for the King's Royal Rifle Corps just sent a form to Blackburn's family briefly indicating that he had been reported missing, adding: 'The separation allowance and allotment now being issued to you will continue to be issuable to you for a period of 30 weeks from the above date.'[65] This stark and distressing form, which was widely used, must have caused great anguish to the recipients.

Today it is rather different, two senior non-commissioned officers break the news to the serviceman or woman's family at home. Helena Tym remembers how they came to tell her about the death of her son Cyrus:

> I'll never forget that man's face. What a shitty job telling people that they've just lost a son, thousands of miles away from home in a dusty land we'll never visit or even care about. What were the details, when would we know? All sound was muffled. All I could see was my ruined family, and feel a blind panic. Nothing will ever be the same again, oh God. They were so sad, these two men, with pain behind their eyes. They referred to their notes, unable to make eye contact. How do you tell people such awful news and it not kill some part of you. After they left – I don't know how long they stayed – the glue descended. I think we were given a name, someone who would come and see us, look after us, guide us.[66]

During and after the First World War, support, such as it was, came from family and friends, and possibly a charity worker from the regimental association or the Soldiers' and Sailors' Family Association. Many people were unwilling to approach charities because of their deserved reputation for patronising and high-handed upper-class volunteers. D. Allan Hay, secretary of the Association's Glasgow branch, told the Annual Meeting in September 1917:

> For the most part our workers in different parts of the country have been representatives of what I may call the better off classes. We all know the amount of suspicion and distrust which was working in the minds of the great industrial population before the outbreak of war. But they realised when this Association spread its network intensively through the country that it was in no spirit of patronage that the voluntary workers of the Association defied their enemies to safeguard the homes of soldiers' wives and dependants who in countless thousands of cases found in

our workers real friends, real encouragement in time of anxiety, financial difficulties and worry.[67]

Although they meant well, their advice was generally of little value, except in the purely practical matters of sorting out pensions and allowances.

Certainly, Mrs Macnaghten's agonies over the disappearance of her husband Angus near Ypres were undoubtedly made worse by letters from relatives and comrades of her husband, who assured her that he was still alive. Macnaghten's fellow officers reassured her that he was alright. A postcard marked 'urgent' and dated 30 October from Captain Victor Fortune, the battalion adjutant, reads: 'Angus was captured yesterday, but is quite safe and from questioning a fellow who escaped they were v. kind to him so no need to worry.' Captain Guy Hamilton also sent a card: 'He is captured I know and I hope unwounded. But there is a possibility he was hit in the leg, which would not be serious... He is safer now than he was before.'[68] On receiving the postcard Mrs Macnaghten wrote to her aunt that she was 'so *utterly* thankful'.[69] A month later another officer, Ian Colquhoun, wrote encouragingly: 'I am certain he must be alright. I saw some of the regiment today and they were quite hopeful about him.'[70] Captain Macnaghten's sister Lettice contacted her sister-in-law after interviewing a survivor of the attack in which Angus had been killed: 'It was perfectly awful hearing all the man said, but both Wilcox [the housekeeper] and I are rather disinclined to believe him... He actually said he had seen a grave at La Ferté with A's name upon it, dated Nov 5th. I *absolutely refuse* to believe it.'[71]

Today, families of service personnel killed in action are in contact with trained counsellors to help them come to terms with their loss. Mrs Tym was assigned Warrant Officer Ian Tindall, a man with decades of service in the British Army and senior enough to be able to make things happen: 'He has been our source of information throughout this awful journey, the bearer of both good and bad news, utterly reliable and compassionate, making this whole process as smooth and painless as he can.'[72]

Then the widow or mother had to deal with matters that she might barely understand, but were increasingly important in dealing with a soldier's death in wartime. As Thomas Laqueur suggests: 'This ... modern Charon of a bureaucracy ferried men from the world of the living to the world of the dead.'[73] This could be very confusing for families unused to completing even the simplest form.[74] It was not always straightforward to make head or tail of the paperwork that had to be completed in order to get a pension or sort out allowances and, inevitably, it was easy to make mistakes. The family had might have to submit claims and where appropriate arrange probate and negotiate with the War Office for the return of a man's possessions.

By 1914, Britain was a fully literate society. This literacy gave families some confidence to be able to enter into a dialogue with the authorities about the disappearance of their sons and husbands and also to uncover other information about how and why their men had vanished. Naturally there was a gap between those who had regular dealings with bureaucracy and those whose communications lay largely within the family. In the Australian Red Cross Society Wounded and Missing Enquiry Bureau file about Private Frank Vasey, for example, there is a gulf between the hesitant way in which Vasey's mother approached the Bureau for information about her missing son and the formal, rather brisk letter written by her brother E. J. Woods, who worked in the Engineer's Office of the London and North Western Railway about his nephew. Pleasingly, however, Woods got a fairly blunt brush-off from the Bureau, while Mrs Vasey received a number of helpful replies from Vera Deacon and her staff at the Bureau.[75]

Letters such as the ones from Mrs Vasey often spell out the personal circumstance of the correspondent to earn the sympathy of the officials to whom they have written. Widows will mention their marital status, while mothers and wives stress their connection with the missing. They all indicate whether other family members are in the forces.

Regimental offices dealt with preliminary issues (notification of death, burial details, continuation of separation allowance) while the Ministry of Pensions (Widows and Dependents Branch) in London dealt with pension claims. Details of the soldier's will and the consequent distribution of back pay, allowances and gratuities to the beneficiaries were the responsibility of the War Office.[76]

Matters were of course complicated because for the families of the missing because there was no absolute certainty that the man was dead. It was agreed that the separation allowance would continue for 26 weeks from the official notice that a man was missing and then if no further news had been received altering the position, then a pension would be paid to the mother or widow. It might take more than six months for a man to be declared deceased 'for official purposes', often because the individual had in effect been forgotten by the War Office. Occasionally, the separation allowance might continue to be paid for years after a man's decease. In January 1921, the Ministry discussed the case of Private W. A. H. Ruel, Yorkshire Regiment, who had been reported a prisoner of war on 27 May 1918 and subsequently to have died in August 1918. His death was finally confirmed in a letter to Mrs Ruel in February 1920, but a year later her allowance was still being paid. It was agreed to move her across to a pension and say nothing more about the matter. Subsequent correspondence revealed that there were several hundred similar cases.[77]

The initial letter indicated the amount of separation allowance to be paid, the date it ended and the amount of pension to be paid thereafter. But at a time of shock, inevitably this was a lot for the family to take in. Virginia Wyndham, who was a Pensions official in Gloucestershire, wrote to her brother in February 1916:

... the work doesn't get any easier. I have responsibility for an entire district with about 1000 cases, though of course the number increases every day on account of the men who have fallen. The saddest part is when a man is reported missing, as they could of course be only wounded and in a hospital somewhere, or a prisoner, but until they get the B104-82 form confirming they are killed there is nothing we can do to help. Everything is about having the right form. One knows as they stand in the queue if they have lost someone. They stare ahead and avoid talking to anyone and when they reach the counter they just hand over the form. When I began I wanted to be kind and ask is this your father, your son, your brother, your husband. But we are so busy and after a time one becomes quite detached, rather like the form itself. It is so formal and seems so heartless when a man has bravely made the ultimate sacrifice.[78]

5

INFORMING THE RELATIVES

> Once these were men who, having marched where they were ordered, and having done what commanded, after endurance and suffering, fell, and were lost.
>
> Henry Williamson, *The Wet Flanders Plain* (Faber, 1929)[1]

The grief of the relatives was one thing, but the official reaction to a man going missing was rather different. Max Pemberton attempted to reassure his readers that the War Office and the Army as a whole was doing its absolute best to trace missing men. He summarised the processes that were gone though in order to locate an individual soldier:

> In the first place, let it be understood that no such report is made until the officer commanding has made exhaustive inquiries on his own account. The lad went over; was seen in the fight; he did not return. In many cases some soldier who was near him can give a fairly true account of what happened. He saw the poor fellow struck by a shell; he is sure he is dead. Or, again, the man fell and did not rise—or he may have been plainly cut off from his party, and is obviously in the hands of the Germans.[2]

Passing the word back

After each battle or trench raid there would be a roll call, Frederick Manning in his novel *The Middle Parts of Fortune* recreates one such roll call after the Battle of the Somme:

> 'Redmain' was the name called out and at first there was no reply. It was repeated. 'Has anyone seen anything of Redmain?' 'Yes sir,' cried Pike, with sullen anger in his voice. 'The poor bastard's dead, sir.' 'Are you sure of that, Pike?' Captain Malet asked quietly, ignoring everything but the question of fact. 'Are you sure that the man you saw was Redmain?' 'I saw him, sir. 'e was just blown to blazes, 'e was a chum o' mine, an' I seen 'im just blown to blazes.' Then, with a temporary roll established the men returned to camp.[3]

Geoffrey Malins, the director of the film *Battle of the Somme*, described a battalion which had returned from the frontline on 1 July: '... in one little space there was just two thin lines – all that was left of a glorious regiment (barely one hundred men). The sergeant stood there with a notebook resting on the end of his rifle, repeatedly putting his pencil through names that were missing.'[4]

It was not always clear, at least initially, who had been killed and who was missing, presumed killed. Captain Kenelm Digby, the adjutant of the Coldstream Guards battalion in which Lieutenant Hugh Williamson served, confessed to Williamson's parents that for three days after the action in which the officer lost his life, he really did not know 'whether to report [Williamson] as "Missing" or "Killed"'. He had similar problems with another officer and nearly sixty men, none of whom had been confirmed dead.[5] The battalion war diary, written by Digby, graphically describes the bitter and chaotic nature of the attack on the enemy's lines, in which fourteen officers (out of seventeen) and 469 other ranks (out of 690) were killed, so it is little surprise that there was much confusion about the casualties.[6]

Many men initially thought as being missing had actually been wounded and ended up in casualty clearing stations and were eventually transferred to hospitals behind the front line. It was also common enough for soldiers to be separated from their units and who would eventually find their way home. Max Pemberton reassured his readers:

> Nothing is more surprising than the way in which a wounded man will drift sometimes away from his unit. He may hardly know what he is doing at the time, may crawl from crater to crater, lie there for hours, and then sleep the sleep of utter exhaustion. In the end some roving ambulance may pick him up, and he will be carried to a base where some days may pass before he is discovered.[7]

This of course would please the soldier's comrades, as Alfred Burrage remembered his feelings when his pal Dave rejoined his unit after having been posted missing:

> Of course, I am delighted beyond words, but in some odd way I am a little cross with him. I am conscious of having wasted a lot of emotion on the old devil, and I have now got used to the idea of his being dead… He is the only 'Missing, believed killed' who has turned up again. So, glad as I am, I can't help feeling that he might have had the decency to remain dead… he has just arrived in the nick of time to save me from posting a letter to his father, saying that he died quite painlessly and quoting some very noble 'last words' which I had invented for the occasion.[8]

If circumstances permitted, search parties might be sent out into No Man's Land looking for missing men. Occasionally they might find a wounded man, but all too often the men had already been absorbed into the mud. Corporal J R Mercer, East

Lancashires, wrote to the family of one of his men, Private Frederick Wells, who had gone missing in a trench raid on 25 October 1916:

> We called the roll soon after and found we had four men and the officer missing. The officer came in next day, he having been lost near the German trenches. The following night, another man and myself went out to try and find the missing men, but it was of no avail. We found one, and he was a Liverpool man, who had been shot through the head. We buried him in a soldier's grave. We could not see any sign of your son and the other men.[9]

It was not uncommon for men to be awarded gallantry medals for searching for missing men. In September 1917, Sergeant A Gibson, Highland Light Infantry, for example, received the Distinguished Conduct Medal:

> For conspicuous gallantry and devotion to duty during a raid upon enemy trenches ... afterwards going voluntarily into No Man's Land to search for missing men. He went right back into the enemy trenches whilst the bombardment was still going on, setting a magnificent example of fearlessness and great devotion to duty.[10]

The War Office

Responsibility for the keeping of casualty records was shared by War Office, which was responsible for officers, and regimental record offices, which dealt with non-commissioned officers and privates. This looked simple on paper and it was how the War Office had traditionally operated in wartime. However, it was a recipe for disaster when record offices had to deal with hundreds of thousands of men, who were always being transferred between regiments, becoming casualties or, more happily, being commissioned. It was inevitable that the War Office soon became the dominant partner in the relationship, probably to the relief of the always under-staffed regimental record offices.

Details of casualties arrived at Horse Guards Parade who then passed the information to the appropriate regiment, as well as to the press and other interested bodies. Enquiries from the public naturally tended to be directed to the War Office as few people knew to whom to write. The Red Cross and other agencies also preferred to deal directly with Whitehall. It is little wonder that the post-war review of the War Office's Casualty Branch recommended that everything be centralised within the department.[11]

The main Casualty Branch (CS.2) grew from 'nine men and a boy' in August 1914 to perhaps 1500 clerks, supervisors and managers by the end of 1918. Seven hundred clerks just maintained the card index, while hundreds more engaged in correspondence with the public, the Army in France, compiling the casualty lists, and other duties too numerous to mention.[12]

A separate Casualty Branch (MS.3 Cas Officers) just for officers opened on 12 August 1914 with two retired officers, Captain Stanton, who dealt with correspondence and interviews, and Major Stewart who despatched notifications to the next of kin. In addition, there were two ex-soldier clerks who checked lists, raised cards and circulated reports of deaths.[13] Again, it experienced massive growth over the following four years. By the Armistice roughly a hundred clerks, three-quarters of whom were women – were serving in the officers' branch. Initially, many of the staff were wives of officers who volunteered their services. Again, much of their work involved the preparation and circulation of casualty lists and dealing with enquiries with the families of officer casualties. Colonel Capper, who took over command of the branch in 1917, thought that two-thirds of the 900,0000 entries on officers' cards referred to correspondence with the next of kin. Although officers were supposed to provide

Informing the Relatives

details of next of kin, not all did, while others 'gave a friend or a lady of the heart'.[14]

The first communication to the next of kin was supposed to come from the War Office. On the receipt of the information about a man being killed, wounded or being posted missing King's Regulations stated that a telegram (for officers) or letter (other ranks) was to be sent to the next of kin.[15]

In *Mr Britling Sees it Through*, H. G. Wells describes how the novel's hero receives the telegram notifying him of his son Hugh's death:

> He opened the telegram hoping as he had hoped when he opened any telegram since Hugh had gone to the front that it would not contain the exact words he read; that it would say wounded, that at worst it would say 'missing', that perhaps it might even tell of some pleasant surprise, a brief return to home as the last letter had foreshadowed. He read the final, unqualified statement, the terse regrets. He stood still for a moment or so staring at the words.[16]

In working class Wishaw, Mary Morton's mother received a telegram. Her neighbours gathered around:

> They sensed it was bad. Often telegrams were sent to wives to let them know their men were coming home. Then everybody laughed and joked, but not this time. Expectantly they crowded round. Kirsty lifted the yellow paper and read out in her rich Irish voice, these words 'We regret to inform you that Sergeant George Morton has been reported missing, believed killed in Arras, France on or about 20th February 1916. Further information will be forwarded by letter.' There were gasps and sighs from the women. Mama broke into fresh sobbing saying, 'What is going to happen to us, why him?'[17]

Some mothers thought they had a special bond with their son. They felt that they would know instinctively if something had happened to him. Lady Violet Cecil, whose son was killed on 1 September 1914, noted in her diary for that day '7am rifle fire'. On both 4 and 5 September – before the news of his disappearance reached her – she reported 'bad fainting fits', which left her unable to stand all day. And on the 5th, after receiving the news that George had been wounded in the head and missing: 'my darling, darling boy – I see him all the time with some terrible irreparable injury in his beautiful face and suffering – suffering.' But even she admitted a few weeks later: 'To think that he should have been dead nearly three weeks and I not know it.'[18]

If it a soldier was notified as being missing, there was always hope that he was still alive. This hope – however remote it was in reality – sustained many a family. Perhaps the dear boy had fallen into German hands. But in the weeks and months that followed the telegram, the uncertainty about a loved one's fate could cause great stress and anguish. However traumatic, the formal notification of a loved one's death was at least clear. The man had died and had been buried with the appropriate funeral rites. For the widows and mothers of the missing there could be none of this. It is no wonder that so many sought more definitive news of their sons and husbands and fantasised that he had been mislaid by the Army somewhere and would one day just turn up. As H. G. Wells writes in *Mr Britling Sees it Through*: 'Missing's a queer thing. It isn't tragic or pitiful. Or partly reassuring like "Prisoner". It just sends one speculating and speculating.'[19]

The blunt nature of the official communication inevitably led to demands for further information. Mr Britling's secretary Teddy is posted 'missing and wounded'. Teddy's wife Letty telegraphed the War Office seeking more information about her husband's wounds: 'At any rate,' she said, 'they could have answered my telegram promptly. I sent it at eight. Two hours of scornful silence.'[20]

The War Office was ill-equipped to deal with such correspondence. No figures survive about the numbers of enquiries, but they were certainly in their high hundreds of thousands. It was estimated that on average each card maintained by the Officers' Casualty Branch contained details of two or three items of correspondence.[21] Occasionally, families supplied information of which the War Office was unaware, usually when they had received a field postcard from their son or husband indicating that they had arrived in a prisoner of war camp, and no official notification from the Germans had yet been received.

In most cases the War Office was unable to able to help further. Often because they had only received very basic information from the frontline. Michael Durey suggests that the 'official military response to relatives of the missing was based on a rigid bureaucratic policy that did not avoid expressing a heart-breaking realism when necessary, but could also show some flexibility and sympathy.'[22] Reading the officers' personal files at The National Archives one has a sense that the clerks in the Casualty Branch did their best to answer letters from relatives patiently and as honestly as possible. In most cases they were only able to point out the obvious – that they either had no further information – or gently suggest that all the evidence suggested that the dear one had been killed.

A typical case was that of Second Lieutenant Sidney Orme Rothe. In one of the last actions of the Battle of the Somme his battalion was ordered over the top near Serre Road. Three officers and fifteen other ranks were killed, and eight officers and 133 men were reported missing: Rothe's body was one of those which were never found.[23] Over the months following his death the War Office conducted a courteous correspondence with his widow Frances.[24] For well over a year Mrs Rothe refused to accept that her husband's disappearance meant that in all probability he had been killed. On 2 February 1917 she wrote asking for contact details of Sergeants Jennings and Blair from her husband's platoon, who were also wounded on 13 November 1916: 'I am hoping that they have some information...' At the end of the month, she sought the name of the battalion medical officer whom she planned to contact about her husband's death.

On 4 March the War Office wrote to her that: '...no further information has been received since he was reported missing ... and his name has not appeared on any German list yet received.' Mrs Rothe continued to seek information about her husband's fate by other means. The Red Cross found a possible witness to her husband's last minutes. Lance Corporal T. H. Tucker told a Red Cross searcher on 10 April:

> 2nd Lt Rothe was in charge of my platoon... He went over with us at Serre on November 13th and got hit close up at the German wire. The stretcher bearers saw him there and spoke about it to me when we were in rest. They couldn't get near enough to the wire to bring down stretcher cases, and they said that the Germans were coming out and taking in our cases.

Unusually, the War Office dismissed Tucker's statement. On 18 September they pointed out that he had: 'no personal knowledge of the fate of this officer. The particulars he mentions are not considered of a sufficiently definite nature on which to base a special enquiry.'

On 8 August she wrote to the War Office:

> I have had a report from the Red Cross that my husband was wounded close up to the German wire and the Germans were seen to be taking in our cases. In these circumstances it seems to me, more than probably, that my husband is an unreported prisoner of war... I feel sure that there are ways and means by which you could extract information from the German government about my husband, who undoubtedly fell into their hands, and whether he is alive or dead, it would be some comfort to know the truth.

The War Office replied five days later they 'have no ground for believing that an officer could be a Prisoner of War for so long a period without news of him being received... I am to say that this officer was originally reported wounded and missing 13th November 1916, and later this report was confirmed.'

Almost a year after husband's death Mrs Rothe wrote again to the War Office on 25 October:

> I have heard from one of the men of my husband's platoon, now a Prisoner in Germany, that he last saw my husband lying wounded on the field by machine gun fire... I understand that two special search parties, in addition to the ordinary burying parties, went out on that night to search for my husband and did not find any trace of him. Under these circumstances taking into consideration that the objective which they failed to take on that day was taken on the next day, something would have been found of him, had he died of his wounds.

On 14 November 1917, almost a year to the day after the disappearance, the War Office wrote to Mrs Rothe enclosing a witness statement from Private W. Taylor who had become a prisoner of war on 19 April 1917 and presumably had responded to an appeal circulated by the International Committee of the Red Cross: 'Lt Rothe was in charge of my company during the attack on the 13rd Nov. When about ½ mile from the village he dropped saying he had two bullets in the chest. He died about 5 mins afterwards.'

This was the confirmation that Mrs Rothe needed to finally accept her husband's death, although she queried the delay in sending Taylor's statement and, in an attempt to save face, requested: '... that a systematic search is made of the graves in the Serre cemeteries and let me know whether my husband's grave has been registered there or in any cemetery in the neighbourhood.'

War Office staff were always stretched and as the fighting was several hundred or even several thousand miles away, it was next to impossible to discover much more about the fate of individual officers and men. By the middle of 1917, the families of the missing were sent a two-page leaflet, *Missing Officers and Men*, explaining in simple terms the steps being taken to trace their boy. The War Office stressed that '... an endeavour is being made to cover broadly the whole field of possible witnesses of the missing soldier's fate and if he unfortunately met his death upon the battlefield to place his relatives in possession of definite information upon the subject.'[25]

The letter to the families of ordinary soldiers had also been amended to read more positively:

> The report that he is missing does not necessarily mean that he has been killed, as he may be a prisoner of war or temporarily separated from his regiment. Official reports that men are prisoners of war take some time to reach this country and [for men] captured by the enemy it is probably that unofficial news will reach you first.[26]

This must have reduced the number of enquiries received by the authorities.

In addition, a number of newspaper articles were placed in the press in the hope of placating relatives. In general and encouraging terms they described the processes being taken to find the men by the War Office and Red Cross, both on the battlefield and in the prisoner of war camps, and also stressed the possibility of a man's survival, even though no information had yet been received.[27] Although done for the best of reasons, this would come back to haunt the authorities after the Armistice.

It was not so easy when you received the letter or telegram indicating that your boy was missing. Did this mean he was still alive and, if so, where was he? Of course, in perhaps three-quarters of cases 'missing' was in effect code for 'we cannot locate the body', but their families at home could not know this. It was impossible to tell families the truth, even if the bureaucracy was able to explain what had happened to their loved ones.[28] Stephen Graham, who was serving with the Guards on the Western Front in 1918, wrote that he 'formed the opinion, which was afterwards completely confirmed, that "missing" very often meant *dead and unburied*, and that an unburied British soldier if he belonged to a unit which had passed on was almost inevitably reported "missing".'[29]

If further information reached Whitehall, the next of kin would eventually be contacted again. Generally, this was a letter confirming that a body had been located and buried or, more often, that a period of six months for officers or longer had passed since the man had gone missing and as there had been no further news it was now presumed for 'official reasons' that he had died, although the body had yet to be found.[30] But it might be several years before the Army Council finally concluded that the soldier was indeed dead.

In April 1919, well over a year since her husband was posted missing, the War Office wrote to Mrs Stephenson, the wife of Sergeant Edward Stephenson, Machine Gun Corps: '... it is regretted that no further information has been received in this Office and that he has not been traced as a Prisoner of War. Under these circumstances and in the view of the lapse of time, it is feared that the chance that he may be still alive, is now very small.'[31]

Two months later Mrs Stephenson received a curt form from the Machine Gun Corps Record Office informing her that the 'Army Council have been regretfully constrained to conclude that he is dead...'[32]

The six-month period was settled on after pressure from solicitors who needed to sort out deceased clients' legal affairs and life insurance companies wishing to pay out on policies.[33] It also fitted in well with the payment of widows' pensions and other allowances, which were arranged in six-monthly cycles.[34]

And it allowed a formal death certificate to be issued and the payment of any back pay, gratuities or other allowances due to the deceased.

The letter must have also given closure to most families that the authorities had done all they could to trace their relative and that their loved one had died on the battlefield. In *Mr Britling Sees it Through* Teddy's wife Letty: '... went about the village in a coloured dress bearing herself confidently. Teddy had been listed now as "missing, since reported killed", and she had had two letters from his comrades.' This was a public display: in her heart Letty remained convinced that her husband was still alive: '"Presently, we will see his name in a list of prisoners," she said, "He is a wounded prisoner in Germany."'[35]

As well as writing, it was possible to call at the War Office to seek information. Colonel William Capper recommended that the individual dealing with the enquirer be an officer of rank: 'It means everything when interviewing members of the public. The public is very touchy. It dislikes civilians and does not think kindly much of junior officers, but will take anything from senior officers and go away without a grievance after being interviewed by a colonel.'[36]

Early in the war, Lady Isabella St John had not heard from her son for a few weeks. Nor had she heard from the War Office and was determined to find out what happened: 'Any actual knowledge, I thought, would be easier to bear that my present anguish of uncertainty.' She decided to visit the War Office one Sunday evening. On arrival she was amazed at how busy the Office was. On being directed to the Officers' Casualty Inquiry Office she found 'a bare and desolate room' with a single official 'whose business it was to attend to questions such as mine'. He was 'patient but, oh, so painfully slow,' searching through 'the great folio in which were recorded the names of those killed or wounded in recent battles'. As the official went through the casualty lists, Lady Isabella began to fret:

> For where, or what, is my soldier now? Wounded? Missing? Dead? Wounded, certainly, missing certainly, since unidentifiable at the War Office, dead? Ah I had still to learn. To no better purpose than this had been all the strenuous struggle of his young life? For this had I brought my son into the world? That ... he should now be missing, dying or dead where never I could reach him. How could I bear it?[37]

She was advised to go home and: 'to account no news as being tantamount to good news, and so on and so forth ... and with this was bowed out to take to myself what comfort I could from the promise of official inquiry and information.'[38]

In 1920, the Williamsons visited the War Office to talk about the search for their son. It was an amicable meeting, but it did not resolve anything. The official who saw the couple minuted that: 'It is hopeless to argue with them, or with Mrs. Williamson at any rate.' The couple were certain that their son was still alive.[39]

One of the concerns of the grieving was the impersonal nature of the bureaucracy, whether it was the War Office, the Army or even the Red Cross. However, it was necessary, as Michael Durey notes:

> A bureaucratic, regulatory response was inevitable to avoid complete chaos. Moreover, for the clerks – many of whom were unfit or recovering veterans – the bitter experience of closing files on multitudes of solders who seemingly had just vaporised required the development of a sense of detachment that needed to be buttressed by a set of policy rules that helped to reduce the emotional stress that the department's daily work must have caused.[40]

Without understanding how difficult providing such an answer might be, families found that these institutions could not answer what appeared to be a simple question: what exactly had happened to their son or husband? Sometimes the Red Cross and other agencies could help, but in most cases, there could be no certainty over a man's last few minutes. And, indeed, when the next of kin received some new piece of information about their loved one, it was not always easy for them to comprehend what they had been told.

What was as bad was the feeling that somebody who was priceless to you with all his charms and foibles was nothing more than a name and a number to the War Office. As has been pointed out, an individual casualty was a tragedy, the loss of thousands was a statistic. The anonymous mother who wrote a plea to her missing son could not understand why he had been issued with an identity tag:

> …surely there has never been such sorrow over just one number. Do you remember how angry I was about those figures on your identification disc, when I first noticed them on your wrist – how I hated you being a number at all? And how you said that… 'Why so long as I'm Number One to you, what in the world does it matter what number I am to the Army?'[41]

Searches for the missing sometimes stressed details of the man being sought in the hope that it would jog the memory of potential witnesses. Rudyard Kipling wrote that his son's clothes had been marked with his name. And the relatives of Rifleman Ernest Blackburn, King's Royal Rifle Corps, stressed that their boy 'was very well known in his connection with the Ebenezer Congregational Chapel, Dewsbury'.[42] The mother of Allan Tennant circulated newspapers and YMCA canteens with letters and posters about her son. Every piece of literature mentioned that 'in his pocket would be a brown leather chess case.'[43] In reality, such information made little difference. But it gave the missing soldier a personality: he was not just a number.

Mistakes

Keeping track of all six million men who served in the British Army, as well as the hundreds of thousands who were in the Royal Navy and Royal Air Force, was of course a nightmare. It was bad enough when it came to working out pay and allowances, but it was ten times worse when it came to providing details to the next of kin of a man's death, capture by the enemy or being wounded. Getting facts wrong might cause serious distress or unwarranted joy. But with so many men in uniform it was inevitable. The press liked to claim that the War Office was a hive of inefficiency and bureaucratic nonsense, which they condemned as 'red tape'. Even in the midst of war, editors relished the opportunity to expose errors in official reports that listed soldiers as missing or dead.

Robert Graves was once declared dead. And Rowland Fielding was recorded as having died four times.[44] The official weekly casualty lists almost always included entries for men previously erroneously reported missing. In the list for 16 October 1917, for example, A. Butler, South Staffordshire and J. Bryce, Sherwood Foresters, had both 'previously reported wounded and missing now reported neither wounded nor missing' and S. Campbell, York and Lancaster, was 'previously reported missing, now rejoined.'[45]

In his account of the work of the Red Cross in France Harley Granville Barker discussed the consequences: 'Once a mistake was made, a man killed and buried by register, though he comes up smiling and salutes his company in the flesh, it is the world's work to resurrect him on the roll of the British Army.' He stressed how the Graves Registration Commission checked and then rechecked the records of deaths: 'each graveyard has its plan, each grave marked on it, no later shifting of the crosses can cause confusion.'[46] But it cannot have been reassuring to the families to whom a man had been mistakenly reported killed or missing.

One missing man, both in body and in the records of the Imperial War Graves Commission, was Private Edgar Oswald Gale, East Yorkshire Regiment, who went missing in action on 18 August 1916. Although this fact was recorded on his service record it wasn't until 1978 that his name was etched on the Thiepval Memorial.[47]

In February 1919, the case of Rifleman Ernest Russell, Rifle Brigade, came to the attention of the *Territorial Services Gazette*. His mother had apparently been informed that he was a prisoner of war and had been sending letters and Red Cross parcels, 'to none of which she has received any reply, not have they been returned.' The War Office and the Army's Graves Registration Units blamed each other, saying that the confusion was because there was another casualty with the same name. Russell was killed on 21 March 1918, and is now commemorated on the memorial to the missing at Pozières. But rather oddly, a man with the same name, regiment and service number appears in a register for the POW camp at Merseburg in June 1918.[48]

Letters from commanders and comrades

One of the unsung heroes of the Great War was the Army Postal Service. It took no more than two or three days for letters and packages to arrive in the trenches and any replies to be received at home. The efficiency of the postal service was a major factor in keeping the morale of British soldiers high by providing a direct link between Tommy and his nearest and dearest at home.

If regular letter writers at the Front fell silent, this might be a sign that something had happened to them. Lady Isabella St John's son, an officer in the Royal Scots, wrote home every four or five days providing 'cheery and detailed answers' to her daily letters. Having not received a communication for a fortnight she became increasingly worried about him, although she told herself that she, 'a person of acute and accurate premonitory intuitions, had had no instinctive intimation of there being anything wrong with him.'[49]

Families of men killed in action would normally receive a letter from his commanding officer or the unit padre describing the circumstances of his death. The reader was normally reassured that the man had died quickly and without pain, often while engaged in an act of bravery. And that, of course, he was a trusted and popular member of the unit. It was easier to accept when you knew that your loved one had a last resting place. Lieutenant Norman Collins, Seaforth Highlanders, remembered that 'We always tried to write a nice letter to the mother or father because we felt for them.'[50] The reality might be very different to that described in the letter – being buried by a shell or a slow agonising death in a casualty clearing station. In these circumstances who would want to know the shocking nature of their loved one's last few minutes. Most families were happy with the explanation given, which allowed their boy to die as a war hero. Mrs Marion Hemming replied to the Revd Victor Tanner after he had offered condolences on the death of her son Lieutenant Frank Hemming, Worcestershire Regiment: 'It is a great relief to us to think that our dead son did not suffer, but was killed instantaneously and _was_ all you say, and we are proud to be the parents of such a son. Nevertheless, the blow is a terrible one to bear.'[51]

Canon N. C. Crosse, who was a chaplain with the Devonshire Regiment, wrote:

> In the case of those other than officers, such letters had an immense importance. If an officer was killed the CO [Commanding officer] and usually one or more of his company officers were pretty sure to write to his home and give details. But in the case of other ranks this was by no means always the case. Thousands and thousands must have been killed on active service under circumstances which were perfectly well known to their comrades, but the next of kin

received nothing more than the cold official fact notified by the War Office. This scanty information a padre could often forestall and usually supplement by the addition of a few details, which made all the difference to a man's home.[52]

Probably more treasured were letters from the man's comrades. Soldiers' letters to the grieving families of their missing were inevitably less fluent, partly because of the subject matter but also because they were less confident writers. But they were always much more welcome, because the sympathy was more heartfelt and, within the bounds of censorship and the wish to spare the feelings of the family, more information was provided. The writers were also aware of the anxiety that the parents and wives of the missing must be feeling. Private Alfred Burrage, Artists Rifles, remembered that: 'Most of us had the addresses of one another's people in order to write the usual letter in case the worse happened.'[53]

However helpful the correspondent might have thought he had been in writing to the family of a missing man, it was not always taken the right way by the next of kin. During the summer of 1918 Stephen Graham found some letters on a corpse. He wrote 'a carefully constructed missive' to the writer. He received a letter from the lad's father asking for more information as 'he had not been heard of for a long while.'

> By that time, however, the boy's body with seven others had been into one hastily dug grave; the names but not the units nor the numbers had been printed on one cross. I then informed the father of his son's death, and of the exact locality of the grave. In due course of time the father replied that I must be mistaken, for his son had been reported as being wounded and missing.[54]

It wasn't just a man's comrades who would write to the family. Complete strangers might get in touch with snippets of information. In May 1918, Miss Beatrice Lord of Leicester wrote a long letter to the mother of Private Henry Bellerby, Machine Gun Corps. She had received a letter from her boyfriend, a stretcher bearer who was a prisoner of war:

> He asks me if I will write to you and tell you about your son. He says in the trench where he was a shell burst ten yards away from him and killed 4 men and wounded 3, and one of the unfortunate ones was your son. My young [man] says he found this photo on him, and asked me to write to you as he couldn't himself (letters being so limited). I'm so sorry Mrs Bellerby, I didn't like to send you such sad news, but perhaps you have heard from other quarters. I hope you have, it will be a bitter blow I know. I have a brother that we have not heard anything of since the 21st March. Well, we have had the official news that he is missing since that date. We would welcome <u>any</u> news of him. I think it is best to know the worse than be left in suspense.[55]

Relatives sometimes contacted their boy's unit in search of further information. The commanding officer or adjutant would normally try to be as helpful as they could, although the additional evidence supplied might be very limited, particularly for ordinary soldiers who were normally no more than just a number to staff at battalion headquarters. Constraints over military secrecy and the need to spare the enquirer's feelings could reduce the information provided. Mrs Hemming asked the Revd Tanner for more information, 'could you tell me a little more about our dear boy's end.' She realised that the padre might not be able to help directly but wondered whether any of her son's fellow officers might have witnessed the death. Tanner replied, that 'as far as I can gather death was due to the shock of the explosion and was therefore instantaneous. None of the splints of the shell seem to have struck him.'[56]

Royal Flying Corps units in France were advised not to help enquirers. G. H. Foukes, the Corps' Adjutant General, wrote to Squadron commanders in October 1917:

> Cases are continually coming to hand where Commanding Officers of fighting units <u>officially</u> report officers and other ranks as "missing" and afterwards <u>un</u>officially inform relatives that death can be assumed though the body was not actually found. As contradictory reports lead to much discontent at home and unnecessary correspondence, it has been decided that in all cases of 'missing', no further statement should be made to the relatives beyond informing them that all possible enquiries are being, and will be made ... it should be carefully explained, that in the light of past experience, a mere expression of opinion is of no value, unless backed up by the evidence of some <u>reliable</u> eye witness.[57]

However, information from infantry battalions could be more forthcoming, particularly if the event was still fresh in the mind of the person replying to the enquirer. Second Lieutenant Hugh Bird, Royal Fusiliers, went missing during the German advance in March 1918. It was assumed that he had been killed. His brother wrote to the battalion commander seeking more information, who replied on 13 April 1918:

> I wrote about a week ago to your brother's wife telling her all I could – which I am sorry to say is very little, for we were fighting a very hard rear-guard action when your brother was killed by a shell. This is practically all I can tell you. In fighting a rear-guard action it is very difficult to get one's wounded back – the gallant boys who are killed cannot possibly be looked after and buried; they are simply left where they fall. This was your brother's fate.[58]

In fact, Hugh Bird, although badly wounded, had actually been taken prisoner. It took several months for the news to filter back to his family, by which time a memorial service had been held for him.[59]

The receipt of letters both official and unofficial inevitably led to the desire to find out more. For some grieving relations like the parents of Hugh Williamson and the widow of Sidney Rothe, the War Office appeared to be nothing more than an unfeeling bureaucracy. They were unable to understand the complexities of modern warfare. What they asked about the fate of their loved ones seemed simple but was in fact almost impossible to answer. Indeed, as parents and widows dug deeper, the less obvious the answers often seemed to be.

This urge was a key element of the grieving process, made worse for the families of the missing because of the uncertainty. There were other places, official as well as unofficial, for the families of the missing to approach. But it was rare for any additional information to come to light.

6

THE SEARCH FOR THE MISSING

"Have you news of my boy Jack?"
Not this tide.
"When d'you think that he'll come back?"
Not with this wind blowing, and this tide.
Rudyard Kipling, 'My Boy Jack' (1916)[1]

The information that a relative received depended in part on the needs of the war, but as importantly on the persistence and the social class of the enquirer. In almost every case, of course, the search proved fruitless. But to an extent this did not matter. Trying all avenues might assuage the guilt you felt about the loss of your loved one, and who knows, just possibly there might be some clue that proved he was still alive. The reasons behind Hazel Macnaghten's frankly obsessive search to discover the fate of her husband Angus is less certain, but their relationship had been extremely close. It did not help that, for the best of reasons, her friends encouraged her by telling her that they felt that Angus was still alive and suggesting ever more bizarre avenues she could follow in her search. Nor were his fellow officers and men able to agree about the circumstances of Macnaghten's death in October 1914.[2]

Even the most obscure embassy or organisation might find themselves besieged by letters from families of the missing seeking news about their menfolk. In January 1917, the neutral Spanish placed news stories in the British press advising enquirers to contact the War Office in London rather than the authorities in Madrid: 'This practice is due to a misapprehension as to the real nature of the humanitarian work undertaken by His Catholic Majesty.'[3]

And although relations often received detailed information about the fate of their loved ones, it was not uncommon for enquirers to refuse to believe the evidence. Hazel Macnaghten refused to listen to the sage advice offered by an Anglican bishop: 'I fear however that if your husband had survived, he would have found some means to let you know it since Oct, 29th. It grieves me to write it but that is what experience tells me in this sad, sad war.' Instead, she believed a letter from a friend of a friend about her son who had written after eight weeks in German hands: 'It shows how news may come even after such a long time...'[4]

Rudyard Kipling was lucky in that he was able to piece together considerable detail about his son's last days using his unique connections across politics and the military. According to Thomas Pinney, Kipling and his wife 'were never to learn where his body might lie, but through their persistent inquiry they were able to learn almost every circumstance apart from the location of this grave'.[5] Few other parents would gain such knowledge. That said, in some cases the next of kin received all the facts, but did not recognise that this was so.

There were various alternatives to the War Office to which relatives could turn. The most important of which was the British Red Cross Society.

The British Red Cross
The Red Cross (and its partners the Order of St John) was heavily involved in so many aspects of the war effort that they effectively

became a branch of the government. They provided, and ran, hundreds of auxiliary hospitals helping soldiers recover from their injuries, supplied volunteer orderlies and nurses, knitting bandages and providing ambulances to carry the wounded. Not the least of their work involved sending parcels of food and clothing to British prisoners of war in Germany and other countries.

It was almost inevitable that the British Red Cross Society became involved with the search for the missing. *The Red Cross*, wrote in April 1915 that:

> In any appraisal of Red Cross work made on lines of strict utility the search for missing men could scarcely hope to hold its own with ambulances and hospitals. But as a measure of pure mercy it has several characteristics which raise it to a level in some respects beyond the reach of utility. It is quite true that the missing man is almost certainly dead, wounded or a prisoner. To place whichever is the fact beyond doubt is not to say that any physical good is necessarily accomplished. Nevertheless, mental misery is often more acute in its way than bodily pain; and in war that is the lot of soldiers' relatives who, in volume of distress, suffer a great deal more than the soldiers themselves.[6]

From mid-1915, the War Office advised families seeking information about men who had been reported missing to contact the charity for further help. To modern eyes this seems odd, but Lord Northcliffe argued: 'No department of state could hope to touch the human chord which gives this work its greatest value. It would be wrong to expect an already over-worked War Office to busy itself collecting small personal details, yet it is just these details for which all those who have suffered the great loss yearn so wistfully.'[7]

The Red Cross was able to undertake this work in part because they were a trusted intermediary between the combatants.[8]

The Search for the Missing

It helped that despite the pressures of the war national societies generally worked harmoniously together for a common humanitarian good. In May 1916, for example, when Sir Arthur Lawley met Prince of Max of Baden of the German Red Cross in Berne, they agreed that 'the names of missing officers or men should be sent to the German Red Cross, who would make enquiries in the same way as is at present done by the searchers in the Wounded and Missing Department.'[9]

This Department emerged from the same lack in the provision of services by the British Army as did the Imperial War Graves Commission. Its founder, Lord Robert Cecil, told *The Times* in April 1915:

> We divide our cases into three main categories; soldiers who have disappeared and whose friends are unable to learn anything about them; soldiers who have been reported wounded; and soldiers who have been reported missing. There is a fourth category for inquiries concerning the whereabouts of the graves of the men who have fallen.[10]

Although Lord Robert praised the close links with the War Office, in practice Whitehall was often unable to answer letters from relations in any meaningful way. In the early months of the war, one or two individuals and organisations tried to meet the demand. They were either exposed or overwhelmed by the mass of enquiries. The need was met by the Red Cross. The Wounded and Missing Enquiries Department formally opened in April 1915. It was established to become 'the clearing house for all enquiries received from the public and also for all reports collected by the searchers in hospitals at home and abroad.'[11]

The Red Cross's work actually began in the early weeks of the war, when volunteers in their Paris office began to compile a card index of casualties based on lists published in *The Times* or provided by the French authorities. During October and

November 1914, they 'received 1088 enquiries about missing men and about 800 callers about wounded men', of which they were 'able to satisfy a large number'. Volunteers also sought to interview men returning from the trenches, which proved to be 'a most difficult part of our work' as many soldiers reached hospital in 'such a nerve-racked condition that their evidence has to be checked and counter-checked by questioning other men.'[12]

In addition, volunteers from the Paris office under Fabian Ware sought, with moderate success, to identify the graves of fallen men and in some cases individual bodies. This was eventually taken over by the War Office's Graves Registration and Enquiry Unit.

Initially enquiries were only conducted after a member of the public had contacted the Red Cross, but in July 1916 it was decided to research each man once his name had been passed to them. 'By that time ... it was proved that such special enquiries [were] often too late for fruitful search; and it was judged best to begin enquiring for every missing man as soon as he was so reported.'[13] In addition, many people wrote to the Department for additional information about the circumstances of their husband's or son's death, even after they had been officially told that he had been killed in action. During its almost four years of existence it dealt with nearly 350,000 enquiries from members of the public.[14]

Data about the missing was obtained in several ways, from lists supplied by the War Office, by circulating questionnaires to prisoner of war camps or writing directly to prisoners asking for any information they might possess about missing men in their units.[15] Lastly and perhaps the most important, volunteers – known as searchers – visited hospitals and rest camps in the hope of interviewing men who remembered the last minutes of missing comrades.

Initially, there were twenty volunteers in the Department, plus a team of paid typists. By late 1918 the number had risen to 150 men and women who maintained the index and replied to enquiries from the public, together with a team of 1200 searchers who combed the hospitals at home interviewing patients about their comrades who had gone missing and another 300 who worked overseas.[16]

The lists supplied by the War Office came in several forms. For the most part they were published daily casualty lists with additional details of a man's battalion and company. The Red Cross's Prisoner of War Department also received lists of prisoners of war from the German Red Cross and the ICRC in Geneva. Details of each man was added to the card index. Enquiry lists were compiled, which were given to searchers and placed in YMCA and other refreshment huts for men to look at while they were having a cup of tea. However, this did not prove to be successful: 'Reports of value were never obtained except by direct questioning.'[17]

Lists of missing men were also circulated to prisoners of war camps through the embassy of the protecting power or by the ICRC in Geneva. Initially this was done by charities such as the Princess Victoria League in Geneva and the Bern International Peace Commission, but with limited success.[18] The compilation of such lists was taken over by the Red Cross's Central Prisoners of War Committee established in September 1916: 'In this way we were able to reassure the minds of many hundreds of enquirers who would otherwise have had to wait a much longer time for news that their relatives were, though prisoners, at least in the land of the living.'[19]

The searchers interviewed wounded men seeking information about those who had gone missing. They visited hospital wards and convalescent homes for information. This was largely in France at first, but increasingly volunteers visited hospitals in England and the other theatres of operations. *The Times* estimated that during the War five million soldiers had been asked about missing, fallen and wounded comrades.[20]

Conditions in the early months of the war were chaotic as hospitals and reinforcement centres were constantly being set up in Boulogne, Rouen and other centres well behind the front line. Ian Malcolm and the other searchers found it almost impossible

> ... to find and to visit hundreds of men who might have been able to give us information, since they was hardly time for us to find out that they were in Boulogne and to reach the hospital before we learned that they had been sent back to England. The only chance was to have a searcher ready to visit each ship as it was filled, and to gather such news as he could from the invalids in their bunks before the anchor weighed for home.[21]

The work was monotonous and hard going. Ian Malcolm thought it was only

> ... the deep pleasure of assisting by a 'find'; to relieve one single aching heart that enables our searchers to continue this work for months at a time, steeped as they always are in an atmosphere of pain, and listening for hours to stories of heroism and tragedy that will never be surpassed.[22]

One labelled his job the 'pursuit of the illusive bone'. Going from bed to bed, searchers typically found only five useful patients for every hundred approached. There was no way around this.[23] However, *The* Times felt: 'The information which they gave would not otherwise, in nine cases out of ten, have reached the inquirers at all.'[24] The writer E. M. Foster, who was based in Alexandria, thought that the work was 'depressing in a way, for one does get news about the missing although it is generally bad news.'[25] In most cases nothing could be found out about the man, and where there was information, men often remembered that comrades had just vanished over the top or into an enemy trench.

The writer Harley Granville Barker wrote about a typical searcher's routine in a hospital:

This man is not well enough to talk. This man is well enough; and being well enough would like to. What regiment? What company? Does he know any of these names. Smith? Yes, he knew Smith, a little dark chap with a yellow patch in his eye. Killed last February at Ypres. Ah, but this Smith was not missing till May. Well there was a Smith in B Company killed last February, a dark little chap with a yellow patch in his eye. Does he remember his number? No, he's afraid that he doesn't; it might have begun with an 8 – but it might not. But he knows he was killed, for he helped to bury him. Not much use this, but the searcher makes a careful note, for stranger things happen then that a man reported missing in May should be found to have been buried in February.[26]

Witnesses of course were unreliable. Most had been traumatised in some way by their experiences in the frontline. The man interviewed might omit some of the facts, include erroneous details or perhaps tell the searcher what he had himself had been told. John Lucy of the Royal Irish Rifles, whose brother went missing a few yards from him on the Aisne in September 1014, found the 'yarns' he was told by his brother's comrades hard to believe. 'The troops, I am sure,' he later wrote, 'did not lie deliberately, but their imaginations in the stress of battle often played strange tricks on them.'[27]

And the longer the time since the event the less reliable a man's memory was likely to be. In the case of Lieutenant Angus Macnaghten, Black Watch, who went missing at the end of October 1914, Private Gibson was interviewed in the Imperial Hospital, Boulogne on 21 January 1915. 'I saw Lt Macnaghten lying down wounded in the dead. I was close to him ... but I was soon taken into the barn and saw him no more.' However, another witness, Lance Corporal Mackay, interviewed on the same day, categorically stated that he was 'captured at Ypres. Informant knew Macnaghten and enquired about him specially, and was told by a man who had actually seen him captured.' The interviewer noted that: 'Several other NCOs of the Black Watch ... gave me the same story, which I have heard several times before.'[28] Macnaghten was actually killed on 29 October 1914.

To overcome these difficulties the Red Cross tried to find at least three separate accounts of a man's death, although this was not always possible: For weeks and months many an enquiry may hardly bear fruit, but any report worth making is sent round to each office, docketed, collated and little by little the contradictions are sifted down and good evidence built up. The stark facts will appear quite suddenly sometimes.[29]

It was easier to find men who remembered an officer or an NCO's death, as they were often well known to a large circle of men under his command than for ordinary soldiers who might be recognised only by others in their platoon, or, in some cases, had just only just joined the battalion and were known by almost nobody. In the case of Private Frank Vasey, Australian Imperial Force, who was killed at Pozières on 25 July 1916, two witnesses spoke of him being killed by a machine gun bullet while charging the German lines. But a third claimed that he had been struck by a shell while taking rations up to the line.[30]

The parents of missing men naturally tended to believe witnesses who thought their son was still alive. Lieutenant Horace Walpole, a fellow Coldstream officer, told Lieutenant Williamson's parents that he had talked to him on the battlefield about midday, some hours after their son must have been killed.[31] Yet one of Williamson's NCOs reported to the War Office, a report which was forwarded to the parents, that his officer had been 'killed by a Minenwerfer which buried him under a mound of earth as high as a house!'[32]

It was up to the Red Cross to evaluate these testimonies. Enquirers would be sent copies of the searchers' reports, although they might be edited to minimise inconsistency or to hide some of the more shocking circumstances of a loved one's death.[33]

It was almost impossible to lay down general rules; each case had to be considered on its own merits. The very eagerness with which the relatives of a missing man naturally grasped at any information that seemed give hope of his safety, and their equally natural desire to find flaws in any evidence of death, made it advisable that reports should be accompanied with some sort of guidance for their interpretation. This was especially the case in dealing with less educated correspondents, who were of course, by far the greater number.[34] It was the Department's primary objective to extinguish such 'hope deferred which maketh the heart sick.' The only way of doing this was by telling the truth as accurately as possible.[35] As Jay Winter observed:

Many [enquirers] yearned to share the last moments of their man; to know what he knew; and at least for a moment to feel what he felt. This kind of identification with the fallen required a more human and to a degree a more brutal disclosure of information than the state or the army provided.[36]

Where no report could be compiled *The Times* noted 'an attempt was made to compile for the benefit of enquirers a general account of the action where their son or husband was last seen.'[37]

From 1916 the War Office also began to operate a similar system, but here the expectation was that the missing man was no longer alive. They wrote to potential witnesses, enclosing a form entitled 'Evidence as to Officers or Men on Missing Lists'. The informant was instructed that they should 'give fully your reasons knowing him to be dead, e g whether you saw him buried. In all cases you should state your reason for being certain as to the identity of the officer or solder referred to.' It would have been hard for a witness to write that they thought that the man might be alive or had been captured by the enemy.[38]

The Red Cross's Wounded and Missing Enquiries Department also received enquiries from German families seeking information about their missing menfolk. They included enquiries about German civilians interred and uninterred across the world, including settlers in South West Africa, naturalists in Abyssinia, and sailors who had been taken off captured merchant ships. One man was even 'successfully traced to a farm on the Congo'.[39]

The real importance of the Department was undoubtedly psychological. In part, like other aspects of the Red Cross's work, it showed the human side of officialdom in time of war, but it also provided reassurance to relatives that everything had been done to trace their loved ones. Harley Granville Baker in describing the work of the Department argued, rather patronisingly: 'It is a merciful work this Red Cross department is about, bringing certainty of good or ill to the wives and mothers and fathers of the fighting men as, helpless and ignorant, unwilling and patient, they sit at home.'[40]

In the final report on its wartime activities the Red Cross concluded:

> The appreciation shown [by enquirers] was more than enough to make the necessity for the organisation clear. It would have been quite impossible that relatives should have remained content with the mere official report of casualties.[41]

International Committee of the Red Cross

The International Committee is the centre of the international Red Cross movement. Based in Geneva, it is made up of self-appointed businessmen from the Swiss canton. The Committee was founded by Henri Dunant in 1863 to care for the wounded in battle. As well as the Committee there was a network of separate national organisations, such as the British Red Cross Society. During the First World War the Committee sought to monitor the adherence to the Geneva Conventions of 1907 by the belligerents with mixed results, although they are now remembered largely for their work with prisoners of war. This

Above: 1. An Australian pipes & drums band play during a Last Post ceremony at the Menin Gate in July 2016. (Kenneth Zirkel/Wikipedia)

Below: 2. John Heaviside Clark, 'The Morning after the Battle of Waterloo on June 19, 1815'. (Deutsches Historisches Museum, Berlin/Wikipedia)

3. Roger Fenton's photograph of British graves on Cathcart's Hill, Crimea. (J Paul Getty Museum, Los Angeles)

4. Office sign for Clara Barton's Office for Missing Soldiers, Washington DC. (Author)

Above: 5. Constant shelling destroyed the drainage systems which had kept dry what became the Western Front. Tens of thousands of men drowned in the evil-smelling mud which resulted from this destruction. This is Hooge Wood near Ypres on 29 October 1917. (Frank Hurley/Wikipedia)

Right: 6. A gravestone to two of the four unknown German soldiers who lie in Tyne Cot cemetery near Ypres. (Nancy W. Beach/Wikipedia)

Left: 7. German message about the shooting down of pilots and observers from 13 Sqn RFC on 5 December 1915. The translation reads 'With regard to the BE no 4092 and other aircraft brought down after a violent fight in the air. The pilots and observers, 4, met with an honourable flying man's death and were buried yesterday with all military honours.' (The National Archives TNA AIR 1/967/204/5/1097, p9c)

Below: 8. A statue of a grieving woman at the Canadian National War Memorial at Vimy Ridge. (Xavier Alphand/Northern France Tourist Board)

9. Veterans remembered the thick mud, which could suck the unwary to a horrible death. (Author)

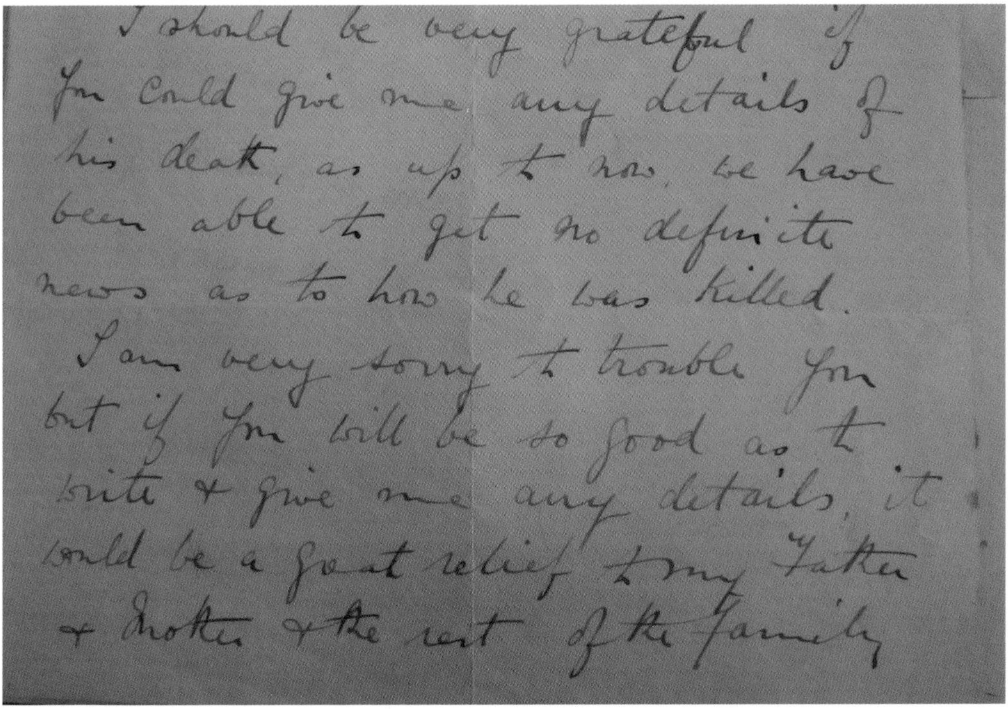

> I should be very grateful if you could give me any details of his death, as up to now, we have been able to get no definite news as to how he was killed. I am very sorry to trouble you but if you will be so good as to write & give me any details, it would be a great relief to my Father & Mother & the rest of the family

10. Relatives of the missing would write to men they thought had witnessed the disappearance of their loved ones. (Author)

Above: 11. Edwin Martin, 'A Cemetery in France' (1918). (Wellcome Collection Reference 45163i)

Left: 12. The card containing details of correspondence with the brother of Sidney Rothe. (International Committee of the Red Cross)

Above: 13. Inside a German prisoner of war camp in the early days of the First World War. (International Committee of the Red Cross)

Below: 14. The 1,200 volunteer employees of the Prisoners of War Agency outside Geneva's Museum Ruth in 1918. (International Committee of the Red Cross)

MISSING SOLDIERS Column

¶ Enquirers should write us briefly, giving full name of missing soldier, with rank or number, battalion, and regiment, and any other useful information. Enquirers must also give us their own name and address for publication.
¶ Notices written and inserted FREE.
¶ Enquirers should inform us when missing soldiers have been traced, so that we can cancel notices at once.
¶ Relatives should address communications to "The Missing Soldiers Column," Dundee Courier, Albert Square, Dundee.

15. The *Dundee Courier* was one of many newspapers which published appeals from relatives for information about their missing family members. (Dundee Courier, 2 September 1915, p1. British Library Board)

LIEUTENANT ANGUS MACNAGHTEN.

Miss Macnaghten, Bittern Manor, Southampton, is anxious to obtain information regarding Lieutenant Angus Charles Rowley Steuart Macnaghten, of the 3rd Battalion Royal Highlanders (Black Watch), who was officially reported missing some weeks ago. Lieutenant Macnaghten, who was serving at the front with the 1st Battalion, is a grandson of the late Sir Francis Workman Macnaghten, Dundarave, North Antrim.

16. The appeal made for information about Lieutenant Angus Macnaghten, Black Watch. As with so many such appeals nothing useful was received. (Belfast News Letter, 2 December 1914, p10. British Library Board)

Above: 17. Graves of five officers who died during the Siege of Mafeking. (Wellcome Collection)

Right: 18. The First World War memorial to the dead at St Mary's Church, Twickenham. Twickenham had one of the highest proportions of missing men of any town. This is due to coincidence rather than any other reason. (Author)

Above: 19. Lord Plumer speaking at the dedication of the Memorial to the Missing at the Menin Gate, Ypres 24 July 1927. (University of Victoria Libraries/ Wikipedia)

Left: 20. A display of photographs of the British soldiers who disappeared during the Battle of the Somme at the Thiepval Museum. (Author)

Above: 21. The carriage carrying the body of the Unknown Warrior passes down Whitehall. (Marian Mollett)

Right: 22. The Cenotaph as it appears remains the simplest and most impressive memorial to the losses of the two world wars. (Author)

Left: 23. Many grieving families memorialised their sons and husbands. William Barker was killed during the last few weeks of the War. His name appears on a family gravestone in the Fulham Cemetery in Kew. (Author)

Below: 24. Will Longstaff's 'Menin Gate at Midnight' also known as 'Ghosts of Menin Gate' (1927). (Australian War Memorial/Wikipedia)

Above: 25. The Tomb of the Unknown Warrior in Westminster Abbey. (Mike/Wikipedia)

Below: 26. A grave plaque for a man at the Taukkyan War Cemetery near Yangon, Myanmar. The cemetery has a memorial to 27,000 men who went missing during the Burma Campaign. The plaques are made of bronze to better weather the brutal local climate. (Wikipedia)

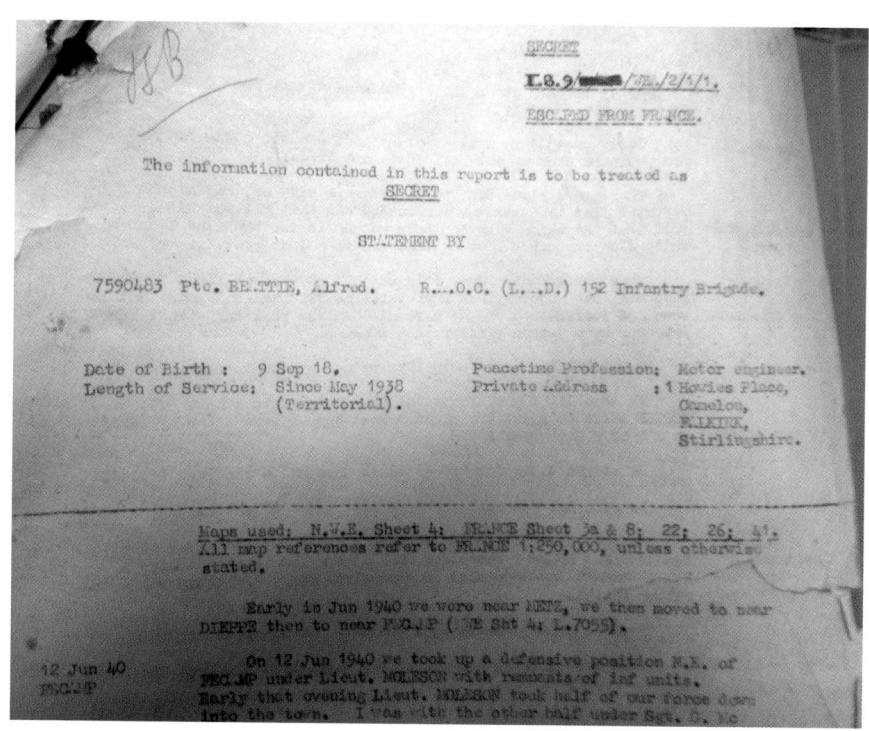

Above: 27. The evaders report for Private William Beattie, RASC the only soldier known to have evaded capture by the enemy after the Fall of France in June 1940. (TNA WO 208/3348/1)

Below: 28. Soldiers awaiting rescue from the beach at Dunkirk. The British authorities hoped that some at least of those left behind managed to hide from the Germans with local families. However, most ended up as prisoners of war. Other men drowned as they made their way to the ships and their bodies were carried away by the tide. (Imperial War Museum IPY 68075/Wikipedia)

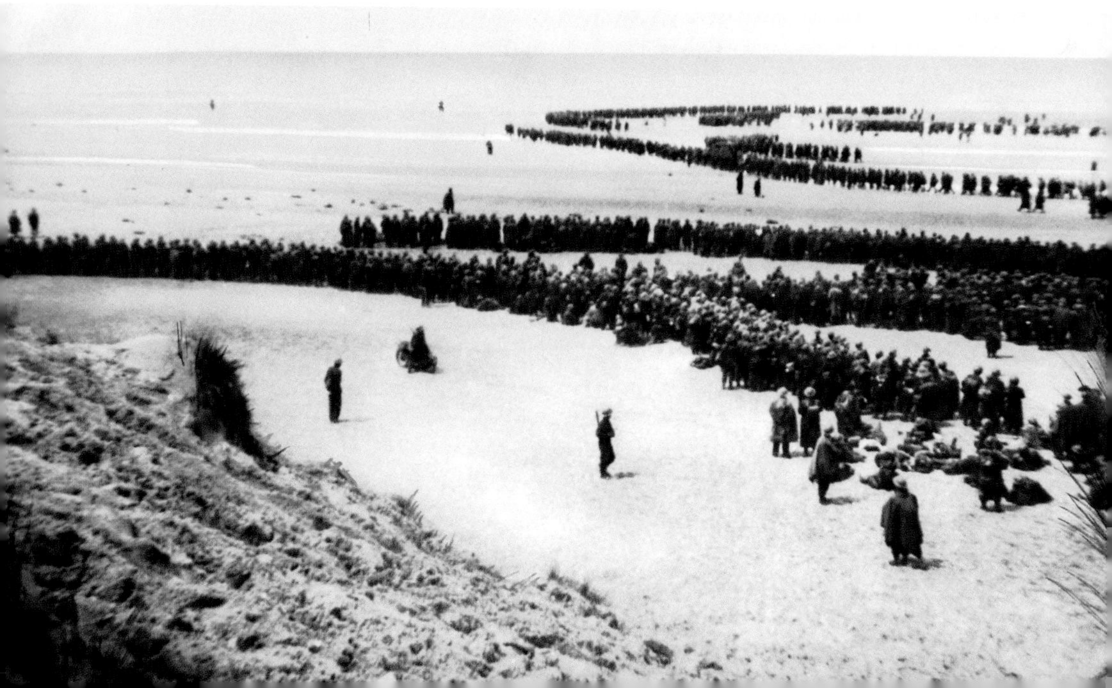

Right: 29. A wreath commemorating the American Missing in Action/Prisoner of War campaign at the Vietnam Memorial in Washington DC. (Author)

Below: 30. The RAF Memorial to the Missing at Runnymede. The names of 20,000 airmen and airwomen who lost their lives during the Second World War and have no last resting place are commemorated here. (Author)

Left: 31. A photo of the SOE Agent Roland Alexandre who was almost certainly murdered by the Nazis at Gross-Rosen concentration camp in May 1944. (TNA HS 9/21/4)

Below: 32. Israel's Garden to the Missing in Action on Mount Herzl in Jerusalem. (Author)

did not have any standing in international law, but it was accepted by the belligerents because they saw the benefits. It probably helped that the Committee was technically nothing more than a small group of Swiss citizens, with little control over the national societies.

At the outbreak of war, an International Agency for Aid and Information on Prisoners of War was quickly established in two small rooms in Geneva, with the intention that it should share lists of wounded, dead and prisoners between the belligerents. On 4 September, it received its first list of names: 29 wounded French prisoners.[42] By the end of October they were dealing with 3,000 letters a day from anxious relatives across Europe. The Agency soon filled the city's Musée Rath with an army of volunteer clerks. Letters and parcels by the thousand arrived in Geneva in the hope that they would be forwarded to missing or imprisoned loved ones. By 1918, 120,000 people had visited the city to ask for help in tracing missing relatives. The German writer Stefan Zweig wrote after a visit: 'Outside from one end to the other of our world, the crucified heart of Europe bleeds from innumerable wounds. But here the heart still beats... For here ... resounds another eternal feeling – human pity.'[43]

The Committee's work was recognised as being of great value. The Foreign Office in particular found the ICRC useful, as the Committee had access to the authorities in Turkey and Bulgaria, so were able to provide information about prisoners in these countries that would otherwise be nearly impossible to obtain.

National governments were asked to send copies of the prisoner of war lists to Geneva for use by the ICRC. Details from the lists were incorporated in a vast card index. The services at Geneva were not just used by governments. Individuals seeking information about loved ones who had gone missing also contacted the Committee. In March 1915, Edouard Naville, a member of the Committee, wrote to *The Times* that several thousand letters were being received each day from families across Europe. In providing basic details about the man and when and where he was supposed to have gone missing, enquirers were asked to write briefly 'and in a legible hand':

> It is requested that no photographs be sent nor personal description be given; also that news of individual prisoners should not be asked for on the strength of photographs in groups, since people have a habit of sending out [such photographs] thinking that in such groups they recognise one of their relatives. This is almost invariably wrong, the photograph being of some quite different individual. No inquiry should be made unless the person has officially been reported missing... Only next of kin should submit enquiries.[44]

In most cases the ICRC was unable to help individual enquirers because the men they sought information on had not been captured by the enemy. The wife and brother-in-law of Lieutenant Sidney Rothe, for example, are noted in the Committee's card index having written several times to Geneva in 1916 and 1917 on the off chance that he was in German hands, but without success. A year later the mother of Private Allan Tenant also contacted the Committee.

Other Sources

Most families were satisfied with enquiries to the War Office and the Red Cross and may perhaps also have contacted the missing man's comrades, but there were other avenues available to the determined. It seemed sensible to insert newspaper classified advertisements in order to contact the man's comrades, who might have information or, even if they could not help, at least provide a tangible physical link to the man and his last minutes on earth. But occasionally the search took a ludicrous turn.

The Search for the Missing

By the First World War every newspaper carried a wide range of classified advertisements, for everything from patent medicines to jobs, theatre shows, appeals for lost dogs and lonely hearts. They were a relatively cheap and easy way to pass on news, sell goods and services or seek information. For many readers small ads were the reason why they bought the paper. It is little wonder that they were a plot device used by Conan Doyle and other novelists.[45]

It was natural that families soon began to insert appeals for information about missing men into both local and national newspapers. The response rate would have been very low, but individuals must have thought that it was worth the few pence the ad cost for the feeling that they had left no stone unturned. Indeed, some newspapers, such as the *Dundee Courier* printed the appeals for free, which the paper saw as a contribution to the war effort. And no doubt it did the paper's circulation no harm.

The potential advertiser had a wide choice. Local newspapers had limited local readerships, but it was worth advertising here (and cheaper too) if your boy had joined a local regiment or pals battalion, where all the men came from a particular area. However, advertising in daily regional or national newspapers attracted a wider and more affluent readership, so if you were trying to discover the fate of an officer it might be worth trying there. Advertisements in the *Manchester Guardian* and *The Times*, for example, were overwhelmingly for officers, while those in the *Dundee Courier* and *Liverpool Daily Post* were largely for non-commissioned officers and other ranks.

The text which appeared in the advertisements varied little, in part because they were rarely more than 25 words long. Naturally, they gave details of the missing man, his regimental number, battalion (and often the company he was in), date of disappearance, and perhaps where he was last seen. One of the first was inserted by the widow and the sister of Lieutenant Angus Macnaghten in December 1914 in various provincial newspapers in Scotland, Hampshire and Ulster, where the officer had had family connections. The notice in the *Belfast Weekly News* reminded readers that: 'Lieutenant Macnaghten who was serving at the front with the 1st Battalion is a grandson of Sir Frances Workman Macnaghten, Dungrave, North Antrim.' In most cases there were no replies. However, Mrs Macnaghten was eventually contacted by a Red Cross nurse in Dorset, one of whose patients had told her that he had seen Lieutenant Macnaghten taken prisoner.[46]

Occasionally, enquirers sought more information about how their son or husband had been killed. For Lance Corporal William Craig, Seaforth Highlanders, the advertisement in the *Dundee Courier* said that 'Chum reports him wounded in the face 25th September 1915. Not heard of since.'[47] Most advertisers were looking for local men, although William Craig and his family came from Coatbridge in Lanarkshire. The spouse of Private Peter Mclean, Black Watch, wrote: 'Last letter from France dated 22 September. Information would be welcomed by his anxious wife.'[48]

Such was the demand for these small ads that a magazine began to specialise in them. Before the war the *Territorial Service Gazette* mainly ran Army Council Instructions and amendments to King's Regulations together with news of rifle shooting matches and social events for officers and NCOs; but by 1916, the editor increasingly included appeals from relations of territorials and other soldiers who had gone missing overseas. An attraction to potential correspondents was its claim that the *Gazette* was 'posted to the members of regiments serving on all Fronts and is circulated in all Military Hospitals'.[49]

Much more space could be allocated to each appeal, sometimes with details of correspondence with the War Office and elsewhere, and there is often a photograph of the missing man. Enquiries appear to be largely for Londoners. In many cases enquirers were not really expecting to receive a reply but were venting

The Search for the Missing

their frustration with what they perceived to be a bureaucratic and uncaring system. When Mrs F. M. Champion of West Norwood received a polite brush-off from the commandant of the returned Prisoners of War Reception Centre in Ripon when she attempted to seek information about her missing husband Private Percy William Champion, London Regiment, the editor commented, somewhat unfairly, that this was 'another instance of the soullessness of Whitehall, where a dead or missing soldier is of no account.'[50]

The *Territorial Service Gazette* was not a patch on *Les Recherche des disparus*, a weekly newspaper that was first published by the French Association for the Search for the Missing in February 1915. Its motto was: 'As long as the search has turned up nothing, we will pursue it with all our means.' Containing casualty lists as well as appeals from the families of the missing, it was widely circulated within France. Unfortunately, publication was suspended in December 1917 through lack of funds and a shortage of paper, but the association promised that the search would carry on.[51]

Did the advertising work? In a few cases it must have done. Occasionally newspapers printed thanks from readers for information supplied. The editor of the *Territorial Services Gazette* advised the father of Private R. C. Phelps, Middlesex Regiment, to place a notice in the *Hackney Gazette* seeking information about his son who was a member of a local battalion. As a result, he was eventually contacted by a Lance Corporal Thakes, a returned prisoner of war who passed over some of Phelps' possessions, including a war bond.[52] Annie Allard advertised for months for information about her husband George. Eventually a reader wrote to tell her that he had been the last person to see George alive: he had been killed outright by a shell.[53]

The *Territorial Services Gazette* made a point of including success stories. As the result of seeing an appeal in the magazine a returned prisoner of war contacted the family of Private Arthur Hainzinger, London Regiment, providing details of how their son had died. He had received a severe spine injury, the result of British shrapnel minutes after having been taken prisoner by the Germans.[54]

A few individuals went further and tried to insert appeals in enemy newspapers. This was of course illegal under the regulations on trade with the enemy. But there was a way round it: the *Continental Times*, a pro-German propaganda newspaper for Americans in Europe which was widely circulated in prisoner of war camps.[55] Although published in Berlin, the *Continental Times* had an office in Amsterdam in neutral Holland. Several British families took advantage of this and paid for advertisements, include the family of Second Lieutenant Cecil Gennings, East Surreys, who advertised in the issue of 15 December 1916 giving a contact address in Amsterdam.[56] The Foreign Office commented:

> This would be a highly objectionable method of advertising for missing prisoners. It would be unpleasant to prosecute the relations of missing men, but if anybody in England has, even indirectly, paid for the advertisement about Second-Lt Gennings, they would undoubtedly lay themselves open to heavy penalties.

The Foreign Office passed the issue to the War Office, which had far weightier matters to attend to and the subject seems to have been quietly forgotten.

The American Embassy

After the War Office and the Red Cross, the next most popular place to turn to was the American Embassy in London. On the outbreak of war they took over responsibility for British interests in Germany. The Embassy would forward requests for information to colleagues in Berlin who would make enquiries of the military authorities there. Newspaper reports suggested that lists of prisoners were 'furnished intermittently by the German government through the United States embassies in Berlin and London'.[57] This encouraged families to write directly to the Embassy seeking information, although lists were the same as received by the War Office. Hazel Macnaghten duly contacted the London embassy, stressing her great anxiety about her husband and urging them to 'take compassion on her'. She received an unhelpful reply explaining the lists.

A week or so after receiving news that his son Lieutenant John Kipling, Irish Guards, had been posted, Rudyard Kipling wrote to Walter Page, the American Ambassador in London seeking his help in tracing his son. He provided a full physical description adding: 'He is short-sighted wearing gold spectacles. He wears small gold signet ring with monogram JK. All his clothes are marked.'[58]

The American and, after the United States declared war in April 1917, the Dutch embassies received at least 11,000 enquiries from members of the public relating to Prisoners of War in Germany and another 7400 enquiries relating to prisoners in the other Central Powers, notably Turkey. which they forwarded to the Foreign Office. These figures are on the low side, as detailed records were not kept until spring 1915.[59]

Because of the increase of letters to embassies and other bodies, particularly those in Germany, the War Office increasingly advised families of missing men not to contact them:

> Individual enquiries sent to Germany in missing cases have been found by experience to produce no correct information that was not already in the possession of the War Office and, as ... the placing of names of the missing is done by the War Office automatically, and it is therefore not necessary for relatives to take any steps to ensure that official enquiries in Germany are set on foot. It is particularly requested that letters should not be sent to

the Netherlands Legation or to the Foreign Office as applications of this description cannot be dealt with.[60]

Private eyes, conmen and enquiry bureaux

In the early months of the war German private enquiry agents were occasionally hired by British relatives in search of their missing boys.[61] In late September the British politician Alfred Milner used one to try to find his friend's son George Cecil. The detective thought that the officer might be found wounded in a prisoner of war camp in Aachen, although when the Dutch consul investigated he found this was not the case.[62] Another private eye, Otto Lange in Berlin, was employed on occasion by the International Committee of the Red Cross in Geneva to investigate missing Allied servicemen in Germany, although how much use he was is not known. The Committee passed one of his letters to the War Office who was investigating the fate of Second Lieutenant G. H. F. Power, Middlesex Regiment. Herr Lange was unable to help with the officer but provided details of two Irish privates also called Power who had been taken prisoner in May 1915.[63]

Where there are vulnerable people there are people who prey on that vulnerability. This immutable rule applied to the families who sought information about their missing sons and husbands during and after the First World War. In some ways it is surprising that there were not more scams perpetrated, particularly during the early months of the war when there was much uncertainty over the fate of the missing.

There were several legitimate organisations and individuals who tried to help, but with little success as they only rarely had access to information that was not already available to the War Office and the Red Cross. Hazel Macnaghten, for example, contacted the Morning Post Prisoners of War Enquiry Bureau, Cox & Cox's Enquiry Office and American Express, which had offices across Europe.[64] In April 1919 the *Territorial Service*

Gazette, described above preposterously patted itself on the back for its hard work, for otherwise

> ... the present 'missing' soldier scandal would have been considerably accentuated. The War Office has relied on [the Gazette, the Red Cross] and other organisations to care for and investigate the prisoners of war questions, and what success has been attained is entirely due to voluntary work and not to any effort of the War Office.[65]

The *Gazette* claimed success in tracing a number of men, including Private Stanley Hastilow, London Regiment, whose mother 'had done so much to use the *TSG* in tracing missing men'. Hastilow, a repatriated prisoner of war, returned home safely in December 1918.[66] There is nothing to suggest the magazine made any difference at all, but it is possible they helped Mrs Hastilow approach the International Committee of the Red Cross in Geneva.

Several conmen leached off the relatives of the missing. Frederic Page Gaston, an American journalist, during the autumn and winter of 1914 claimed to have special access to prisoner of war camps in Germany. For a fee he would 'search' for individual British prisoners who did not appear on the official lists. This seems to have been a development from his plan to 'supply' parcels of food and gifts to those incarcerated. To be charitable he was, perhaps, initially meeting a demand from relatives who wanted to help their men, but he was soon promising services he could not deliver.[67] The *Daily Graphic*, for example, published an interview with him in which he unwisely boasted that:

> I have already organised in Germany a comprehensive searching service. No doubt there are hundreds perhaps thousands of officers and men who have been wounded and placed temporarily

in peasants' cottages, farmhouses and hospitals and other places where they are for the time being lost to those at home.⁶⁸

He added that these prisoners were forbidden to write home. In a relative's frantic search for news, who would not believe him? Eventually he became such a nuisance that the American Ambassador in Berlin, James W. Gerard, asked British newspapers to warn readers that they should avoid 'confiding anything in this man. He has no connection with the Embassy and I will not even permit it. He has been required to leave Germany and Belgium by the German authorities. I most earnestly beg the British public and the friends of prisoners to have nothing to do with him.⁶⁹

On a smaller scale, Harry Whiting of Kew stole £114 from widows and mothers through his MMA Company which offered to trace missing officers. 'He 'replied to persons advertising for relatives missing in the war, stating that through his organisation and agents he had the opportunity of tracing men not available through the usual channels.' He charged three guineas for a search and two guineas for expenses. Whiting was eventually sentenced to four months imprisonment.⁷⁰

A private in the Royal Army Medical Corps, John Johnson perpetuated at least one heartless fraud. During the summer of 1918, he contacted a Mrs Eleanor Ruffell on seeing a report her husband was missing on the Western Front. Johnson claimed to be a comrade of George Ruffell, and offered to go and find him, if Eleanor would pay his expenses, Four pounds was duly handed over, but no work was undertaken. When brought to trial, Jackson said that a fellow soldier had told him that Ruffell was dead. Eleanor immediately collapsed in court, this being the first news she had received of his fate. Johnson was sentenced to three months imprisonment.⁷¹

It must have been fairly easy to engage in fraud of this kind. The *Territorial Service Gazette* included a letter from 'a broken -hearted mother' who had been visited in May 1919 by 'an apparently crippled soldier' who claimed to know her son, who had been admitted with serious wounds to the same prisoner of war camp. With the son's dying breath he told the soldier to contact his folks in England. The man heard the surname as being Ashley or Askew, 14th London Scottish, living in a place called 'Waltham something'. By trial and error he had found the correspondent living in Walthamstow.

'I showed him my boy's private photo ... the one in Scottish dress. "Yes". He said "he could swear that was the young fellow he had buried in Strasburg camp...Well, what could I do but believe him? With combined similarity of name address, he gave, I never doubted for one moment that it was not my dear boy he had seen die.'

He asked for 27 shillings for expenses but would not stop to meet the correspondent's husband. This made her suspicious and he was sent away with just five shillings.[72] No doubt he was not the only person engaged in this scam.

7

THE IMPERIAL WAR GRAVES COMMISSION

The men don't fear death any more, we have made our peace with the thought of our own demise. A much heavier burden is the fear to be forgotten in foreign soil – an inglorious end for any soldier.

Unknown German Officer[1]

The Imperial War Graves Commission (IWGC) became the repository of the hopes of many families of the fallen. It was established in 1917 under Sir Fabian Ware to preserve the physical remains and the eternal memory of the British and Commonwealth war dead. Renamed in 1960 as the Commonwealth War Graves Commission (CWGC) it continues to care for the graves and memorials of the men who fell in both world wars. This included the design and construction of the cemeteries which lie along the Western Front and in theatres of operations elsewhere across the world, from 1921 the exhumation and reburying of the fallen in these cemeteries, and finally, and most perhaps importantly for the families of the missing, the erection of memorials to the fallen.

In the years after the Armistice the Commission became a huge undertaking, negotiating with the mayors of French and Belgian villages for suitable land for cemeteries, engaging local building contractors to construct them as well as finding the appropriate British architects to provide suitable designs. Not the least of its work was its dealings with the families of the missing. In an appearance before the Public Accounts Committee in 1927 Sir Fabian Ware said:

> I do not think there is any need for me to tell the Committee that the anxiety and interest taken by very many of the relatives of the missing is poignant. I mean, they are always asking if you cannot 'find their boy,' or if 'something cannot be done'.... I was only asking the porter this morning, and he said that people are always dropping in to ask where a grave was, or whether anything is known about a missing person. The other inquiries are from relatives, by letter.[2]

For the families of the missing there was always hope that the body would be found. Sir Fabian told the Select Committee that bodies were still being recovered from the battlefields 'at the rate of something like 100 a week... Last year there were about 5000 new identifications, which is a very considerable number.'[3]

The gathering of bodies, their identification and the subsequent registration of their names was initially more or less left to private individuals and the British Red Cross. By the summer of 1915, following pressure from Fabian Ware, the Army had taken over the work of the Red Cross and established the Directorate of Graves Registration and Enquiries (DGR&E), tasked with identifying and burying the dead in cemeteries and dealing with the next of kin. Sir Douglas Haig recognised the importance of the Directorate's work:

> It has [been of] extraordinary moral value to the Troops in the field as well as to the relatives and friends of the dead at home. The mere fact that these officers, day after day, visit the cemeteries close

behind the trenches, fully exposed to shell and rifle fire, accurately record not only the names of the dead but also the exact place of burial, has a symbolic value to the men that it would be difficult to exaggerate.[4]

Initially, men were buried more or less where they fell on the battlefield. Where possible a marker would be left to help searchers find the body or bodies. The grave markers could be constructed with any immediately available pieces of equipment, from upturned enemy rifles to aeroplane propellers and wooden ration boxes. In a letter of March 1915, Lieutenant D. Allen remarked that there were a number of graves in the Ypres sector where a cross had been made with a Huntley and Palmer biscuit tin, listing the dead soldier's name, rank, and the date of his death. Burying parties were required to note details on a piece of paper, placing it in the neck of an upturned bottle or similar vessel which could be placed in or on the grave.[5]

Burial parties in wartime

The failure to clear the battlefields undoubtedly affected the morale of many soldiers as they could see with their own eyes what might so easily be their fate.[6] Fabian Ware wrote in June 1917 of the effect of having so many unrecovered bodies:

> We are on the verge over here of serious trouble about the number of bodies lying out still unburied on the Somme battlefields. The soldiers returning wounded or on leave to England are complaining bitterly about it and the War Office has already received letters on the matter... This kind of scandal will be used immediately and with great effect by the pacifists, and by others who are endeavouring to assist the enemy by obstructing the proper prosecution of the war.[7]

It was an almost impossible task to retrieve bodies from No Man's Land. There were just so many corpses and the terrain in which they lay was hardly conducive to their recovery. John Masefield described one small area near the Leipzig Redoubt at Thiepval after the Battle of the Somme:

> Other places are bad and full of death, but this was deep in mud as well, a kind of chaos of deep running holes & broken ground & filthy chasms, and pools & stands & marshes of iron-coloured water, & yellow snow & bedevilment. Old rags of wet uniform were everywhere & bones & legs & feet & heads were sticking out of the ground, & in one place were all tools of a squad just as they laid them down; in order & then all the squad, where they had been killed & the skull of one of them in a pool & nearby, the grave of half a German, & then a German overcoat with ribs inside it, & rifles & bombs & shells literally in heaps... Such a hell of a desolation all round as no words can describe.[8]

Even so, after each battle burial parties were sent into No Man's Land in order to retrieve or bury bodies, for reasons of morale, hygiene and humanity. Men would have on their gas masks and probably sandbags on their hands to guard against infection from corpses. Charles Carrington wrote: 'After a battle you buried your comrades and saw to it that their graves were marked with a wooden cross and a name. if you had time, and if it was not too dangerous, you did as much for other British dead. The enemy came last in priority, and more than once I have cleared a trench of its defunct tenants by throwing them over the parapet where someone might or might not find and bury them when the battle was over.'[9]

Lieutenant George Craike, Highland Light Infantry, remembered one such party going out after the Battle of Loos:

> One frosty evening practically the whole of our company, including the captain himself, were on a special burial party to dispose of a

large number of the 7th East Surreys who had been killed between the 25th and 27th of September [1915]. We crawled out of the trenches with caution in small parties, and dealt with the dead by simply pulling them into depressions in the earth, or into shell holes. This was not a pleasant task and occasionally the arms disengaged from the bodies. However, the bodies were placed as far as possible in these holes and covered over with a light layer of earth, this earth being brushed or dug in by entrenching tools. All this work had to be done on all fours, for to stand erect was courting disaster. In addition, the very frequent Very lights of the Germans necessitated instant stillness... The work was slow, laborious and difficult. Before the bodies were actually covered over, the main task was to retrieve the identity discs. These discs were found round their necks and were cut off, collected and in due course sent back to headquarters.[10]

Whole bodies were sewn into blankets. In a ghastly type of jigsaw puzzle, body parts that seemed to belong together were placed together and buried as a complete human being, although often it was impossible to confirm his identity. Private Alfred Burrage, Artists Rifles, was detailed to remove bodies from a trench:

> We picked up unspeakable things with our hands, putting them into sandbags. Strangely enough, the actual experience was not so revolting at the time as it seems in retrospect. I could not have endured it before, I could not endure it today; but I derived an odd sort of comfort to find that I could endure it then.[11]

In areas where the front line had moved forward, more systematic searches could be made for the dead. During 1915, Grave Registration Units, part of the Directorate of Grave Registration and Enquiries under Fabian Ware were set up to identify bodies and then to ensure they were buried in cemeteries in such a way that the remains could be found again. By 1917 there were 23 such units attached to individual Army headquarters in France and Flanders. Instead of being allocated to specific areas they were sent where they were needed to clear battlefields as best they could, where they worked with burial units provided by infantry regiments. By the beginning of 1918, there were 800 such cemeteries across France and Belgium with some 300,000 graves.[12]

Work continued after the end of the war. In 1927, Sir Fabian Ware noted that between the Armistice and September 1921, 204,650 bodies 'were taken from the battlefields and reburied in cemeteries set aside to receive them'. The vast majority of these had already been buried in individual graves or small graveyards and were just being 'concentrated' in larger and more manageable cemeteries.

There was a particular need to move the bodies of the 150,000 or so men who lay in isolated or small clumps of graves, in order to return the land to its owners and to allow the reconstruction of the devastated areas to proceed. They soon became a point of interest to tourists. In his guide to the Western Front, published in 1920, Lt Col Lowe wrote: 'The little crosses in the hillside mark the rest billets of our ... comrades of the trenches. They really haven't left us: they are only on ahead, like scouts finding the way.'[13]

Some of the first tourists to the Western Front were Marjorie and Elsa West who visited the area in May 1919. Outside Ypres, the sisters found that:

> Every now and then also came an English Cemetery with its plain wood crosses, everyone bearing a small metal plate inscribed with the name and rank of the dead, but some also with the touching words 'To an unknown Soldier'... There are also isolated graves still scattered here and there over the field, marked sometimes by a mere tin hat and bayonet or by rough nameless crosses like the ones we saw.[14]

As well as concentrating known graves the units had to go over the battlefields to exhume and identify the bodies they found there. It was perhaps the most difficult and draining work that service personnel were expected to undertake in the aftermath of the Great War. Each body had to be carefully examined in order to identify it. This might involve feeling inside a body that had been damaged by shellfire or partially eaten by rats. In the months after the Armistice, when many bodies had decomposed only a little, the corpse's flesh often came away when touched.[15]

Sir Laming Worthington-Evans explained to the House of Commons that:

> In the spring of 1920, the work was very easy and rapid owing to the number of surface indications, but since then in the cases of, approximately, 90 per cent of the bodies found there was no surface indication. These invisible graves were found by various local indications recognised by the experience of the exhumation parties.

Even in the best of conditions it would not have been an easy task, but their task was made ten times worse by the devastation that was still to be found on the Western Front and extending many miles either side. Marjory and Elsa West were taken to a wood at Bourton near Cambrai:

> Here and there over the field we came across isolated graves and white fragments of bone, but whether horse or human we could not tell. They said that the fewness of German and English graves was accounted for by the fact that often as fast as they were made, they were blown to bits by bombardment. It was a gruesome wood, shattered and broken.[16]

The process of exhumation was simple on paper, although much more difficult on the ground. A Survey Officer selected

500-yard squares to be searched, indicating to the Burial Officer the anticipated number of remains based on the records, which were often inaccurate. In one map square 'information reported eleven isolated graves, careful search reveals 67. In another area in one fortnight no remains found under four per cent of crosses erected.' In the end experience indicated where to dig. Indeed, the IWGC noted 'Unless previously experienced men are employed, 80 per cent of the bodies which remain to be picked up would never be found.'[17]

William McBeath of the Australian Graves Detachment found that the thicker the flowers in an area, the more horrible it was underfoot. In his first week, his unit exhumed and reburied around 200 bodies in the area around Villiers-Bretonneux. 'You could hardly think there were so many graves in the fields.'[18]

His colleague Major Alfred Allen even used a divining rod in order to locate bodies. The English writer John Oxenham wrote that 'When all hope of finding a body has been given up by everyone else, one can turn to Major Allen as a last resort. In eight out of ten cases Allen solves the mystery setting the seal of certainty on lingering hopes and doubts at home.' Sometimes the ground that had been gone over many times by burial parties would yield its secrets when Major Allen used his divining rod. According to Oxenham, the major found 70 to 100 dead men a week, mostly in freshly cleared areas.[19] Inevitably, there were doubts about the Major's skills. Matters came to a head over a botched exhumation of an Australian officer near Fromelles. Allen failed to locate the body, although he found five other British corpses. A subsequent court of enquiry was inconclusive.[20]

The work of exhumation units came to an end in mid-July 1921. To cheers, Sir Laming Worthington-Evans told Parliament that the: 'battlefield area [had] been systematically searched at least six times' and in areas where fighting had been particularly heavy 'as many as 20 times'. The British would leave it to local farmers to report any bodies they found to the authorities.[21]

In fact, the work of the units was unfinished. Worthington-Evans had to admit in a written Parliamentary answer that 'the number of missing officers and men still unaccountable for is approximately 93,800.'[22] The incompleteness was graphically but probably inadvertently exposed in a story about the devastated areas that appeared in the *Illustrated London News* the week after the announcement. Among the pictures of the reconstruction work there was a photograph of skulls lying on the ground at Hooge Crater.[23]

Over the next fifteen years, 38,000 more bodies were recovered. Sir Fabian wrote that they were 'still coming to light at the rate of twenty to thirty a week... About 20 per cent have been identified and it is still possible to identify from 10 to 15 per cent of the bodies discovered.'[24] Visiting Hill 60 near Ypres in July 1927, the journalist H V Morton came across a guided tour. The guide 'stopped and picked up a bone, and placing it against his chest said "that is a breastbone." A young English girl took it in her hand and looked at it. I felt sorry for all of us. The war has gone. Its memories have gone.[25]

For identification purposes, a careful examination of pockets, the neck, wrists and braces for identification tags was required. Officers of the Labour Companies who were undertaking the work were told:

> It has been found advisable to impress upon [the men] that the work is of vital importance, having regard to the number of men still missing, many of whom can be found and identified if the work is carefully done ... the greater the stress laid upon the need for identification, the greater the pride the men take in the work.[26]

Most men were identified by their identity disc as the authorities had intended. British ones were made from stamped leather and were worn round the neck. They provided the soldier's name, his regimental number and unit, as well as his religion, usually CE for Church of England. Many men also carried unofficial ways of being identified such as aluminium discs or bracelets which they wore round their necks or on their wrists, while others took their pay books into battle or wrote their details on the back of family photos. Not every soldier wore his identity tag in the first place. Perhaps the first missing casualty of the war, an unknown gunner, was buried at Le Cateau in late August 1914 having been shot by a French sentry. Staff Officer Wyndham Childs had the task of arranging his burial:

> It was impossible to identify the man at the time, for when the unit to which he belonged moved they very stupidly took away his identity disc, so I had no idea who he was. I had great difficulty in arranging the poor fellow's funeral ... as a nameless person cannot be buried in France without considerable formality.[27]

At Tyne Cot, 61 per cent of men who were recovered from the Passchendaele battlefields for reburial at the cemetery were identified by their dog tag. Other ways might be through a man's pay book, army kit which had been inscribed with the owner's name, and personal possessions, such as wallets, letters and cigarette cases. Private T. Morrow, Royal Inniskilling Fusiliers, for example, was described as being an 'Unidentified', but a letter from his father in Belfast was used to establish his name. Private H. T. Breakwell, Royal Welsh Fusiliers, had made every attempt to keep hold of his groundsheet as it had his name written in each corner.[28]

Despite the best efforts, it was always difficult to identify individual corpses, but it was possible. One such success was Private Frank Sowden, Devonshire Regiment. In January 1920, the *Western Times* wrote that Mrs Alice Sowden of Exeter had received news of her husband Frank, who had been reported missing on 26 October 1917 and was later presumed killed in action: 'In the process of exhumation of isolated graves his remains were found and reinterred in Hooge Crater Cemetery.'[29]

Fewer than one in three of those uncovered at Passchendaele were eventually identified. The ravages of war and time had destroyed what evidence there had been. The burial registers occasionally contain notes such as 'Bones in sandbag' or 'Remains badly shattered.' Of the 6848 unidentified men listed in the Tyne Cot burial returns, about half can be identified as being British, Australian or Canadian, generally from scraps of uniform. Another third also have details of their regiment by some detail on their uniform, perhaps a button or shoulder strap. For an otherwise unknown soldier in the Worcestershire Regiment there was a 'photo in locket (lady and baby)'.[30]

The methods for identifying soldiers' bodies retrieved from the Western Front have not changed very much. Steve Arnold of the Commission's Human Recovery Unit told Lord Ashcroft in 2019 that when a body is found:

> We cordon off the area and then we look for artefacts that are associated with a certain country – boots, badges, buttons, belt buckles, webbing equipment and weapons that will point to whether they are Commonwealth, French or German. We are also looking for shoulder titles, which will point to a particular regiment... If we can eventually put a name to someone's remains, then that's the perfect scenario, but we realise that is very hard.

The only additional tool is DNA, and that depends on having some rough identification of the body in the first place before undertaking matches with living relatives.[31]

The work undertaken by the Labour Companies was not always of a high standard. In 1919, the historians of the Labour Corps, John Starling and Oliver Lee, note that 'speedy clearing up of the battlefields was probably of higher importance, for sanitary and other considerations, than minute accuracy in establishing the identity of the bodies that were found.' Receiving little guidance, the Exhumation Companies, 'obsessed with the idea that their reputation depended on their concentrating the highest possible number of bodies in the shortest possible time ... often paid little heed to the essential matter of identification.'[32] An Australian newspaper report in November 1920 led the IWGC to conduct an audit of the burials at Hooge Crater Cemetery. 135 graves were reopened and examined. The results were damning: some graves were empty, while others contained sandbags, crosses recorded incorrect burial details, and others were mixed up; and Dominion soldiers were recorded as being British. The Commission, perhaps charitably, concluded that the exhumation party had worked without adequate instruction.[33] The shoddy work is still evident today: sixty per cent of the graves at Hooge are for unknown soldiers.

Memorials to the Missing

Much of the work of the Imperial War Graves Commission in its first few years concerned the construction of cemeteries where the fallen could rest. By 1937, the Commission had constructed 970 cemeteries containing 600,000 headstones, at a cost of £8,150,000, which Gavin Stamp reminds us was about one-third of the cost of one day's fighting during the Battle of Passchendaele.[34]

Commemoration of the missing required a different solution, either for recovered bodies that could not be identified, or the names of tens of thousands of men for whom no bodies could be found at all. No such thing had been attempted in previous wars. There nearest equivalent were memorials to men lost in naval disasters at sea. In 1919, Rudyard Kipling wrote a pamphlet about the cemeteries that were being planned on the battlefields to reassure the grieving that their loved ones were not forgotten. There was a short, rather tentative section about the provision of 'Memorials to the Missing':

> This matter is naturally of the deepest concern to the relatives of those whose bodies have never been recovered or identified, or

whose graves, once made, have been destroyed by later battles. Their number is not small, and Sir Frederic Kenyon has suggested that the best way to record their memory would be to place a tablet on the walls or cloisters at the cemetery nearest to the spot where it is presumed they lost their lives. In the case of officers and men in the Flying Corps, the place of whose death could not be known within many miles, the tablet might be placed in the cemetery nearest to the camp from which they had started on their last flight. But in any case, relatives may be assured that the dead who have no known resting-place will be made equal with the others, and that each case will be dealt with upon full consideration of its merit as regards the size and the place of the memorial.[35]

There was considerable debate within the Commission about how to commemorate the missing. It was relatively easy to deal with exhumed but unidentified bodies, which were laid to rest in graves in a cemetery near where they fell. Their last resting place is now marked by a standard headstone with appropriate epitaph, generally Rudyard Kipling's phrase 'A Soldier of the Great War/Known unto God.' The epitaph appears on just over 180,000 headstones.[36] Occasionally the phrase may be varied if additional information is known about the deceased. The most common variation is 'believed to be buried in this cemetery' or if a specific unit was identified his regiment will also be given. Until his body was positively identified in the 1990s John Kipling's headstone in St Mary's Advanced Dressing Station Cemetery at Loos had 'A Lieutenant of the Great War/Irish Guards' engraved on it.[37]

It was much harder to decide how to commemorate the men whose bodies were never retrieved. In an ideal world each man would have been commemorated individually. Certainly, this is what their families would have hoped for. But the sheer numbers and the uncertainty in many cases of where exactly a man fell meant that this was not possible. The Australian government originally insisted on a grave and a gravestone for each casualty, whether there was a body or not. The matter was raised at the Commissioners' meeting on 15 April 1919. The Australian representative Mr Box said: 'Their idea is that every man, whether you get his body or not should be entitled to his six feet by three in the Cemetery and to his cross [and] on it should be simply the record of his death – killed in action on such a date – and not going on to say that his body has never been found, or anything like that.'[38]

The other commissioners were largely opposed to the proposal. Rudyard Kipling said that it gave him 'the creeps'. In the end the Australian proposal, which was entirely impractical, was quietly dropped.

The debate then centred around placing tablets listing the missing in the cemeteries nearest where they were thought to have fallen. This proposal eventually fell through because it was not always possible to know even very roughly where a man might have disappeared.[39] Finally, it was decided to honour the missing in a series of memorials at sites near where the fighting had largely taken place. Ware later wrote the intention that the decision would: 'give effect to the desire of relatives that ... the Missing Dead should be permanently commemorated individually and by name, as near as possible to the places where they fell.'[40] However, later critics such as Stephen O'Shea have suggested that they are nothing more than 'stone ledgers of the lost [whereby] the State through its punctiliousness, can be absolved.'[41] Gavin Stamp thought that the memorials asserted 'the significance of each life, however callously that life may have been squandered by those in authority.'[42]

Even a century after the Armistice the memorials remain impressive but inevitably impersonal, reminders of the brutality of the Great War. One wonders how the grieving parents and widows must have felt. Surely, many must have wanted more for their loss than just a name high up on an arch in a country which not all could realistically hope to visit.

Ware proposed that twelve new standalone memorials be erected along the former British sector of the Western Front commemorating the fighting either in a particular area or in a particular battle, such as the battles of the Somme or the operations around Ploegsteert.[43] The French were unhappy about the proposal at a time when financial restraints meant they were unable to provide equivalent memorials of their own. In end, four memorials specifically dedicated to the missing were built in France (Thiepval, Arras, the Cambrai memorial at Louverval and La Ferte-sous-Jouarre) and two in Belgium (Ploegsteert and the Menin Gate in Ypres). In addition, there were national memorials for the Canadians at Vimy Ridge, the Australians at Villers-Bretonneux, and Indians at Neuve-Chapelle.[44]

There was a danger that the resulting memorials to the missing would be too triumphalist, acting as much as memorials to British victories as to the sacrifices of war. The Commission's architectural advisor Sir Frederic Kenyon warned: 'It will confuse and obliterate the grand idea which our cemeteries are intended to embody if it is intended to make them serve the turn of battle memorials also.'[45] In fact, the memorials rarely show any such sign and are the better for it.

The Menin Gate's architect Sir Reginald Blomfield's stated intention was that the memorial should 'symbolise the enduring power and indominable tenacity of the British Empire'.[46] Rudyard Kipling's inscription on the memorial itself hints at its dual purpose: 'To the armies of the British Empire who stood here from 1914 to 1918 and to those of their dead who have no known grave.' This narrative did not sit well with the increasingly anti-war feelings of the late 1920s. Perhaps only over the past decade or so – in the twilight of Britain's Imperial decline – has there sometimes been an echo of triumphalism during ceremonies around the sounding of the Last Post at the Menin Gate.

Visitors to the Menin Gate in the late 1920s and 1930s were reminded more of the futility of war, rather than the great British battles in which those on the memorial had died for. A press release issued by the IWGC to British journalists before the Gate's opening stressed that the press should avoid seeing it as a kind of Arc de Triomphe, a celebration of military might and triumph. This would, the release stressed, rightly be seen as an 'offence to the next of kin of all those whose names are inscribed upon, and who, no doubt, consider it purely as a Memorial to their Dead, and in no sense a Monument of Victory.'[47] A guide to Ypres advised visitors: 'This is not an *Arc de Triomphe*, but a gateway of eternal memories, a shrine of the might of the British Empire, and perhaps, when millions of our people have seen it and read some of it, it may be the gateway of '"Never Again".'[48]

The two most important memorials to the missing on the Western Front are those at the Menin Gate in Ypres, which commemorates 54,000 men who went missing in the Ypres Salient, and the Thiepval Memorial for 72,000 men who disappeared on the Somme. They are very different.

The Menin Gate, Ypres

Both the National Battlefields Memorial Committee and the IWGC identified Ypres as a key site for a memorial in the months after the Armistice. The Committee gave the following reasons:

1. Practically every division on the Western Front passed through Ypres at one time or another;
2. In its immediate neighbourhood there was continuous fighting from the beginning to the end ...
3. Its defence stands to the British Army as that of Verdun to the French ...
4. Many thousands of men lost their lives in the salient.[49]

They recommended that the memorial be where the former Menin Gate had once stood. Through it passed the road to the small town of Menen, but more importantly it was the main road out of town used by British troops on their way towards the trenches that had surrounded the town to the east.[50]

The eminent architect Sir Reginald Bloomfield was commissioned to design the memorial, of which he was very proud, writing in his memoirs that it was 'perhaps the only building I have ever designed in which I do not want anything altered.' The Gate is based on the French military architect Vauban's entrance to the fort at Nancy. It was an inspired design on a relatively long and narrow site incorporating the names of the missing in the Ypres salient in a long-vaulted stone hall. The critic Geoff Dyer thought that it '...belies its own scale and you wonder whether it is really as big as it seems. Everything about the memorial suggests that it should work powerfully on you, but its effect is oddly self-cauterising.'[51]

Work began on the memorial in 1922. It was dedicated by Field Marshal Lord Plumer on 24 July 1927, in the presence of King Albert of the Belgians. There were thousands of mothers and widows of the missing in the crowd. Dominiek Dendooven suggests that 15,000 pilgrims were present.[52] Hundreds of thousands more listened to the ceremony on the wireless, as it was the first overseas outside broadcast made by the BBC.[53] Lord Plumer said:

> One the most tragic features of the Great War was the number of casualties reported as 'Missing, believed killed'. To their relatives there must have been added to their grief a tinge bitterness and a feeling that everything possible had not been done to recover their loved ones' bodies and give them reverent burial. But when peace came, and the last ray of hope had been extinguished, the void seemed deeper and the outlook more forlorn for those who had no grave to visit, no place where they could lay tokens of loving remembrance. The hearts of the people throughout the Empire went out to them, and it was resolved that here at Ypres, where so

many the missing are known to have fallen, there should be erected a memorial worthy of them, which should give expression of the nation's gratitude for their sacrifice, and their sympathy with those who mourned them. A memorial has been erected which in its simple grandeur, fulfils this object, honour we are assembled here today. He is not missing, he is here.[54]

The numbers of widows and mothers present is not known. However, 700 widows and mothers were provided with passages by charities such as St Barnabas and the British Legion. The press interviewed several of the women present:

'Oh, my dear boy. How glad I am to be here the spot where he fought and died for King and country,' said Mrs. Raemers, a woman of 70, from London, who proudly wore her dead son's three medals. Mrs. Susan Hardy, 21, Priory Road, Chiswick, said her boy, Gwynne Hardy, of the 2nd Grenadier Guards, was killed in 1914. She was overjoyed at the opportunity of joining in the great tribute. She could not have made the crossing had it not been for the assistance of the St. Barnabas organisation. 'I have a pension of 12s week,' she said. "That would not have paid my passage.' These were utterances typical of the courage in the British mother's heart. Many of the women carried wreaths of roses and garlands of lilies symbolical of the crown of victory.[55]

'It was wonderful. The Menin Gate has given us the feeling that our lads and what they did are remembered,' [said] Mrs Amelia Powell of Birkenhead. 'For months after my boy was reported missing we hoped and hoped until at last we had to realise he was gone.'[56]

Only a very small proportion of women who could have been at the ceremony were present. For most it was very expensive to travel to Belgium and the press stressed how difficult it was for a woman to go by herself. Hazel Macnaghten, whose husband is commemorated there and who spent many years trying to trace his whereabouts, was among those who did not attend. She certainly had the means and confidence to travel, but to have visited the memorial would surely have been the final acceptance of his death, a step she was unable to take.

Inevitably writers had different views of the memorial and how future generations would come to see it. The Austrian writer and pacifist Stephan Zweig visited the Menin Gate a few months after it was dedicated:

> In its really Roman simplicity this monument to the six and fifty thousand is more impressive than any triumphal arch or monument to victory that I have ever seen, and its impressiveness is still further increased by the sight of the heaps of wreaths constantly being laid there by widows, children and friends. For a whole nation makes its pilgrimage every year to this common tomb of its unburied and unreturning soldiers.[57]

The war poet Siegfried Sassoon was not persuaded. Having visited the Menin Gate in July 1927, he wrote in 'On Passing the New Menin Gate':

> Who will remember, passing through this Gate,
> the unheroic dead who fed the guns?
> Who shall absolve the foulness of their fate –
> Those doomed, conscripted, unvictorious ones?
>
> Crudely renewed, the Salient holds its own.
> Paid are its dim defenders by this pomp;
> Paid, with a pile of peace-complacent stone,
> The armies who endured that sullen swamp.
>
> Here was the world's worst wound. And here with price
> 'Their name liveth for ever more' the Gateway claims

Was ever an immolation so belied
As these intolerably nameless names?
Well might the Devil who struggled in the slime
Rise and deride this sepulchre of crime.[58]

Sassoon's views were very much in a minority. The writer – and veteran of the Ypres Salient – R. H. Mottram, realised that the memorial was not for the present generation:

If it were only for those of us who remember so well, there would be little need of that great arch... But we must remember that we are a dwindling number. Who will march though that gate ten and twenty years hence, and with what knowledge? No, the names are well graven up there on so solid a structure. For the day will come that they will be but names and the arch will be their only memorial.[59]

Writing in 1977, Gavin Stamp summed up what many, perhaps most, visitors to the Menin Gate feel today: '... the daily evening sounding in Blomfield's Menin Gate of the "Last Post and Retreat" echoing in the great hall its remorseless decoration of columns of names, can still induce anguish, outrage and a sense of hopeless loss in the visitor.'[60]

The Memorial to the Missing of the Somme, Thiepval

The memorial at Thiepval honours the 72,161 men who who were posted missing on the Somme between June 1915 and 20 March 1918. It offers a very different response to the loss of the missing than the one in Ypres. This is largely due to the architect chosen – Sir Edwin Lutyens – who also designed the Cenotaph in London. And whereas Reginald Blomfield was largely a traditionalist, Lutyens was an idiosyncratic radical genius.

Thiepval was commissioned by the IWGC in 1928 and opened in 1932. It was constructed on the one of the most devastated areas of the Western Front. Standing high on a bluff above the battlefield, the memorial can be seen from all over the Somme. Nothing, however, prepares the visitor when they come up close to it, for it is far bigger than they might have expected. They are dwarfed, humbled even, by the experience. To me at least, the Memorial is curiously uninvolving. Unlike the Menin Gate, it is more about the building than the tens of thousands of men it commemorates. Stephen O'Shea loathed it: 'The closer you get to the oft-glimpsed edifice, the more repulsive it becomes in its Lego-like gigantism... The mammoth block of stone and brick is an in your face reminder that something hideous occurred in the vicinity.'[61]

Geoff Dyer commented: '[It] seems almost ugly, in its hulking intensity dominating the landscape for miles around ... the monument has none of the vulnerability of the body, of its terrible propensity for harm. Its predominant relation is to the earth – not, as is the case with a cathedral to the sky.' [62]

Jay Winter is more positive: 'Lutyens brilliantly managed to create an embodiment of nothingness, an abstract space unique among memorials of the Great War.'[63] But the most enthusiastic of all was Gavin Stamp, who felt that it was the 'ultimate British war memorial... The visitor stands beneath a high stone vault resting on solid brick walls, but is mostly conscious of space and sky'.[64] Certainly, with the exception of the Canadian memorial on Vimy Ridge, no other memorial from either world war makes such an impact.

The memorial was opened by the Prince of Wales and the French President, Albert Lebrun on 1 August 1932. It was a surprisingly low-key event. The Prince's speech was anodyne and the press coverage was muted. Few papers sent reporters to cover the event, relying on agency coverage. There were very few grieving parents and widows in attendance: it was now nearly sixteen years after the Battle of the Somme. The *Manchester Guardian* suggested that there might have been as few as 3000.[65]

The *Daily Herald* and other papers included advertisements for package tours almost up to the day of the ceremony, but there seems to have been few takers. Thiepval was even more difficult and expensive to get to than Ypres; and Britain – and Europe – was in the midst of the Great Depression. Again, the ceremony was broadcast by the BBC, so many pilgrims who in brighter days might have considered making the journey just tuned in.

Perhaps more importantly, attitudes to the war itself had changed. Lutyens' grand statement about the tragic losses of the Great War now seemed out of touch with the modern world.

Today, however, the Memorial has never seemed more important. Since the late 1990s there has been an exponential increase in tourism to the Western Front by individuals, tour groups and above all school parties. The smaller, more intimate Menin Gate has struggled to cope. The much larger site at Thiepval swallows up the largest of school groups, even if it doesn't have the immediacy that the Last Post ceremony offers. The visitor centre and museum provide an excellent introduction to the memorial and the men commemorated here, and offers an interpretation of what their sacrifice means in the modern world.

The memorials in France and Flanders and the recovery and reburial of the dead meant little to most widows and wives. Most would never be able to travel overseas and the chance of a man's body being identified was small. Instead, grieving was largely conducted at home, with public sentiments focussed on two very different memorials within a few hundred metres of each other in London.

8

MEMORIALISING THE MISSING

> In Loving Memory
> Of Those
> "Reported Missing"
> Who, Unknown, Unseen,
> Unrewarded, Gave Their
> Lives For Their Kindred
> Memorial plaque in the Union Jack Club, London[1]

In November 1920, hundreds of thousands of sombrely clad men and women patiently shuffled down Whitehall past the Cenotaph and the Tomb of the Unknown Warrior marking the death of the fallen. Commentators at the time suggested that mourning for their dead sons and husbands could be focused on the Cenotaph and, in particular, the Tomb of the Unknown Warrior, because it was just possible that the body there, whose burial had been performed by the highest in the land, was their child or spouse. Visitors could therefore set aside their grief because it was here that he lay. In modern terminology, the very act of passing the Cenotaph and the Tomb would in some miraculous way offer closure to the grieving. And for some this was the case. Andrea

Hetherington suggests that: 'The popularity of the Tomb of the Unknown Warrior showed the need amongst many of the bereaved for some kind of ceremony analogous to a funeral for their own missing relative.'[2]

Thursday 11 November 1920, a fine but misty day, saw the unveiling of two memorials in the heart of Imperial London dedicated to those who had been killed during the First World War. The Cenotaph, from the Greek for Empty Tomb, in Whitehall was dedicated to 'Our Glorious Dead', a contemporary newsreel called it 'the Shrine to our Soldier's Souls', while the Tomb of the Unknown Warrior, as the name suggests, was specifically dedicated to those servicemen who had no known grave. The inscription on the Tomb reads: 'A British Warrior Who Fell In The Great War 1914-1918 For King And Country. Greater Love Hath No Man Than This.'[3]

Both were the result of an overwhelming desire by the public for a permanent and national focus for their grief. This took two forms: an austere non-denominational memorial designed by the most eminent architect of the age, and a tomb inside the Anglican church's most famous place of worship. The politicians were eager to meet this demand. However, as unemployed ex-servicemen all too often pointed out, such memorials were considerably cheaper than supporting those who had survived, or paying widows' and disabled men's allowances at a decent rate.

However, not all grieving mothers, fathers or widows by any means mourned at the Cenotaph or the Tomb or, indeed, at local war memorials. For many, such ceremonies brought back memories they would rather forget. Stephen Cooper did not remember his grandmother, the widow of Private Arthur Cooper, Sherwood Foresters, who was 'blown to bits' on 12 April 1918, attending any remembrance services: 'She said "I don't need that to remind me of Arthur."'[4] In Leeds, Sapper Reginald Wright went missing at the end of March 1918. His widow Maud was clearly very bitter about his death, refusing to have anything to do with the IWGC and she chose not to have Reginald's name added to the memorial in Headingley where she lived. His details were only added in 2017 after a campaign by Reginald's grandson Graham.[5] Such reactions to a loved one's death cannot have been uncommon. Of the entries in the Commonwealth War Graves Commission's records of the war dead for the 532 Fowlers who died on the Western Front, 326 (61 per cent) contain additional information provided by the men's families. Of the remaining 216 men, whose relatives did not supply entries, the majority are to be found on one of the memorials to the missing. Their grieving families perhaps felt that without a body to mourn then there was little point in replying to the standard requests sent out to relatives by the Commission.

The Cenotaph

The historian Eric Homberger wrote that between the wars, 'The Cenotaph stood for a sacrifice of a generation "for King and Country" and was a reminder of the indebtedness of the living to the dead.'[6] The Cenotaph soon came to symbolise all those who lost their lives in the service of their country, now marked by the annual Remembrance Day ceremony. However, the importance of its counterpart, the Tomb, has faded as the missing men themselves were forgotten.

Three weeks after the signing of the Peace Treaty with Germany, Britain celebrated the successful conclusion of the Great War with a now almost entirely forgotten public holiday, Peace Day – 19 July 1919 – with processions, fetes and fireworks. The centrepiece of the celebrations was a procession of troops from the victorious nations along the Mall marching past the King at the Victoria Memorial outside Buckingham Palace. For many the highlight of the procession was at the new Cenotaph memorial in Whitehall, where the marchers turned their eyes towards it and saluted as they marched past as a mark of respect to the deceased.

It was a last-minute addition erected at the last moment, over the objections of the Prime Minister, who feared it would reek too much of Catholic symbolism for the tastes of the staunchly Protestant British people. An initial proposal was to erect a large cross near Admiralty Arch, but this did not find much favour.[7] The monument was designed by Sir Edward Lutyens, seemingly almost on the back of an envelope, although in fact he had already been working on a design.[8]

The temporary structure immediately became popular with the public, in the way that few other buildings or memorials have. It clearly met an unexpressed need for a national place for remembrance. Eric Homberger suggested that:

> The circumstances of its conception ... suggest that this brilliantly successful focus for the most deeply held emotions of the inter-war period was conceived almost as an afterthought, and that it was the people not the government who made it such an unparalleled object of respect.[9]

Allen Greenberg argues that the simplicity of the Cenotaph embodied the 'acceptance of death and a sense of the fragility and uniqueness of each individual ... perhaps the one part of the peace celebration that spoke of nothing but death, of duty well done, and remembrance.'[10] Gavin Stamp wrote that it

> ... speaks though pure form and deep cultural resonances. This slim pylon, which makes no attempt to compete with the height of the surrounding government buildings, somehow managed to articulate the inarticulate grief of a wounded, damaged society... Lutyens knew better than to resort to tendentious symbolism, whether religious or national or military.[11]

Within an hour of the unveiling in the early hours of 19 July, the *Illustrated London News* reported: 'A little group of bereaved relatives of ones in the war gathered ... and laid at its base their tribute to 'The Glorious Dead'. So their wreaths remained all the while the great pageant passed by, silent witnesses to the private grief that all underlies all public rejoicings over Victory.'[12]

Within days, tens of thousands of bunches of flowers and wreaths were placed on the monument by those still grieving. A large majority of the mourners, but certainly not all, were women dressed in black. The press said that they were mostly mothers, perhaps a simplification. Fathers, sisters and widows grieved as much, but this did not suit the sentimental message that the press wanted to convey. They came to Whitehall because their sons and husbands, nephews and cousins, had no burial place close to home.

The nation's grief centred now on Sir Edward Lutyens' simple plaster and wood Cenotaph: an accidental memorial, simple and severe. It is possible of course that any monument to the dead, whatever form it took, would have met the need of the families of the war dead. Like the Menin Gate, there is something oddly homely about it. Allan Greenberg suggests that 'by relying on understatement, by confronting the elemental tragedy of individual death, his monument ennobled the grief and passion of a nation's mourning.'[13] In thanking the architect for his work, the Prime Minister wrote a few days after the rededication:

> The Cenotaph by its very simplicity fittingly expresses the memory in which the people hold all those who so bravely fought and died for their country. How well it represents the feeling of the nation has been manifested by the stream of pilgrims who have passed the Cenotaph during the past week.[14]

In the days after Peace Day there grew up a feeling that the Cenotaph should be made permanent. Within two days a letter appeared in *The Times* calling for the monument 'to be retained either in its present form or rendered in granite or stone'.[15] Despite concerns from Westminster Council about the danger to traffic of its location, Sir Alfred Mond, the First Commissioner of Works, asked the Cabinet on 23 July to agree to erect a permanent 'replica of the present design' on the same site, otherwise 'the monument itself would lose its appropriateness having been designed for a special position and for a special occasion.'[16] The Cabinet approved and Lutyens was duly approached to undertake the work. He was pleased to be asked: 'It was decided by the human sentiment of millions, that the Cenotaph should be as it is now, and speaking as the designer I would wish for no greater honour, no more complete and lasting satisfaction.'[17]

The Cenotaph was bitterly opposed by the Church, because of its lack of Christian symbolism. The *Catholic Herald*, for example, dismissed the Cenotaph as: 'nothing more or less than a pagan monument, insulting to Christianity ... a disgrace in a so-called Christian land.'[18]

The Tomb of the Unknown Warrior was the Church of England's riposte to the Cenotaph, offering a clearly Christian burial within the greatest church of the Anglican community. The proposal came from David Railton, the Vicar of Folkestone, and it was championed by the Dean of Westminster, Herbert Ryle. Even the funeral service was resolutely Anglican, making no concession to other denominations, let alone other faiths.[19] Stephen Graham later recalled Sir Edward Lutyens saying of the Cenotaph:

There was some horror in Church circles. *What!* A pagan monument in the midst of Whitehall! And that is why we have a rival shrine in the Abbey, the Unknown Warrior, but even an unknown soldier might not have been a Christian, the more unknown the less sure you could be.[20]

After the success of Peace Day the authorities expected that there would be few commemorations of the first anniversary of the

Armistice. On Whitehall huge crowds, however, gathered around the temporary Cenotaph, now looking rather tatty. The King and Queen laid a wreath, as did the Prime Minister. *The Times* reported noted that at the first stroke of Big Ben announcing the hour of eleven: 'Here and there an old soldier could be detected slipping unconsciously into the posture of attention.' There was a sudden sharp sound of a woman's sob, and *The Times* reporter saw 'streaming eyes of all too many a man', which attested to the 'genuineness of the moment.'[21]

And almost as suddenly as everything had stopped, the nation resumed its everyday activities.

The unveiling of the Cenotaph

Armistice Day in 1920 was centred on a funeral. On that day, the 'Unknown Warrior of the Great War' was laid to rest at the end of the West Nave in Westminster Abbey. At the same time the Cenotaph, rebuilt in Portland Stone, was rededicated by the King.

For many the most memorable feature was the queue of women in black or grey who snaked all the way down Whitehall from Trafalgar Square to Westminster Abbey. The press again assumed that they were largely mothers mourning their sons, but there is little evidence to suggest that this was actually the case. Many must have been widows of the fallen. But as the *Daily Mail* noted, among them were 'a few fathers, with grey moustaches and grey hair and an air of proud grief.'[22] Mixed in were groups of veterans who had brought wreaths in memory of fallen comrades. *The Times* reported that thousands of employees at the Slough Motor Depot contributed a penny each towards a wreath to be placed on the grave of the unknown warrior.[23]

Perhaps a hundred thousand passed the Cenotaph on Armistice Day itself, with hundreds of thousands more during the days following. Many mourners brought wreathes or bunches of flowers to lay at the Cenotaph. Surviving photographs show that the memorial was surrounded by flowers, and the authorities became concerned about clearing the huge pile of rotting blooms. The *Manchester Guardian* described how 'The women in the crowd with flowers raised them above their heads so that they could be helped to get into the road and so one saw all along Whitehall the black mass suddenly blooming in white blossom like hedgerows in April.'[24]

Perhaps half a million over the following weekend walked down Whitehall and another half million by the end of November. It was calculated that 170 people per minute were passing the Cenotaph to pay their respects, while 'many thousands ... contented themselves with walking more quickly along the pavement saluting the Cenotaph from that distance.'[25]

There seems to have been little awareness in their minds of the mourners about the different representations of the fallen at the Cenotaph – for all who had died during the war – and the Tomb of the Unknown Warrior in Westminster Abbey – commemorating those who had no known final resting place. Perhaps this was reinforced by the fact that there was no separate queue for the Abbey. Not everybody who paid their respects at the Cenotaph visited the Tomb, but a very large number seem to have done so.

The Tomb of the Unknown Warrior

On 11 November 1920, the British 'Unknown Warrior of the Great War' was laid to rest at the end of the West Nave in Westminster Abbey. This event, unique in British history, was marked by great symbolism reflecting the nation's continuing mourning for the lost men of the Great War and empathy for the grief still felt by the mothers and wives of those who had fallen for their country.

The idea is usually thought to have first come to an Army chaplain, the Reverend David Railton, when he noticed in 1916 in a back garden at Armentières a grave with a rough cross on which were pencilled the words 'An Unknown British Soldier'.[26] In August 1920, he wrote to the Dean of Westminster, Herbert Ryle, suggesting that such a memorial to the unknown soldier be erected in Westminster Abbey. Railton had wondered how the 'unknown' as well as the 'known' could be commemorated. Writing much later, rather oddly in the third person, he said:

> I do not know and I do not think he is sure himself as to the time when an idea came to him by which he thought all these longings and desires could be more fully satisfied... He had been speaking at a Church Parade one day, in praise of certain fallen comrades. When he was riding from the that parade to another he was wondering how the 'unknown' as well as the known could be sufficiently honoured in the minds of Englishmen. The idea that came brought great joy to him... In truth he felt that most people would simply laugh at the notion of taking the moral remains of an Unknown Soldier or Sailor back to Blighty to be enshrined in the heart of London.[27]

The lack of a funeral, however cursory, and a grave, denied hundreds of thousands of relatives at home the chance to accept the finality of death. Perhaps a single body of an unknown man could be brought from the battlefield to fill the gap left by a father, brother or son. A loved one who could be made to symbolise and fill that void in many family's lives. Railton was concerned that the idea, and the whole ceremony, might seem mawkish and perhaps inappropriate in the post-war world. But Dean Ryle approved of the idea and wrote to the King and, David Lloyd George, the Prime Minister proposing the such a memorial. The King was initially cool to the idea, but soon came around.[28]

The politicians seized on the concept. Lord Curzon was enthusiastic:

> The ceremony of burying in the Abbey an unknown soldier, whose remains should be borne in honour through London and then interred in the Nave, has not merely this emotional, sentimental and dramatic aspect, but would also offer a worthy and highly esteemed tribute to those who fell in the War, and strike a chord of deep feeling in the hearts of the nation.[29]

According to one of the *Daily Herald*'s readers, H. J. Gillespie, the unknown warrior was 'the man who changed the world – and died in the doing of it. His country buries him where it is accustomed to bury its most famous men.'[30] The Communist *Workers' Dreadnought* grumbled that Railton had 'conceived the idea of performing this ceremony to keep green the memory of the poor and lowly, whose lives were sacrificed without note in the great capitalist war... Our rulers seized upon the chaplain's proposal and exploited it to the full for their own advantage.'[31]

Rather unusually at a time when there was generally little planned involvement of the middle or working classes in public events and ceremonies, the organisers were well aware of the *Workers' Dreadnought*'s argument. The committee organising the event was determined that the burial of the unknown warrior would be one at which ex-servicemen and, in particular, the widows and mothers of the fallen would be present in large numbers, alongside the King and representatives of the armed services. They stressed that 'fashionable Society should be excluded' from Westminster Abbey.[32]

This worthy intention proved difficult to enforce. The Dean of Westminster 'felt strongly' that the nave should be reserved for the 'chief mourners and the procession', that is the members of the Royal family and the senior officers who had escorted the coffin into the Abbey. In the end the Dean was slapped down by the Cabinet, which insisted that the 'bereaved were more deserving of consideration in respect of accommodation in the Nave than those who had taken part in the procession.'³³ During the planning of the ceremony attempts by MPs and peers to attend were successfully resisted; in the end, only members who had lost sons during the War were present.

Tickets were eventually allocated by ballot to 3,200 relatives of the deceased at the Cenotaph (for both men and women), 2,374 in government offices overlooking Whitehall (women only), with another 1050 mothers and widows in the Abbey itself.³⁴ Seats were offered to women in three categories: those who had 'lost a husband and all their sons or an only son', mothers 'who have lost all or their only sons' and finally widows. It was decided not to make any special allowance for mothers and widows who had just one son or only their husband missing.³⁵ In the end, space was found for 190 women who had lost husbands and sons, 600 mothers who had lost all their sons or only sons, and 360 widows.³⁶ Not everybody who applied received a ticket. The *Daily Graphic* journalist Rita Strauss recorded the thoughts of one widow:

> One slender little woman in black who come up from the country with her ten-year old boy burst into tears when she heard she could not be admitted. 'I did write for a place, and had no answer, but I did think they would help me and it would be all right it if I came up.' She sobbed. 'My husband was Quarter-Master Sergeant of the Royal Fusiliers ... he was wounded three times badly enough to be excused from service, but each time he volunteered again. The last time he never came back.'³⁷

The body was chosen from four unknown British servicemen exhumed from four areas on the Western Front where the fighting had been particularly severe: the Aisne, the Somme, Arras and Ypres. It was decided to find somebody who had been killed in 1914, largely for the practical reason that the remains would have decomposed more than those of a man who had been killed later in the war.[38] As a result the body is likely to be that of a pre-war regular soldier, rather than a reservist or conscript.[39] And because of the large numbers of troops from the Raj serving in France and Flanders in the early months of the war, there is a reasonable possibility that the unknown warrior is Indian. The remains were brought to the chapel at St. Pol on the night of 7 November. The General Officer in charge of troops in France and Flanders, Brigadier General L. J. Wyatt, with Colonel Gell, went into the chapel alone, where the bodies on stretchers were covered by Union Flags. They had no idea from which area the bodies had come. General Wyatt selected one and the two officers placed it in a plain coffin and sealed it. The other bodies were reburied at St Pol.

Next day the body was escorted to Boulogne to rest overnight and then the coffin was placed inside another which had been sent over specially from England made of two-inch thick oak from a tree at Hampton Court Palace, lined with zinc. Within the wrought iron bands of this coffin was placed a 16th-century crusader's sword from the Royal Armouries' collection. The coffin arrived at Platform 8 at Victoria station late on 10 November, where it lay in state overnight guarded by a platoon of Grenadier Guards.[40]

Next morning, the coffin was placed on a gun carriage drawn by six black horses and began its journey through the crowd-lined streets, making its first stop in Whitehall where the Cenotaph, newly rebuilt in Portland stone, was unveiled by King George V. Here the King placed his wreath of red roses and bay leaves on the coffin. His card read: 'In proud memory of those Warriors who died unknown in the Great War. Unknown, and yet well-known; as dying, and behold they live.' One observer saw that among the watching masses hats removed as the silent crowds 'uncovered' at the approach were not returned to heads, even twenty minutes after the procession had passed into Westminster Abbey. It was as if the extended emotion and the indelible memory of the coffin had brought a near total paralysis.[41]

The carriage made its way to the north door of Westminster Abbey, a few hundred yards away. The coffin was carried into the church on the shoulders of pall bearers made up of generals and admirals, followed by George V, members of the Royal Family and ministers of State. The funeral service was kept as short as possible as the King stood to attention throughout and also to avoid straining the emotions of the relatives to breakjng point. Philip Gibbs stressed how the mourners: '... sat without the distinction or rank as lot arranged them places, titled ladies next to charwomen, artisans by city merchants, for all had equal title to be there, the gift of a son or brother to the country.'[42]

One of those present Mrs Annie Macbeth, who lost two sons killed on the same day on the Somme, wrote in the *Daily Mail*:

> We tried all we know to find their resting place but those who were with them when they fell said the whole place was a shambles and unrecognisable. To add to our sorrow, we could not tend their graves. Today bought the sadness of a revived sorrow, but with a splendid consolation. If tears came to me during this service, as they came to many, they were mingled with gladness, for in that beautiful building sad music thrilled my soul. I felt very near to my lost boys... Being among other sufferers like myself and knowing that in the homage done to the bier of the Unknown [Soldier] our lost ones were being honoured was of infinite consolation, it was with a full heart that I left the Abbey.[43]

Another mother wrote in homage to her dead son, as if he were the soldier buried in the Abbey: 'I never understood what "Death swallowed up in victory" meant until I watched your father by your grave. The honour, glory, splendour of your funeral made all memories golden for him and, for the time at any rate, took all the sting from death.'⁴⁴

Herbert Thompson, a resident at St Dunstan's Home for Blind Ex-Servicemen, had similar feelings:

> The ceremony in the Abbey left an indelible impression on my mind – a feeling of ineffable sadness and melancholy, yet there was a message of inspiration and hope. I felt as if the spirit of the Unknown Warrior had whispered in my ear, 'Courage, brother, hope on.'... I came to the Abbey glad that I had been chosen from among so many. I went away sorrowing but with a message of hope locked in my heart.⁴⁵

Opposition to the ceremony was muted. Ex-servicemen as a whole seem to have been little moved by the Tomb and the ceremonies around it, perhaps they were too aware of the numbers of their comrades remaining on the battlefields. Their constant complaint was that more should be done to help the survivors rather than the dead.⁴⁶ The *Workers' Dreadnought* thundered:

> As they exploited the Unknown Warrior in his lifetime, our rulers now exploit his corpse. They seek, by the splendour of his burial, to turn the eyes of the people from the fact that his comrades who escaped death, but came back broken in health, or failed to find employment on returning, have been treated by the Government and the employing class with grudging stinginess and vivid neglect... In life our capitalist rulers exploited the Unknown Warrior, ruthlessly forced him to be the cannon-fodder in their ambitious and mercenary quarrel, and at the same time used his sufferings and death as the bait to draw his brothers into the battle-line and to quiet the discontented murmurings of his class.⁴⁷

More typically the Labour supporting *Daily Herald* was initially opposed to the interment of the Unknown Warrior, describing it as being: 'the emotional doping of the people', but later was persuaded to change its mind by the strength of the reaction of its readers: 'As we stood there in silence, while the muffled drums began to whisper, as it were a million miles away and grew into the sound of a rushing wind, the stone atrocities faded, the vulgarity and bad taste were forgotten, the pomp and circumstance forgiven.'[48]

The pacifist Winifred Holtby thought the ceremony to bury the Unknown Warrior both stagey and hypocritical, and something of a sop to those could not summon the strength or vision to carry on. A decade after the ceremony, the writer and war veteran Alfred Burrage called the Tomb 'the crowning example of hypocrisy':

> I don't mean the nation was insincere – indeed, I am sure the proceedings were a consolation to those near and dear to many of the missing – but the Generals who came to weep crocodile tears over the poor fellow's shrine were the very people who had made his life unendurable, while he was alive, and probably one of them was responsible for his present condition.[49]

What is clear, however, is that both the Tomb and the Cenotaph touched the hearts of millions. By the end of November 1920, it was estimated that one and a half million people had visited the Abbey to pay their respects.[50] The emotional outpourings exceeded those for Diana, Princess of Wales in 1997.[51] The queues were largely female with a few fathers and brothers among them: the event was organised for and attended by women, even though, as we have seen, grief affected fathers and brothers as much as did their wives and sisters. Rita Strauss interviewed some of the women as they queued along Whitehall waiting to go into the Abbey. One was 'a girl of 21, who didn't look more than 16, and whose husband had been killed just before the Armistice. "I'm going to put my wreath on the Unknown Soldier's grave and if I've got to wait here all day I'll do it in the end."'[52]

There was huge public interest in the events of 11 November 1920. How could there not be? Perhaps three million families had been affected in some way by the war. And if they personally were not affected, most people would have known families who had been. The Great War had scarred everybody's life in one way or another.

This interest is shown in massive newspaper sales reporting on the dedication of the Tomb. The *Daily Mirror* sold just under two million copies – a record for the paper at that time. The *Daily Graphic* claimed that it had to produce several special editions which quickly sold out.[53] As might be expected, coverage was overwhelmingly positive. *The Times*, which produced a special supplement, stressed how the Tomb of the Unknown Warrior acted as a unifying influence in society: '…we were made one people in one act of remembrance … all could mourn him the better because he was unknown.'[54]

The mid-market and illustrated papers marvelled at the simple dignity of the ceremonies and concentrated on the grief of the mourners. The *Daily Graphic*'s front page was a sentimental drawing from the popular cartoonist Bruce Bairnsfather, which showed a mother dressed in mourning and her small son stood by the grave of the unknown warrior. The headline claimed 'What thousands of children are asking today', with the caption reading: 'Is it Daddy?'[55] The paper's star writer Hannen Swaffer wrote that when standing by the Cenotaph, he became aware of 'Women with hungry eyes … and with thirsty ears they sat across the road – hungry for news of a missing soldier, thirsty for tidings of a hero gone away for ever. But there was no sob, no tear!'[56]

P. O'Donovan of the *Daily Express* described the reaction as the mourners left the Abbey: 'One of them handed a few shrivelled blossoms to an attendant. She tried to speak, but for a moment she could not control her sobs. "In the grave," she finally managed to say, and pointed to emphasise her meaning.

"My husband – it's from my wedding bouquet." And with a shaking had the man fulfilled her wish.'[57]

On the same day, the French Unknown Soldier was laid to rest at the Arc de Triomphe in Paris. Five soldiers and five veterans of the Franco-Prussian War of 1870 brought the chosen body from Verdun.[58] Both the British and the French were 'family affairs' – foreign dignitaries and, even Imperial representatives were excluded from Westminster Abbey. As in London, there were long processions of relatives who wished to grieve at the casket and then the grave itself. The *New York Times* reported: 'Every one threw flowers on the grave. Poor women, sobbing bitterly, laid bunches of violets and rich women united with them in the memory of war's griefs, kissing their flowers, laid them beside them. Soon the whole great space below the arch seemed filled with blossoms.'[59]

Over the years Unknown Soldiers were solemnly exhumed and buried with honours in many of the Allied nations. The final such ceremony took place as late as 2004, when New Zealand laid the body of a soldier of the Great War to rest at the National War Memorial in Wellington.[60]

Later years

Local war memorials in the United Kingdom rarely if ever make any distinction between those who were killed in action, died of wounds or sickness, or were posted missing. No matter where they lie now, they were all regarded as having given their lives equally for ultimate victory. It also reflects the fact that in almost every family of the missing it was eventually accepted that their boy had been killed, even though their body had not been found.

The Imperial War Museum's catalogue identifies just a few memorials in the United Kingdom, mainly commemorating individual soldiers, for example, at Christ Church, Nailsea near Bristol a memorial reads:

> Private Frederick Courtenay James Glos. Regt./ Aged 29 Years/ Fourth Beloved Son Of/ W & S Jones Of This Parish/ Reported Missing After The Battle Of Cambrai/ France Dec 3rd 1917/ Greater Love Hath No Man Than This/ That A Man Lay Down His Life For His Friends[61]

Villages and towns consciously or unconsciously wanted to mark Allied victory as well as to mourn the dead. There is little evidence that, except in a very general way, these memorials provided any real consolation to bereaved families. For many widows and mothers of the missing, solace seemed more readily available through the Cenotaph and the Tomb to the Unknown Warrior and the national services which took place around them.[62]

Time was a great healer; or at least it had amnesiac properties. There were great crowds again on Armistice Day 1921, but as the years passed, inevitably the numbers fell way. *The Times* once commented that the 'hysterical emotionalism' of 1920 gradually declined to 'a more reasoned and slightly less emotional response'.[63]

Throughout the whole of the inter-war period Britain stopped as one for the two minutes silence each Armistice Day. However, from newspaper accounts the numbers of mourners attending the service at the Cenotaph slowly began to fall away. In 1923, *The Times* correspondent described the vast numbers of mourners as a 'human sea' who filed 'unbroken all the width of Whitehall' and noted, perhaps significantly, that the mourners wore 'black, dotted here and there with the coloured hats of women'.[64] Five years later, on the tenth anniversary of the Armistice, *The Times* reported: 'Little or no mourning was worn, though many of the women showed the medals of the dead husbands, sons or brothers... There were plenty of multi-coloured hats.' There was still a 'dense and immovable crowd [that] seemed to stretch from one of end of Whitehall to the other.' For the first time the ceremony was broadcast nationally: 'The microphone picked up some incidental sounds which broke down slightly the sense of solemnity, but which yet helped to complete in the mind the picture of the vast assembly.'[65] It brought the ceremony into the lives of many who would never be able to attend themselves.

There was also a new sense of reconciliation. Writing in the *Radio Times* Henry Williamson spoke of 'the things, done in the name of honour of patriotism ... we should scorn and cast out of ourselves, and so forget; and when that has been done we shall remember that the sun is universal ... and that all men are like ourselves.'[66]

In November 1933, still 'a great column of ex-Service men and women moved forward to salute the Cenotaph. The day belongs to those who served as well as to those who fell [followed] by the first of the long faithful one of men and women who year after year bring their flowers to the monument in memory of those who "Shall not grow old, as we that are left grow old."' The 'pilgrimage', as *The Times* described it, 'went long into the night' and even into the following morning.[67] The ceremony in 1938 took place in the shadow of war. The correspondent in Whitehall thought that 'the King and his people assembled around the Cenotaph to unite in remembrance and to resolve afresh to work hard and constructively for peace.' At the service by the Tomb of the Unknown Warrior in Westminster Abbey, the Dean of Westminster asked the congregation to 'remember in silence and in sympathy the Jewish people in their troubles.'[68] There is no mention of the crowds of mourners which had been the feature of previous years.

At the same time, Mass Observation undertook a survey of the public's attitude to Armistice Day. It found that the events meant very little to most people, and for some brought back distressful memories. One interviewee who had lost her husband during the war clearly found the day stressful: 'It brings back memories, my husband was killed in it. It makes me miserable all day. I stopped at home for the day, listen in... My second husband goes all of a tremble when it comes on, he was shell-shocked then... My poor pop jumps out of his bones at it.'

Another woman said that she 'didn't care for it now. Makes everybody sad, all the poor people who lost theirs. I have an Aunt who lost her lad, it's terrible for her on that day.'[69]

On the outbreak of war in 1939 the ceremony at the Cenotaph was stopped for the duration, and when it restarted in 1946 it no longer had the impact that it had in the 1920s and 1930s. In part this was because Remembrance Day was now fixed as being the Sunday nearest 11 November. As Adrian Gregory says: 'The mood of 1945 was sceptical of the high ideals and high-flown phrases that marked the year that had begun the Silence.'[70] In October 1945, a Mrs M. Harrison wrote to the Prime Minister, Clement Attlee, to protest against the reintroduction of the Two Minutes Silence:

> I do think it is about time that this form of hypocrisy was put an end to. My life has been completely 'silent' for the past 2 yrs when I received the dreadful news that my dearly beloved son was 'missing' from a raid over Essen. Surely there is no need for this 'mechanical' 2 mins silence as many families like my own do not want *reminding* of their grief. I think the harm done to such as us is quite sufficient without the need to emphasis it.[71]

It was not until the mid-1990s that remembrance again came to the forefront of people's minds, as the horrors of the two world wars came to be replaced by a cosy nostalgia for a time when Britain had once been great.

Any history of Britain in the immediate aftermath of the First World War must reflect the grief of families who had lost sons and husbands and the feeling of the sacrifice that their deaths meant to the men who had returned, to the families of the fallen, and to the local communities where they had once lived. It is hard now to understand how prevalent this sentiment was.

Commentators at the time commented on how cathartic the Tomb of the Unknown Warrior must have been to the families of the missing. They stressed grieving mothers and widows could imagine that the bodies of their loved ones were buried, even if their physical remains had not been found and in all likelihood would never be traced. For some no doubt, this was succour enough. The sacrifice of their man had not just been acknowledged, but their special status as being one of the missing was marked in the most public way possible. The Tomb of the Unknown Warrior always seemed linked to women. Perhaps as Adrian Gregory suggests, attendance at Armistice Day services at Westminster Abbey, which centred on the Tomb, avoided 'all the military display at the Cenotaph, which many women appeared to have objected to.'[72] Almost a decade later came another great memorial to the missing at the Menin Gate in Ypres, where many British soldiers died during the Great War. Here, too. the grieving were encouraged to believe this was where their loved ones could be found.

The Tomb of the Unknown Warrior has largely faded into history. The commemorations for the nation's war dead take place at the Cenotaph. In part it is the location, in full public view on London's most important thoroughfare, while the Tomb lies inside a building which many people feel uncomfortable entering.[73]

The British took the Cenotaph – simple, unreligious and austere – to its heart in the way that they rarely have done for any other building or memorial. The Cenotaph suited the national mood in a way that the more religious Tomb of the Unknown Warrior in the end did not. And as memories of the missing men faded, so did the importance of the Tomb. Now tourists just glance at it, or perhaps stop to read the inscription as they shuffle past.

9

CHASING GHOSTS

While in her heart she yearn'd incessantly
To rush abroad all round the little haven,
Proclaiming Enoch Arden and his woes
Alfred Lord Tennyson, Enoch Arden

For many people, Juliet Nicolson suggests, 'The post-war world was in large part a world paralysed by grief.'[1] On the streets could be found the maimed and unemployed selling matches, in the school room and the hospital ward women for whom there were no husbands, and on the living room mantlepiece a photograph of a young man who had fallen on the Somme. Historian David Cannadine argues that inter-war England was obsessed by death and the cult of the dead, 'in the face of bereavement at once so harrowing, so unnatural and so widespread', that the churches and conventional ritual was unable to cope. Instead, there grew up a variety of memorials – national and international, religious and communal – where grieving was focussed. But many families – perhaps most – preferred to grieve in private at home and in their own way. Mrs Jessica Hinds from Tasmania must have spoken for many widows across the British Empire when she replied to an enquiry from the Australian War Memorial to verify her late husband's details so that it could accurately be inscribed on the roll of honour:

> I have filled in the enclosed form as you requested. But at the same time I am not in favour of all this kind of thing, as we wives and mothers do not need them to remind us of those we have lost. I think it would it be more fitting to put the money to better use for those who are living and finding it hard to live these days ... why worry over the dead. I am sure they would not wish it, if they only knew how we who are left are treated.[2]

For some the unveiling the Cenotaph and the Tomb of the Unknown Warrior was sufficient closure, for others it was the unveiling of the Menin Gate. But for many it must have been the letter from the War Office which gently stated that because of the length of time since the man was reported missing, his death must be assumed. Writing to Rudyard Kipling's solicitor in June 1919, J. A. Corcoran of the War Office Casualty Branch concluded that: 'In view of the length of time that elapsed since [John Kipling] was officially reported missing ... the Army Council are regretfully constrained for official purposes that Lieutenant Kipling is dead, and that his death occurred on, or since, the 27th day of September 1915.'[3] Like so many other families who had received similar letters, there followed the necessary business of sorting out his son's financial matters, including the back pay owed for the short period of John's service in France.

Other less well-to-do widows and families had to apply for a pension or an allowance, always a difficult experience. Retrieving the deceased's personal possessions often proved to be a nightmare: they may have been lost or pilfered before they reached home, and for many men they may well have been shared out between his comrades. The wife of Private Arthur Cooper eventually received those of her husband eight months after his death: 'Disc. Photos. Pocket Book. Corres. Religious Book. Cards'.⁴ In the course of time, a message of sympathy from the King, a brass memorial plaque universally known as the 'Dead Man's Penny' and finally his campaign medals would arrive to be signed for before they were handed over.

Rudyard Kipling hinted at the old cliché of time as the great healer in the poem 'London Stone', published in *The Times* on the fifth anniversary of the Armistice, 10 November 1923:

> When you come to London Town,
> (Grieving—grieving!)
> Bring your flowers and lay them down
> At the place of grieving.
>
> When you come to London Town,
> (Grieving—grieving!)
> Bow your head and mourn your own,
> With the others grieving.
>
> For those minutes, let it wake
> (Grieving—grieving!)
> All the empty-heart and ache
> That is not cured by grieving.
>
> For those minutes, tell no lie:
> (Grieving—grieving!)
> "Grave, this is thy victory;
> And the sting of death is grieving."
>
> Where's our help, from Earth or Heaven.
> (Grieving—grieving!)
> To comfort us for what we've given,
> And only gained the grieving?

Heaven's too far and Earth too near,
(Grieving—grieving!)
But our neighbour's standing here,
Grieving as we're grieving.

What's his burden every day?
(Grieving—grieving!)
Nothing man can count or weigh,
But loss and love's own grieving.

What is the tie betwixt us two
(Grieving—grieving!)
That must last our whole lives through?
"As I suffer, so do you."
That may ease the grieving.[5]

Will Longstaff's mystical painting of *Menin Gate at Midnight* attracted many visitors when it went on display in Britain and Australia in 1929. The *Adelaide News* reported that those looking at the painting when it was displayed in the city's Public Library were mostly women: 'They came in quietly, took a seat, and sat looking at the canvas. They seemed in more than one instance to be searching the spaces between the shadowy, helmeted figures for someone there.'[6]

Although published in 1933, after the flood of First World War related memoirs that had occurred in the late 1920s, Vera Brittain's memoir of the loss of her fiancé, brother and two close friends *Testament of Youth* became an instant bestseller. At the close of publication day, its first print-run of 3,000 had sold out. It spoke then to war widows and grieving mothers, and speaks still, about loss and grief and the tragedy of war. The *Sunday Times* called it 'a book which stands alone among books written by women about the war.' When it was later published in America, the *New York Times* reviewer wrote that

Brittain's autobiographical account was 'honest, revealing and heartbreakingly beautiful'.[7]

At Christmas 1923, Kipling's wife Carrie confessed in her diary that it had been the 'best Christmas since 1914'. Almost a decade later, in 1931, the Kiplings attended the Armistice Day ceremony and afterwards Carrie wrote: 'We stand in the street at the Cenotaph, a deeper feeling this year than ever before.' There were times when she felt that memories were fading, then the hurt broke through, as sharp as ever.[8]

Many widows and fiancées of course found new partners. In 1925, when Vera Brittain was considering marriage, she debated with herself about 'the final and acute loyalty to the dead; of how far I and other women of my generation who deliberately accepted a new series of emotional relationships thereby destroyed yet again the men who had once uncomplainingly died for them in the flesh.'[9] In the end, sensibly, she decided to devote herself to the present rather than past.

The persistent delusion

For some mothers and widows there was always the hope – the nagging hope – that their boy was still alive and would miraculously return one day. Popular fiction encouraged this hope. Alfred Lord Tennyson was perhaps the first writer to use such sentiments in his poem *Enoch Arden*, in which the eponymous hero, a seaman, is supposedly lost at sea. In the meantime, his childhood sweetheart Annie marries, but Enoch returns:

> Then he told her of his voyage,
> His wreck, his lonely life, his coming back,
> His gazing in on Annie, his resolve,
> And how he kept it. As the woman heard,
>
> Fast flow'd the current of her easy tears,
> While in her heart she yearn'd incessantly

> To rush abroad all round the little haven,
> Proclaiming Enoch Arden and his woes.

Enoch resolves to leave Annie and and returns to sea. The poem was widely translated and became the basis of a popular film in 1911. As a result, the public believed that such occurrences were possible.[10] During the war there were several press stories about women of missing men remarrying only to find their first husband turning up again. In November 1915, for example, the *Daily Express* reported 'An astonishing and dramatic incident recalling Enoch Arden':

> An officer in the Army was reported to have been killed at the front. His will proved. After an interval his widow became engaged to another officer, an old friend. He was ordered abroad for active service and before his departure the two were married. The second husband is still abroad on service and, now, in his absence, it is learned that the first husband is a prisoner in Germany.[11]

Often in such stories the wife's first husband had been posted missing and although she had never heard from him he was a prisoner in Germany. In one or two incidents – such as with Mary Morton's parents – this proved to be the case. In 1916, Mary Morton Hardie's mother had received a telegram to say that her husband, George, was 'missing, believed killed'. Assuming that he was dead, she took up with another man, Hughie. On 8 January 1919 Mary remembered that one of the neighbours knocked on the door:

> I saw Kirsty standing there and crying. She carried a newspaper in her shaking hand, crying to Mama. 'Holy Mother of God, have mercy on us.' She went on and on, as Hughie, now pale-faced, shook her by the shoulder, saying 'Calm down Kirsty, what is it,

tell me.' Kirsty just pointed to the paper... The headlines stated that another hospital ship had docked at Southampton with 300 prisoners of war. Their names were printed in long columns in alphabetical order. Hughie ran his finger down, stopped, then read out in a hoarse voice 'Morton, George, Sergeant of the 1st Battalion Royal Scots Regiment.' Mama stared at him, then slipped sideways in her chair. He gave her a little water, and when she spoke, she whispered, 'What shall we do' over and over again.'[12]

When George returned to Glasgow, his mother told him the news: 'He was very angry. His face was scarlet, and he said "I've heard about this happening to others, but I never thought it would happen to me."'[13] Mary's parents divorced soon afterwards.

In *Mr Britling Sees it Through* there is a happy ending, when Letty is reunited with her husband, Teddy:

> It was alright. She had always known it was alright (Hold close to him). Except for just a little while. But hadn't she always known he was alive? And here he was alive (Hold close to him). Only it was so good to be sure – after all her torment; to hold him, to hand about him, to feel the solid man, kissing her, weeping too, weeping together with her 'Teddy my love!'[14]

How readers must have wished that they were Letty.

Teddy explains that he had been left for dead in a barn behind enemy lines in Belgium, but although seriously wounded, he makes his way home via neutral Netherlands and then back to England. To readers unfamiliar with the minutiae of life in occupied Belgium, there was a ring of authenticity. It could happen to their boy. Indeed, a handful of Tommies left behind during the retreat from Mons spent years in hiding.[15]

Secret camps

If the grieving could not believe that their boy was dead, then the logical place for him to be was in a German prisoner of war camp. One could persuade oneself that one had not heard from him because although he was now a prisoner of war the paperwork had somehow been lost or that because of German 'beastliness', he was being kept in a secret camp where he was not allowed to communicate with the outside world. In fact, of course, after a few months of relative chaos at the beginning of the war the Germans became meticulous in their record keeping, and the secret camps were nothing more than a myth.

During the weeks after the Armistice ships carrying tens of thousands of released prisoners returned home from Germany. It was a chaotic process. They were greeted by women seeking information about their missing boys. One of the first to return was Jack Rogers. On arriving at Hull, he remembered:

> We climbed aboard [the train] and as we looked out of the carriage windows, up and down the platform were any number of women. These poor mothers were walking up and down the platform, each of them carrying a picture of a missing son or husband. They came up and showed you the picture 'Did you know him? Have you seen him? Was he in your regiment?' And so forth, all up and down the train. You wanted to give them a little hope, to say we had seen them, but no we hadn't, we couldn't tell them anything.[16]

Towards the end of 1918 there grew up that myth that the Germans were keeping British soldiers in secret camps. The basis for the story may have been that many British and French prisoners were forced to work behind enemy lines rather than sent to camps in Germany. In October 1918, the *Birmingham Mail* reported the case of a Grenadier guardsman who had been captured during the Spring Offensive and taken to a squalid compound for prisoners at Marquevilles, one of several camps which had not been registered with the Red Cross and so were unknown to the authorities in Whitehall.[17]

Another prisoner, Private Barnard Brammer, Lancashire Fusiliers, kept a diary of the eight months he spent working behind the German lines. His capture does not seem to have been reported to the International Committee of the Red Cross until August 1918 after he and fellow inmates had protested to the camp commandant, who told them: 'You are not registered, so cannot write home, nor can you have emergency parcels.' Brammer grumbled in his diary that 'it is a gross injustice and we have no means of redress' when 'men who were captured when we were, are receiving their Regimental parcels and have been able to write home for the past 6 weeks.' However, Brammer was finally allowed to write home on 4 August, five months after his capture.[18] In Germany itself, parties of prisoners were often sent to work on detached 'kommandos' in factories and farms that were often some way away from the main camp.

The release of the POWs was very chaotic, with men arriving home in dribs and drabs, so it was not unreasonable to hope that your boy, even if there had been no official notification, would turn up eventually.[19] The press contained the occasional story of soldiers reunited with their families in incredible circumstances. In Southport, for example, the *Manchester Guardian* reported that Private William Holding, South Lancashire Regiment 'has returned from Germany... An officer had written to Holding's wife describing the funeral.'[20]

In letters to the next of kin the government had offered reassurances that one reason they had not heard officially about their boy's fate was that he might be a prisoner of war. It was thus easy to be persuaded that the reason he had not returned was down to German dishonesty. In particular, there grew up a belief that the Germans had maintained that network of secret camps, although their purpose was never made clear. The inhabitants of these camps were supposed to be men whose identities had not been passed either to the War Office or the Red Cross. A variant of this story was that men were being held in hospitals unable to communicate with either their German nurses or British comrades. Cecil Thomas came across one such unfortunate in a hospital in the Ruhr in the spring of 1918:

> There we found a man whose eyes were almost starting out of his head as he recognised something about us which marked us as his countrymen. We stood by him for a few minutes and learnt his story. For nearly two years he had been in that bed having been brought there from the Somme, and during all that time he had received no letter, parcel or communication of any kind from home, but had lain there week after week, year after year, unable to move and never, till then, heard a word spoken in his own language... He did not know that any other Englishmen were in the hospital, or even in the town, and had it not been for a pure accident, and the orderly's sudden thought, he would doubtless have remained in ignorance still.[21]

Others worried about men who had lost their memories who were stranded in German hospitals. But the British Army could find no patients who fitted this category.

In the weeks after the Armistice many widows and mothers contacted the War Office asking that the Germans be forced to disclose the whereabouts of the missing prisoners. Mrs May Elliott of Wimbledon wrote to Lord Lucan's Committee on the Mistreatment by the Enemy of British Prisoners of War, asking them to consider sending a commission of enquiry

> ... as soon as possible throughout the length and breadth of Germany as a guarantee, other than those based on German assurances, that no single prisoner has been left in enemy hands – be it in Hospital or Fortress or Gaol or Camp, in mine or factory or workshop or farm... May I add that though the years have killed

the hopes that people once had their fears remain and it is to this Committee they look to remove them beyond all shadow of doubt.[22]

The Revd John T Penrose of Petworth wrote to Lord Cave, the minister responsible for prisoners of war:

> There are also many examples of both soldiers and civilians who have long been missing, because they were in 'silence camps' and have now returned home. Those of us who have long been convinced that a great number of our missing have deliberately hidden away in Germany, will be only be to glad to think that <u>no stone</u> will be left unturned to discover those who remain.[23]

Gertrude Coleridge, whose son Luke Coleridge had been posted missing in December 1914, pointed out that: 'the Germans concealed all the new German U-Boats in buildings until Admiral Browning discovered them accidentally, just as much may "missing" be concealed until they are driven to give them up. No peace should be signed before.' She enclosed a copy of a letter from her son Derek, who had been told by returning prisoners of war that: 'while speaking <u>about officers</u>, that there are one or <u>two big towns</u> in Germany where their camps are, that they are <u>not</u> allowed even to write to anyone at all, so there may be good luck still.'[24]

This was all nonsense. Lord Lucan's committee noted in January 1919:

> The idea [of secret camps] frequently originates in a cherished, unreasoning belief that the soldier is still alive and must be accounted for somehow; but there are also three clear reasoned lines:
>
> 1. some men have been seen to be captured and have not been heard of again. It is definitely known that some have been killed by the Germans, and some have been struck by our own shells

2. confusion of identity. The War Office are the only authority fully capable of identifying soldiers. This is recognised by the British Red Cross Society, who refer doubtful cases for verification...
3. supposed identification from photographs. This is an exceedingly fruitful cause of error... Twice a figure has been identified as five different men; in one case the real man was known, but in the other he was not. Men missing in France have been identified in photographs taken in Asia Minor. Men have been identified in photographs of prisoners before the date when they were missing.[25]

The truth was that the real reasons lay partly in the delays and confusion in the official paperwork, but mainly in the inability of families to accept that their husbands and sons had been killed. The government was unsure how to proceed. There was clear evidence that there were no secret camps and, in addition, the Germans had co-operated fully. Yet there was always the slight chance that not all the men had been identified. As Dame Adelaide Livingstone, the secretary of the Committee on the Mistreatment of Prisoners of War, pointed out: 'There would be among such relations [of the missing] a very strong and bitter sense of grievance, if, for any reasons of economy and similar considerations there should be any failure on the part of the Government to take all reasonably possible steps.'[26]

On 4 January 1919, Lord Lucan's Committee published a statement printed in many newspapers across the United Kingdom reassuring readers that great effort was being made to contact POWs languishing in German hospitals: 'Instructions have been sent to British representatives to make investigations at camps, mines, asylums and elsewhere in enemy countries and wherever prisoners may possibly be found.' The Committee also described the 'systematic work' being undertaken to identify bodies on the battlefield. And lastly, it reassured readers that no prisoner with amnesia had been found nor was likely to be: 'The War Office and the Red Cross receive many inquiries, which show that relatives of missing men found hopes on the possibility that a prisoner's identity may be untraceable owing to loss of memory.'[27]

The move was welcomed. Dame Adelaide Livingstone wrote to Lord Cave that the knowledge that the Government: 'is prepared to trace the fate of these unfortunate men will prove balm to the hearts of those whose sons or husbands have never been accounted for'.[28]

Twenty search parties toured Germany looking for missing men, but their endeavours proved fruitless. The *Daily Express* described their work scouring hospitals looking for British prisoners who had been left behind. In general, the article concluded that: 'No British have been hidden deliberately, but it is true that many are scattered in various hospitals and it is not easy to find them.'[29] The searchers did not find anybody who had not already been accounted for. The few remaining British soldiers were hospital patients and between 25 and 30 men who preferred for one reason or another to remain in Germany. One party trawled the camps and work commandos of Pomerania and Lower Silesia and reported that although a thorough search had taken place 'not [a] single prisoner of war whose existence was unknown to me and who was willing to leave has been found.'[30]

By February these searches had quietly ended. Of the 150,000 men who had been prisoners, the War Office reported that only eight had turned up unexpectedly: 'All of them had been in hiding in Belgium, and could hardly, be described as being prisoners at all.' However, officially the search for such men remained open 'in the interests of the prisoners and their relatives'.[31]

The Secretary of State for War Winston Churchill told the House of Commons in February 1919 that 'about 64,800' servicemen remained missing, even after trained medical teams had scoured 'every camp, prison, mine, asylum, hospital' in Germany.[32] Churchill grossly exaggerated the numbers, and unfortunately gave hope to those who believed that their boy was among the number. It is possible he meant those prisoners who were still in transit home including from the Middle East, although even then the number he quoted was still much higher than was actually the case. In an attempt to reassure families, he added: 'The suggestion that many of the missing are in Germany in secret camps, asylums etc, has not so far been substantiated ... although every supposed case has been investigated as far as possible.'[33] In a further statement in early April, Churchill said that 121 prisoners had been located, the majority of whom were hospital patients.[34] The search for prisoners, in theory, continued well into 1920, but this work was really a cover for the British Military Mission in Berlin to gather intelligence about Germany and German 'intrigues' in Russia and Eastern Europe.[35]

In early January 1919, Dame Adelaide suggested to Lord Cave that an appeal be launched for information about men who had disappeared in the formerly German-occupied areas of Belgium and France. On 11 January the War Office issued a press notice: 'It is thought that there may be information ... which might lead to determining the fate of officers and men which has not yet been communicated to any of the Government departments or organisations interested.' The notice invited people to send 'reliable information' to the War Office.[36]

The intention was for a small team to investigate the fate of British soldiers thought to have evaded capture by the Germans. Based on the information received, 23 officers and men were identified as possible subjects, although much of the supposed evidence was based on hearsay and wishful thinking. The team would visit Belgium and Northern France to search for information in 'out of the way country districts, where men may most probably have been in hiding, and where information as to their fate might be obtained from local mayors, notables, peasants, parish priests and neighbouring convents.'[37]

The War Office agreed to send Dame Adelaide and a secretary to Belgium. This led to protests from relatives calling for a rather more high-powered delegation to cross the Channel. It was not until July 1919 that Dame Adelaide and two Army officers arrived in France. A further appeal for information was published in the press.[38] There were no prisoners of war to find. Instead, Livingstone and her colleagues devoted their time to identifying British war graves in the rural areas of Belgium and Northern France and the men who lay in them:

> A solitary grave on the road to Elouges was found marked 'Unknown British soldier, Died 24 August 1914'. The man who buried him was interviewed and showed the mission the photograph of a woman which was found in the man's right hand clasped against his heart. At the bottom of the card, which contained a cheerful message from the original, was the name of the hitherto unidentified man. When the work of the mission has been completed in close cooperation with the directorate of graves, the public may rest assured that all that can be done has been done to trace the missing.[39]

The story about the existence of secret camps refused to go away. As late as November 1919 the *Dundee Courier* included one such piece headlined 'Secret Prison Camp – Where Germans still have Allied prisoners hidden'. It told the story of a Belgian who had escaped from one such camp in the Hartz Mountains, having been kept there since the Armistice. The paper noted: 'The most significant feature of this remarkable story is the Belgian's assertion that there are still a number of Allied incarcerated in the hidden camp... If this soldier's story is true some of the thousands of "missing" Allied soldiers of whom no trace has ever been got may yet be discovered.'[40]

Stories about secret camps occasionally resurfaced during the 1920s. In March 1924, for example, the British government had to remind readers of *The Times* and other newspapers: 'No British Soldiers are being detained as prisoners of war, or otherwise, against their will, in any enemy country or elsewhere.' The statement came as a result of an increase in enquiries to the War Office after an erroneous report 'that two Belgian soldiers had escaped from Germany after having been kept as prisoners of war for nine years.'[41]

Loss of memory

Perhaps the thinnest of straws was the possibility that their missing son or husband was in an asylum having totally lost his memory or was otherwise unable to communicate. Of all the millions of men who fought in the Great War there are just three recorded cases of this occurring. In each case the response from grieving mothers and wives was the same. In the words of David Hastings, the appeals for information and the resulting news stories were as if a 'subterranean river of unresolved grief had suddenly burst its banks.'[42] The people who contacted the hospitals, the newspapers or the authorities told stories that conveyed the same anguish composed from a sense of loss, compounded by the uncertainty over the fate of their husband or son, and made worse by the dread that hope so suddenly raised could be extinguished just as swiftly. False reports and rumour had the same effect.

Total amnesia is an extremely rare medical condition usually resulting from traumatic damage to the head. It was not unknown for servicemen to be identified with amnesia or loss of memory, although it was a rare condition. The National Archives at Kew has a dozen or so case files for such men. Private Charles Arnoll, Royal Fusiliers, and Driver Henry Streeter, RASC, for example, received pensions for loss of memory. Private James Stokes, Labour Corps, suffered from both a weak heart and amnesia.[43] But in each case, of course, the name of the amnesiac was known, and each man recovered some or all of his memory over time.

Bowing to public pressure, the War Office set up a branch after the Armistice to deal with enquiries about missing men who might have been abandoned in asylums in Germany. Not a single man was identified. The officer in charge, Major Stirling, bluntly told the *Daily Mail* in April 1920:

> As a matter of fact, there is only one case on our books of a man who has lost his mind remaining unidentified and we shall certainly trace him shortly ... of lost memory cases we have only had four, and for each patient we have had hundreds of inquiries.
>
> It is heart-rending to read the letters we receive, but the cold truth is that the dead are buried and the missing have been found.[44]

As with secret camps, there nevertheless continued to be occasional stories about former soldiers being found with total amnesia. In August 1926 a supposedly deaf and dumb former Tommy was admitted to a hospital in Rotterdam. It was not until the following January that he was identified as Paul Horn, a Hungarian tramp. Horn had been found walking in a confused state along the border between the Netherlands and Germany. The news found its way back to Britain and caused great excitement among relatives of the missing. In October a Sunderland woman Mrs Paul went to Rotterdam to see whether the man was her son, Private James Sidney Paul, Durham Light Infantry, who had disappeared in 1918. The *Sunday Post* reported that she was still uncertain whether he was her son:

> If it is not her boy, there are many other things he has in common with her son that can only be explained as amazing coincidences.
>
> 'I had to write my questions on a slate for him,' Mrs Paul explained. 'Among the questions I wrote was one asking if he remembered a Jimmy Paul. When he came to the word Paul he excitedly pointed to himself. Another question was about

Sunderland. When he saw 'Sunderland', he grew very agitated and tapped his chest with his hands. Then he got a printed chart of all the badges of the English regiments, and ignoring all the others, pointed to the Durham's badge... There was nothing about his appearance to point to his being my son. But it might possibly be that his sufferings in Germany – he appears to have been a prisoner there – has greatly altered him.[45]

Other families were equally interested in the news. The *Sunderland Daily Echo* reported that Mrs Paul had been 'inundated' with letters from people 'inquiring about their own sons or relatives reported missing in the war'. She had, the paper said, replied to forty letters and 'the task is proving too much for her.'[46]

A couple of weeks later the *Lancashire Evening Post* noted that the man in Rotterdam bore 'a striking resemblance' to Lance Corporal Karl Clarence Sutherland, Border Regiment, who went missing on the Somme. His mother had sent family photographs to the hospital in the hope that they would be recognised.[47] Eventually, questions were asked in Parliament. Sir Laming Worthington-Evans, the Secretary of State for War dismissed the rumours, telling the House that the patient's loss of memory 'was quite recent and this is not the case of the reappearance of a British soldier reported missing during the war.' Walter Raine, the MP for Sunderland, stressed the need for the case to be thoroughly investigated as 'much mental anxiety prevailed through the country, particularly among women as the possibility of the man being a relative.'[48] Raine had interested himself personally in the case as several local families had visited the man in Rotterdam in the hope that he was their missing son.[49]

The interest in the missing man reached a crescendo in the first few days of 1927. The British consulate in Rotterdam reported being overwhelmed by letters and photographs sent by families in Britain.[50] Not everybody accepted that the man was not their son. The mother of William Henry Newlove of Hull was not convinced: 'Every mother knows her son,' she told the papers.[51]

When the mystery man's name – Paul Horn – was revealed, Mrs Ann Horn of Bradford thought that the man was George Horn, who was killed at Arras. She told the *Leeds Mercury*: 'George was born on February 18th, 1891. The man at Rotterdam is said to have been at Arras and he says his birthday is February 19th, 1891... Paul Horn says his mother was a little woman... Just look at me.' Mrs Horn was four feet six inches tall.[52]

All hopes were dashed when Horn's identify was revealed 'in startling fashion' to the local police who were interviewing him: 'Suddenly the man made a full confession intimating that he was not a British soldier but a Hungarian. Apparently, he was had neither lost his memory, nor was he deaf or dumb.'[53] It is not clear why Horn had behaved in this way, but perhaps he had begun to take pity on the scores of British families who had visited him in the hope he was their missing son.

In 1930 there were press stories about a John Goulding who had seemingly lost his memory during the fighting of 1914 and had only recovered it again in 1930, by which time he was living in California. Inevitably Hazel Macnaghten tried to get in touch, and no doubt other people did too.[54] Goulding's reply to her letter suggests that although had he lost his memory in 1914, he managed to successfully enlist in the British Army in 1915.[55] Unfortunately, it has not been possible to find anything more about Goulding.

There was another hoax in 1932, this time in Germany, where the grief of the parents and wives of the missing was every bit as great as that in the United Kingdom. In October 1932, *The Times* reported the case of Karl Ignaz Hummel, who had impersonated a former prisoner of war and school friend Oskar Daubmann. Hummel had returned to Freiburg in Breisgau the previous May and 'was received with public rejoicing'. He was subsequently feted, appeared on the radio and 'delivered a great number of lectures on his supposed experiences in French captivity... The parents of the man he had impersonated – who was reported as missing 16 years ago – collapsed today when they heard the news.' Hummel told reporters that he had no idea that his arrival 'would cause such commotion'. He said that the deception 'was due to his desire to obtain a passport'.[56]

Three soldiers – none of whom were British – were actually known to have lost their identities and ended up in asylums. The first was a former Italian soldier unable to furnish his identity after he was arrested in Turin for petty larceny in 1926. He was interned at the asylum at Collegno and his portrait was published in local newspapers. Among the many families who thought they recognised him, one took their claim to a drawn-out trial. One Signora Canella recognised her husband, a distinguished professor who had gone missing at Salonika, meanwhile Signora Bruneri identified her husband, a small-time crook. The putative amnesiac, who chose the Canellas – acquiring a substantial fortune and a loving wife whom he soon made pregnant – was finally identified by fingerprints as being the petty criminal. But the Canella family persisted in their belief against all the evidence.[57]

On 1 February 1918, A French *poilu* was found wandering lost and without any papers on the platform at Lyons-Brotteaux station. He had apparently been one of a group of seriously wounded prisoners of war who had been exchanged with the Germans. He said his name was 'Anthelme Mangin', or at least that is how it was written down. Mangin was later identified as suffering from advanced dementia praecox.

The authorities made considerable attempts to find his family with news stories in French newspapers in 1922. The response was astonishing. Some nursed the hope that their loved one was not one of the 300,000 French soldiers whose bodies had never been identified, but might still be alive in some psychiatric ward. Three hundred families believed, or wanted to believe, that Mangin was their missing son or husband, including several from Quebec and one from Guernsey. They began arriving at the asylum at Bron near Toulouse, desperately hoping he would recognise them. Which of course he did not. Yet many still refused to give up. Eventually some claims went to court.

Eventually he was identified as being Octave Monjoin, who had been a waiter at the French Embassy in London before the war. The clincher came when Mangin returned to his home village of Saint-Maur and although he did not recognise his family, he clearly remembered the village. The *Daily Herald* reported that when he left the family house: 'a gendarme who had been posted outside with special instructions said gruffly to him: "Come along! Get along to school." For the third time the man smiled and walked straight to the village schoolhouse.'[58]

Inevitably, Mangin's future ended up in court. Lucie Lemay, who also claimed him as her missing husband, took legal action against the authorities. By the time the action had been decided against her, Mangin's surviving family members, his father and brother, had died, so he spent the last few years of his life in an asylum in Paris, where he died, probably of malnutrition, in 1942.[59]

Meanwhile eight thousand miles away a returned Anzac was a patient at Callan Park Mental Hospital in Sydney. George McQuay, who came from a small town in New Zealand, was there largely because he was a victim of bureaucratic mix-ups. George had enlisted in 1915 and, despite severe mental problems that included schizophrenia, which led to several periods of field punishment, had served at Gallipoli and on the Western Front. On 5 July 1916, he deserted his comrades on the Somme. His company – the 16th Waikato – had been under severe pressure from the Germans. During the barrage McQuay appears to have been buried alive and this may have set off the events which led to his incarceration. On 2 August he was found wandering behind the lines by British military police, who reported that he assaulted a guard and that his face was contorted, but otherwise he was apathetic. He had little idea about his time in the Army and wrongly gave his name and number as being 2584 Pte George Brown, Australian Imperial Forces.[60]

Clearly unfit for further service 'George Brown' was sent back to Australia where he became a patient at Callan Park. Because he had no family he received few visitors, and became increasingly socially isolated, until in 1928 the local branch of the Returned Services League decided to see whether they could find his family. Details were placed on noticeboards in their clubs and elsewhere. The story was picked up by the press. *Truth*, for example, wrote: 'The Digger who had gone away from Australia's sunny shores as somebody had returned as nobody – a man who has as thoroughly and effectively lost himself as if he had been stranded in the barren wastes of the Sahara.'[61] They provided a physical description and, as with Anthelme Mangin, his photograph was published

As in Italy and France, there were hundreds of responses. The numbers, however, were cut by the wide distribution of McQuay's photographs and a physical description. Families came to the hospital to look at George, something which he naturally found unsettling. It was the photograph which led to him being reunited with his family. The story in *Truth* was read by two of George's childhood friends who lived in Sydney. They visited Callan Park and reminisced with the patient about the old times. In one account, when George was asked who his visitors were, he replied 'Billy Porter! At Taranaki, eating peaches' and chatted with them about a favourite dog they remembered from their childhood.[62]

Truth sent a reporter to New Zealand to give George's mother Emma the news:

In a wave of unrestrained Joy, the mother clasped the photograph to her bosom, cried "Yes, that is my George, God bless him!" and collapsed, completely overcome with the wonderful and almost incredible news that her son lived... When the mother had recovered from the first great wave of emotion she declared her intention of losing no time of getting to Sydney to claim her boy and bring back to the loving arms from which he had been lost for what seemed to her an eternity. This missing boy had come to be regarded with the passage of the silent years as dead and gone for ever. [63]

Of the three 'living unknowns' George McQuay was the only one to be reunited with his real family. He returned home to be cared by them until his death in 1951.

Visiting the battlefields

As we have seen, it was decided early on in the War that all service personnel would be buried in cemeteries near where they fell. The Imperial War Graves Commission responsible for administering the cemeteries argued that: 'One could never explain why Lord and Lady This was able to have a body ... while plain Mrs Smith, a labourer's wife or widow could not.'[64] It was not a popular decision, but it was undoubtedly the correct one.

Apart from a lucky few who could afford to travel to the battle areas to visit their dear one's grave or hunt, unsuccessfully, for any trace of their boy's last moments, most families could only grieve at a remove. Even so, a small number of grieving widows and parents either found their own way to the battlefields or went as part of an organised tour. Some perhaps hoped that they might be able to find some trace of their boy. The Williamsons visited in 1920, scouring the hospitals of the Somme in the hope of finding their son suffering from loss of memory.[65]

One ex-soldier, who took tours out to the cemeteries, told the journalist H V Morton: 'It hurts to see the women who come here hoping to find graves, walking about reading other people's crosses and crying a bit.'[66] At the cemetery at Kleine Zillebeke: Stephen Graham found an Englishwoman going from grave to grave 'diligently examining the aluminium ribbons on which names are fixed to the crosses – looking perhaps for her husband's grave but with an expression in her face and form of "They have taken away my Lord and I know not where they laid him."'[67]

Others were more phlegmatic. One of the first visitors to the battlefields was Mrs E. N. Wheeler who visited her husband's grave at Pond Farm in September 1919: 'We found my husband's grave quite easily, a mass of weeds like all the others. We did a little tidying and took a few photographs. My own wish was to start back the first moment I could, thinking of the walk that lay before us.'[68]

As small cemeteries and isolated graves were closed and bodies moved into larger cemeteries built and maintained by the Imperial War Graves Commission, tourists found them much easier to visit, but somehow also more daunting because of their size. The Williamsons also visited several of the new cemeteries: Mrs Williamson thanked God that 'our son is not in any of your "Pagan" cemeteries.' England's heroes, she wrote, were buried 'like dogs'.[69]

In September 1920, the war poet Beatrix Brice argued in *The Times*:

> ... she wrote for those who cannot go to France. Especially for those who for varying reasons opposed or were afraid of war cemeteries. I have just seen the work at Forceville, and it is the most perfect, the noblest, the most classically beautiful memorial that any loving heart or any proud nation could desire to their heroes fallen in a foreign land. Your own man has a wonderful grave, the nation has a wonderful monument.[70]

10

RECORDING THE MISSING OF THE SECOND WORLD WAR

> A soldier of the 1939-1945 War
> Known unto God
>
> The epitaph engraved on gravestones of unidentified bodies by the Imperial War Graves Commission during and after the Second World War

The Second World War was by every measure the most destructive war in world history. It truly was a world war involving every nation, almost without exception. Military campaigns were staged across much of Europe, Asia and Africa. As well as ground fighting, there were naval actions, and for almost the first time, devastating attacks from the air targeted military personnel and civilians without discrimination.

Millions of combatants and civilians lost their lives during the conflict. Between 70 and 85 million people were killed worldwide. But nobody really knows the real total.[1] The academic Dan Stone thinks that in Europe: 'Somewhere in the region of 50 million combatants and civilians were killed, the majority of them from the Soviet Union.'[2] Russian records were patchy at best. The War Office in 1945 believed that the Soviet Union 'kept no records of their service personnel and made no notification of missing casualties to next of kin'.³ British, Commonwealth and American losses were proportionally low. More residents of Warsaw, for example, died during the War than the combined war deaths of Great Britain and the United States.⁴

British casualties were considerably fewer than in the Great War. The Commonwealth War Graves Commission today cares for 244,906 'identified burials' and another 138,899 names on memorials, a total of 383,805 men and women who lost their lives in the War.⁵ Just over a third of them have no headstone, which is roughly the same proportion as for the First World War. The reasons why, however, are very different.

The biggest change between the two world wars is that casualties across the three services were spread much more evenly. In part this simply reflected the relative sizes of each service. The Army, for example, reached a peak of four million soldiers in late 1918, but just 2.9m in 1945. At the Armistice in November 1918, some 290,000 men and a few women were serving in the Royal Air Force. This had risen to just over a million by May 1945.⁶

The most dramatic change in casualty numbers occurred in the British Army. About 144,000 soldiers died between 1939 and 1945, which is less than 20 per cent of the 674,000 that had occurred during the First World War.⁷ The Army was now much more mobile with far fewer infantrymen bearing the brunt of the fighting than had been the case two decades previously. The Second World War, indeed, was the first war in which there were more service personnel in 'the tail' – electricians, drivers and cooks – than there were in the 'teeth', that is the riflemen, gunners and tank commanders. That is not to say that there was not serious loss of life among the infantry: casualties during the early weeks of the advance through Normandy in particular were very high.⁸

Proportionally, the greatest losses in any British service was in the RAF's Bomber Command. Out of a total of 125,000 aircrew who served during the War 55,573 men were killed (a 44 per cent death rate), a further 8403 were wounded in action and 9838 became prisoners of war.[9] The highest loss rate (one in eight of those who took part) was during the air raid over Nuremberg on 30 March 1944. After the raid more than 700 men were posted as not having returned home, of whom 545 had been killed. Another 160 survived being shot down and became prisoners of war. To put it another way, on a single night, the RAF lost more men than they had during the entire Battle of Britain.[10] Some 20,300 Bomber Command aircrew have no known grave, which is well over a third of the total losses. This was a far greater rate of loss than experienced by any British infantry formation in either world war. They are commemorated on the Runnymede Memorial in Surrey.[11]

Some 51,000 members of the Royal Navy also lost their lives, mainly in securing the trade routes across the Atlantic. During the First World War, naval deaths amounted to 34,600. Regardless of which war they had died in, the vast majority of the fallen have no known grave and are commemorated on the Naval memorials at Chatham, Portsmouth and Plymouth.[12]

Merchant seamen sustained a considerably greater casualty rate than almost every other branch of the services. Deaths reached a peak in 1942 when the U-boat offensive was at its peak. The heaviest losses were suffered in the Atlantic, but convoys making their way to Russia around the North Cape and those supplying Malta in the Mediterranean were also particularly vulnerable to attack. In all, 4,786 merchant ships were lost during the war with death toll of 32,000 lives. More than a quarter of this total were lost in home waters. The names of the 24,000 merchant seamen who have no known grave are commemorated on the Tower Hill memorial for Merchant Navy personnel from both world wars in London.[13]

On the surface the processes for finding the missing were very similar to those developed during the Great War, but the very nature of how Hitler's War was fought meant that how searches for the missing were carried out was very different. As we will see in the next chapter, much more effort was made to find the bodies of the missing than was undertaken after the Armistice in 1918.

The obvious start was, of course, to confirm that a man was missing.[14] It was a similar procedure to that followed in the First World War, Notification of a man's disappearance was sent by his unit up the chain of command to the appropriate branch of the War Office, Air Ministry or Admiralty in London. Here details would be recorded and the man's family informed. An airman or soldier might well be initially posted as being missing. Information received subsequently from the enemy, through the Red Cross or from another source, such as the next of kin, would confirm his death or survival as a prisoner of war. Confirmation of his fate gave peace to his family and allowed the bureaucracy tie up any loose ends. But, as between 1914 and 1918, this proof was not always forthcoming.

Towards the end of the war as the Allies liberated enemy-occupied territory the RAF and the British Army began to organise search parties looking for the missing. When bodies were found they would normally be exhumed and reburied with full military honours in one of the new cemeteries designed and built by the Imperial War Graves Commission. Instead of separate war memorials to the missing, the names of those who were never found are normally commemorated on panels in the cemeteries nearest to where it is believed the serviceman died.[15]

The psychological traumas endured by the families of the missing were the same as they had been during the First World War. However, the authorities were now much more aware of this and did their best to keep the next of kin informed of developments, even if other practical help, such as counselling, was still minimal.

In a strange way the fact that British forces were dispersed across the globe rather than concentrated in a strip of land little more than a hundred miles from London made it easier to accept a husband or son's death. There was now no chance of his miraculously coming through the kitchen door unannounced, if it was known that his aircraft had crashed over Germany.

Unlike the Great War, when the military did their best to exclude the media from the front line, journalists, photographers and film crews were embedded in the forces from the start of the Second World War Although coverage in newsreels, wireless broadcasts and the newspapers was inevitably censored, it provided a real idea to relatives at home of what service men and women were experiencing. This must have made it easier for the families grieving over their lost ones to understand why and how the sacrifice had been made.

Record Keeping

Many of the lessons that were so bitterly learnt during the First World War were applied during the Second. A report on the experiences of the War Office Casualty Branch was drawn up in 1922, although it got rather side-tracked into a detailed discussion of the practicalities of the card indexes that kept details of each man reported missing. Its major recommendation was to merge the separate branches for officers and other ranks and to reduce the role of local regimental and corps depots, thus preventing duplication and speeding up the processing of the information received from the field.[16] The actual plans for the reestablishment of the Branch on the outbreak of war was laid down in the War Office's War Book, however, they permitted themselves to speculate that a few men were still at large.

Better records were kept by each of the services from the start. More importantly, where possible relatives were fully kept informed by the authorities of the fate of their loved ones, from common humanity, but also to stop the wild rumours and press speculation that had blighted the lives of many families of the missing during the First World War. At the end of 1941, for example, 3000 men who had been at Dunkirk had still had not been accounted for. The War Office's Casualty Branch concluded that they had likely died, although their bodies had not yet been found.

In December 1941, E A Kemble, the Officer in Charge of the Branch wrote to Colonel R E Barnwell at the War Office: 'I need not labour the point that consequences painful and even tragic for his family and for himself would inevitably often arise from the reappearance of a "dead" man.'[17] The Branch guessed that if were not already dead, most of the men were in hospital either in England or Europe or, more likely, had deserted from the services at some stage. Even so there was a hope that some soldiers were being sheltered by local people. They estimated that up to eighty men might be looked after in this way. After Liberation in 1944, however, it was found that just one man had evaded capture. And against all the odds he did so in full view of the enemy.

Private Alfred Beattie, Royal Army Ordnance Corps, was a pre-war motor engineer from Falkirk. On 13 June 1940 he was hoping to be evacuated from Dieppe, where his unit was engaged in a rearguard action, although in the interrogation report completed after his return to Britain he pointed out he had never fired a gun in anger. When the town surrendered, Beattie's unit was taken prisoner by the Germans. As the prisoners were being marched towards a camp, he managed to escape and hid in a barn. Later he found a deserted house where there was food and civilian clothes. He made his way towards Brittany from where he hoped to find a boat which would take him to the Channel Islands. At one point he was captured but managed to escape from the German Army barracks at Caen.

Eventually, Beattie decided he had to find work as a labourer. Local people helped him to cross into Vichy France and he was employed on farms in the Auvergne. He claimed to be Belgian, although the farmer for whom he worked for nearly 18 months told him just before he moved on that he had suspected what his true nationality was. Beattie tried to make his way east towards Switzerland, but he was arrested for stealing a bicycle and was spent several months in the prison at Montpelier. After his release Beattie joined a battalion of Belgian workers, where he was given Belgian identity papers. By January 1944 the battalion was based near Cherbourg where they were building fortifications on the Atlantic Wall. He and his fellow workers were liberated by American troops on 22 June 1944. He was passed to the British MI9, where Beattie was interrogated and his story checked out.[18]

Alfred was granted a month's compassionate leave. Beattie's return home was reported in the local *Sunday Post*:

> Without warning, Beattie turned up at the house of his parents at Camelon, near Falkirk. He greeted them with difficulty, for Beattie has almost forgotten his native tongue. In four years he spoke English only on three occasions… Tattooed on his right arm is an emblem and the word 'Mary'—his wife's name. On the left forearm, in a revealing scroll, is printed, 'Bonnie Scotland.' 'In many a tight corner I wish I had not had them,' he told *The Sunday Post*: 'They caused me a lot of trouble, those tattoos'… There was a month's leave for Private Beattie—and that brought its own problems. There was no time to write a letter, telling his folks he was coming home. A telegram, he thought, might frighten his mother. So, Pte Beattie just got on the train, marvelling as he did so at the well-filled shop windows and the well-dressed people he had seen in the streets. The first thing he did, when he got to Falkirk, was to call on his sister, who used to live in Thornhill Road. They told him she had died in 1941. So he called on his brother Tom, who works in Falkirk Iron Foundry. 'If it isn't Fred,' cried brother Tom—and they waited at the bus stop for their father. As they were all on the bus going home, somebody pointed to a seat farther up, and said, 'Alfred—that's your wife.' Yes, it was Mary, whom Alfred had married while on a 48 hours' leave before he went to France. That was Pte Beattie's strangest adventure!'[19]

On the outbreak of war separate casualty branches were created in the Admiralty, Air Ministry (P4 Cas) and the War Office (Cas L). They prepared and regularly published casualty lists, liaised with the International Committee of the Red Cross (ICRC) in

Geneva and the British Red Cross, as well as with the other service branches. Another War Office branch dealt with prisoners of war (Cas PW) recording the whereabouts of individual prisoners from all three services and the Merchant Marine. CAS PW also worked closely with the War Office's Directorate of Prisoners of War and the shadowy Directorate of Military Intelligence Section 9 (MI 9) which assisted the escape of Allied prisoners of war and provided resources for service personnel (especially airmen) to evade capture after they were shot down or trapped behind enemy lines in Axis-occupied countries.[20]

The branches were essentially bureaucratic entities recording the fate of individual soldiers, sailors and airmen. But with millions of files as well as tens of thousands of telegrams and letters arriving every day, mistakes were inevitable. Often the errors were soon corrected, but occasionally they might cause real distress to the next of kin. In August 1945, for example, the War Office wrote to the parents of Private Basil Spendlow, Suffolk Regiment, who had disappeared while on a patrol on the banks of the Maas in Holland in February 1945. They had initially written in April to say that their son's body had been found and buried. But now he was 'still listed as being missing'. It was not until August 1947 that the couple were told that Basil's body had been finally in Mook Military Cemetery.[21]

The War Office Casualty Branch also maintained and published casualty lists. As much of the information received was tentative, they constantly needed to be amended as additional and more accurate news was received. The lists were widely circulated within the service departments and in newspapers, but coverage might be curtailed by the need not to give anything away to the enemy and the more practical problem of the lack of newsprint.[22]

So far as possible the authorities worked with the International Committee of the Red Cross, which, as during the First World War, acted as an intermediary between the warring nations, passing lists of men who had been captured or died while on enemy territory.

They were always known by their German name *Totenliste*. These lists weren't always comprehensive or accurate, particularly as the Third Reich began to collapse in the last year of the war. It might take months to formally confirm a man's death. On 23 November 1944, for example, the Air Ministry told 8 (Pathfinder Force) Group that they had received a 'telegram from IRRC quoting German information states 26/8 [26 August] P/K N T Monk [and crew] captured. Reclassified POW. Kinformed [sic].'[23]

The most difficult nation to deal with was Japan. She had refused to sign the 1928 Geneva Convention that regulated how prisoners of war should be treated. Matters were made worse by the Japanese attitude to the prisoners and civilians in their hands as well as the practical difficulties of operating camps across much of South-East Asia with minimal resources. Lists of prisoners and other information were slow to arrive in London and often partial. Only after VJ-Day was it possible to compile comprehensive lists, often helped by unofficial lists of the deceased which had been kept in secret by Allied medical officers and senior NCOs.[24]

News of the man killed in action, or being posted missing, was of course every bit as traumatic for their family as it had been during the Great War. My sister-in-law remembers how her grandmother never really recovered from the death of her son David, who had initially been posted missing. She had to wait months for the official confirmation of his death.[25]

In 1944, the Revd G H Martin was chaplain to the RAF's Pathfinder Force. As part of his official duties, he wrote to the families of the aircrew who had not returned from sorties over enemy territory offering his sympathy. His papers, now at the Imperial War Museum, contain a fascinating collection of letters from wives and parents of these men describing their feelings and shock after hearing the bad news. Mrs B Baldwin from Erith in Kent wrote: 'You know how absolutely heart-broken I am, nothing seems worth living for. When my dearest went, everything seemed to go from my life.'[26] Another correspondent was Mrs R Simmonds of

Southend who wrote in December 1944 regarding her son who had been missing for two months. The stress and grief were so great that she had been forced to sell her business to move to Southend due to her husband's failing health: 'My husband opened that telegram on that morning: he has never got over the shock. He has developed TB in both lungs and lays in bed still waiting for my son to return.'[27] Mrs N Hosgood was distraught when her son was officially 'presumed' killed, as it was based on the time he had been missing, rather than on official information received. She had tried to find out more, but without success. She wrote to the Revd Martin: 'I feel heart-broken – to my mind this of all things is the most cruel ... never to the know the end of someone dearer than life itself.'[28] But most were more accepting. Irene Wellington of Colchester sought consolation in her brother's courage: 'We owe so much to all the men like him, and it is our duty to be brave in gratitude to them.'[29]

Both the War Office and the Air Ministry took pride in keeping in regular contact with the next of kin. The War Office POW Casualty Branch wrote replies which were intended to be: 'immediately intelligible to distraught and often illiterate persons, to manifest sympathy ... to raise no false hopes and to provide the next of kin any further information obtainable without further application.'[30] It was also stressed that: 'The importance of a correct and sympathetic approach to the next-of-kin cannot be overstated.'[31] In dealing with relatives of the missing:

> The aim must be to keep the relatives informed as fully as possible of the progress of enquiries; to suppress or gloss over harrowing details; to present with reserve any information which has not been wholly substantiated; to take care not to raise false hopes of survival but rather offer a true picture of the prospects as far as they can be estimated at the time of writing.[32]

The work could take its toll on the clerks. One of them, Olive Noble, was deeply affected by her work in the Air Ministry's P4

Casualty Branch, where she had to type up files relating to airmen categorised as being 'missing' or 'missing believed killed'. The files included vivid and explicit accounts of all that was known of what happened to the crew and the aircraft, which gave her awful nightmares. She also imagined the effect of the formulaic official letters that she had to send to the next of kin about the fate of their loved ones.[33]

It was usual for the man's commanding officer or another officer, as well as his comrades, to write letters of condolence, stressing the individual's bravery and popularity. It took six months for the War Office to write to the parents of Private Basil Spendlow, Suffolk Regiment, giving the circumstances of his death. But when they did, they provided a detailed if rather guarded account of his movements.[34] They had already received a detailed if rather strange letter from Captain W J C Ayres, Suffolk Regiment explaining what happened. He is still clearly grieving the death of his friend 'Cray', who was lost at the same time. However, he describes how a detailed search was made of the area once it was safely in Allied hands, but without success.[35]

This did not stop letters from relations to both the War Office and the units themselves asking for additional information, which it was generally impossible to provide. There were complaints about the lack of information and the tardiness of the correspondence.

As happened during the First World War, it was natural to try to find more information about a man's disappearance. Mothers and wives wrote to the unit commanding officer and the Red Cross, but usually without success. Mrs Simmonds had received quite different reports from the Red Cross and from the plane's flight engineer, the latter stating that all six bodies were found in the crashed plane including that of her son, but his letter did not agree with the information supplied by the Red Cross. Who was she to believe?[36] It is clear from the letters written to Revd Martin that the families of aircrew provided an unofficial support network, passing snippets of information and encouraging words between each other, mirroring the closeness of most aircrews flying bomber aircraft.

All three services found that: 'When the British armies suffered reverses the enquiries were for the missing; an advance brought a stream of enquiries regarding casualties; while a period of inactivity in the field invariably brought enquiries about the treatment of prisoners of war.'[37]

There were several exceptions to this openness of communication. The first was when the deceased had committed suicide. Here the next-of-kin was informed that their relation had 'died' without giving any further detail, although the cause of death would be provided on request. In addition, aliases were used in casualty lists and other published documents to prevent the Nazis discovering the identity of enemy aliens (mainly German and Austrian Jews) who had joined the Commandos.[38]

More often relations might not be told about the fate of their loved one for operational reasons, for example when a ship was sunk. The most extreme example of this may be the loss of HMT *Rohna* on 26 November 1943, with the loss of 1,040 American soldiers off the coast of Algeria, the result of an attack by a German glide bomb, together with over 200 British and Indian crew and air defence gunners. This was the largest loss of American troops at sea in a single incident as the result of enemy action. It was not until February the following year that the next of kin were informed and full details were not disclosed until the war was over. Some relatives of the American personnel were not fully informed until 1993, fifty years after the sinking.[39] The initial reluctance to release details of the ship's demise seems to have been British Admiralty policy.

There already had been a scandal in late January 1942 when it was revealed that the next of kin of the crew of HMS *Barham* still had not been told about the sinking of the battleship with 862 lives lost the previous November.[40] To conceal the sinking from the Germans and to protect British morale, the Board of Admiralty censored all news of *Barham*'s sinking. After a delay of several weeks, the War Office notified the next of kin, but they added a special request for secrecy: the notification letters included a warning not to discuss the loss of the ship with anyone but close relatives, stating it was 'most essential that information of the event which led to the loss of your husband's life should not find its way to the enemy until such time as it is announced officially.' Following repeated claims by German radio, the Admiralty officially announced the loss on 27 January 1942 and explained that 'it was clear at that time that the enemy did not know that she had been sunk, and it was important to make certain dispositions before the loss of this ship was made public.'[41]

As well as regularly contacting parents and wives of the missing, the Army and RAF maintained a 'large, well-lit and comfortably furnished' enquiry office at Curzon Street House in London's West End, which was run by 'a woman of sympathetic temperament with experience of dealing with the public in one of London's departmental stores'. An atmosphere of 'sympathetic helpfulness and frankness was built up.'[42]

Techniques for locating the missing were reintroduced from the First World War. Red Cross volunteers, known as searchers, talked to wounded soldiers in hospital about individuals who had disappeared, while battalion commanding officers circulated questionnaires to the missing man's comrades. But it was very rare that anything useful was uncovered. Returning prisoners of war, evaders who had been captured by the enemy and escapers from POW camps were asked about British service personnel they had met during their adventures, although in most cases they knew little more than a man's forename or surname.

More often the mystery was solved when the man's family received a letter or postcard indicating that he was safe and sound as a prisoner, or, less welcome, when a comrade wrote offering his condolences. On 10 January 1945, the Revd Martin received notification that the sister of Flight Sergeant W H Sweet, 7 Squadron RAF had 'received letters from him stating that he is a prisoner of war at Stalag Luft 3.'[43] In his interrogation Private Beattie describes how he gave letters to French girls he trusted to post them home, although none appear to have reached Falkirk.

In general, after a period of six months when no news had been received it was assumed, in almost every case correctly, that the individual had died. But there were occasions where this rule was not applied. After the inevitable confusion caused during the evacuation from Dunkirk in May 1940 and Crete a year later, thousands of men were left behind. Their comrades who had successfully returned home insisted that 'many men had escaped from the line of march after capture and were presumably in hiding.' After the Fall of Crete it took much investigation to identify all the survivors. After a great deal of effort, it seemed likely that all the missing men must have been on HMS *Dido*, which had been sunk by enemy action without any survivors.[44]

After the collapse of Italy in September 1943, tens of thousands of prisoners of war left their camps to make their way to freedom. It took many months for these men to make their way south. During this time the War Office could only guess their fate. Most former prisoners survived their experiences, but inevitably a few died during the journey and were buried where they fell.[45]

In the Far East it was hard to discover what had happened to the service personnel who had been captured by the Japanese or had been killed during the Fall of Singapore. Japan felt no need to supply lists of prisoners as the Germans and Italians did. Some information did make its way to the United Kingdom, although inevitably it was months or even years out of date. In addition, because of Allied attacks on Japanese infrastructure together with an incompetent and cruel bureaucracy it was increasingly difficult to supply the captured territories across South East Asia.[46]

Relatively few official records were kept by the occupiers. In many camps, however, the prisoners themselves maintained registers of the deceased. It was a way of ensuring the dead and the cause of their deaths were remembered, and, perhaps as important, keeping evidence which it was hoped would bring war criminals to justice. Keeping records fairly easy to do as the day-to-day administration of camps was often left in the hands of Allied officers and NCOs.

The most important example of this was the Bureau of Records and Enquiry at Changi prison in Singapore. The Bureau was run by Captain David Nelson, who had been a surveyor in the colony before the war. He started by collecting muster lists from unit commanders of everybody who had been under their command in December 1941, together with details of what had happened to these men where this was known. He also prepared notes about everyone at the camp, recording details of when service personnel arrived and left, and information on missing European civilians.

The use of paper was banned so the records were written on whatever was available, including toilet paper. Rolls and casualty details were recorded for prisoners of war who passed through Changi, some 100,000 by the end of the war. Many of them were sent to work on labour camps in other parts of Asia, including the notorious 'Death Railway' between Thailand and Burma. The Japanese discovered the operation, but surprisingly let the group continue. Nelson's team also undertook the vital job of processing more than two million letters from relatives for PoWs and civilians which began to arrive at the camp in late 1942. When the camp was liberated in September 1945, Captain Nelson handed 710 kilograms of material over to the British authorities.[47]

Among the prisoners at Changi was an Australian, Major A E Saggers, who briefly commanded a group of soldiers fighting a rearguard action against the Japanese which had suffered many casualties. It remained a great concern to Major Saggers that many of his men were listed as 'missing': their fate unknown. In December 1942, he persuaded the Japanese to allow him to take a small party of men to search for their colleagues.

Searchers found a shallow mass grave containing the bodies of British and Australian soldiers. It is most likely that they had been killed during the fighting around the village of Bukit Timah and were subsequently buried in the grave nearby. They were able to exhume and identify nine Australians and collect evidence of identification from other bodies. Details were passed to Nelson, who annotated the nominal rolls appropriately. After the war the grave was located, the men exhumed and reburied in the Kranji War Cemetery.[48]

Some of the missing, perhaps most, weren't actually missing. Often being posted missing was an administrative cock-up. Some form was not completed or an arrival or departure not noted. It might take a great deal of effort to work out what happened.

With the constant posting and cross-posting of men from one unit to another it was easy enough for the unit clerk to forget to note a soldier's arrival or departure. Or the fates of men with similar names were confused. The writer Julian Maclaren-Ross described how his friend and literary agent William Makins was posted dead, supposedly having been burnt to death in Egypt:

> I heard the news from Carlotta Makins [his widow], who [sent me] a press cutting from a Cairo newspaper describing how William C Makins, a journalist on leave from the Middle East Forces, had died from asphyxia in a hotel bedroom set on fire, apparently, by a cigarette left alight whilst he was asleep.

Three years later, Maclaren was drinking in a pub in June 1945:

> I became aware of a tall pale man wearing a long pale mackintosh and grey hat, from under the straight stiff brim of which he'd been staring fixedly for quite a while. 'D'you remember me?' he asked.
> 'No', I replied, sighing inwardly. Here goes, for his long shaven chin jutted like a boot and he looked formidable and severe, bearing all the signs of a fellow seeking an argument or fight.
> 'Makins,' he announced abruptly, 'You've surely not forgotten? I'm Bill Makins.'

'No,' I said backing away alarmed, for a fight was one thing and a ghost quite another. 'Not possible. You are dead.'

'How can I be dead' the ghost of Makins asked, 'when I am standing here?' And despite the beardless chin I recognised that piercing stare and eyes.

'But the press-cutting? I stammered. 'Carlotta sent it me, burnt to death in Cairo.'

'A mistake.'

While I called shakily for scotch, he went on further to explain. W.C. Makin was a journalist and war-correspondent; at the time of his death Makins was Missing Believed Killed, when he'd been taken prisoner by the Eyeties, and the similarity of names had caused this confusion that in a work of fiction would have strained the bounds of possibility.[49]

The most common reason why a man was posted missing was that the correct information had not reached the War Office. Captain F C Thompson, Leicestershire Regiment, was posted missing three times. In April 1940 he was part of the ill-fated British attempt to defend Norway. He lost touch with his unit and was subsequently recorded as missing. However, he made his way across the border to neutral Sweden from where he was repatriated. A year later the regiment was posted to Penang. As the Japanese moved south through Malaya in December 1941, Captain Thompson again lost touch with the unit but managed to escape on a sampan and made his way to Singapore. When the city fell, he was reported missing for a third time. On his liberation from Changi, he was posted to Germany, where he was unfortunately killed in a car accident a year later.[50]

This was a particular problem after the Fall of France, when hundreds of thousands of British and Allied soldiers were hurriedly evacuated from Dunkirk and other ports in northern France. It took weeks to reunite men with their units. Lieutenant Ian Noble was a section commander in the Leicestershire

Territorials. On 10 May 1940 he was surprised by the advancing Germans and with his section slowly made his way to Dunkirk. His son Kerry later wrote:

> During this debacle he had been reported 'missing believed killed'. At this time, my mother was expecting my older brother Ian and was in hospital at Canterbury. The hospital staff kept the newspapers from her and left her blissfully unaware of the drama taking place across the channel... My brother was born on 27 May and, when word of this reached my father, he made his way directly to the hospital. Dishevelled and filthy, dressed in his BD blouse and bell bottoms, he duly arrived at the bedside. My mother's first words to him, still ignorant of this momentous event: 'Christ, Ian, you stink!!'[51]

11

THE SEARCH FOR THE MISSING OF THE SECOND WORLD WAR

'I always thought "missing presumed dead" to be such a terrible verdict.'

Vera Atkins[1]

By contrast with the First World War much more efficient efforts were made to locate the bodies of those who were understood to have been killed in action, but whose burial place was not known. Until late in the war, when victory increasingly seemed in the grasp of the Allies, this was inevitably a speculative process.

As the war progressed there was increasing pressure from the relatives of the deceased whose burial place was not known for more information to be provided. Stuart Hadaway in his study of the RAF's Missing Research and Enquiry Service, suggests that the public was now 'more willing to question the powers that be, than just accept what they were told.' In fact, the next of the kin of the missing of the First World War seem to have been equally communicative, perhaps even more so, in search of information.[2]

The Prime Minister Winston Churchill and Members of Parliament received many letters from relatives calling for action.

A not untypical letter came from Mrs Margaret Leeming from Widnes, who wrote to the Prime Minister in 1944:

> Is it not possible now to get a fuller report from the source [from] which the original report came from in Germany – as to how and where Sgt Tabuner [RAF] was found? Was the 'plane found? Where any identity discs found? Oh! I could go on for ages with the tormenting questions that pursue me day and night ... the terrible suspense is slowly but surely getting the better of me.[3]

There was also a widespread feeling that a decent attempt to locate the missing should be made, unlike that which had occurred after the First World War. Within the RAF, Stuart Hadaway suggests that most senior staff had served during the Great War and a surprising number had lost sons killed in action between 1939 and 1945: 'Their experiences as soldiers and as parents must have had some effect on their actions.' The RAF's most senior serving officer, Air Chief Marshal Sir Arthur Tedder, for example, had been with 25 and 70 squadrons on the Western Front. His eldest son had been a Blenheim pilot when he was reported missing in August 1940. His body was only found and identified by the RAF Missing Research and Enquiry Service (MRES) in December 1945.[4] Although it was increasingly hard to fight against Treasury penny-pinching and the lack of available manpower resulting from the rapid demobilisation of Britain's armed forces, MRES was given adequate resources to carry out their work until mid-1947.

In all three services, there was a sense of duty towards those who had fallen but had no known grave. This was less of a problem for the Royal Navy where the vast majority of deaths were buried at sea, helped by the fact that any bodies of seamen which washed up on shore became the responsibility of the Army.[5] Again in contrast to the First World War, great efforts were made by both the British Army and Royal Air Force to locate the missing. This was particularly the case within the Special Operations Executive

(SOE) and the Special Air Service (SAS). There was a determination to locate members who had gone missing and, especially, to locate and punish the war criminals who had killed them, which was largely absent within the Army and RAF.

The RAF established a Missing Research Service (MRS) in 1942 as a response to pressure from the public. Sir Arthur Street, a senior official at the Air Ministry, supported the proposal: 'It would be bad for morale if the idea were to get aboard that the Air Ministry was disinterested in the fate of people who were no further use to the service.'[6] Initially, the staff consisted of one part-time officer and several clerks. Flight Lieutenant Alfred Sinkinson was the initial commanding officer. He remained involved with the work until the very end. He was known for his well-written descriptions of how individuals were traced. One of the first was for a Pilot Officer Sanders:

> This officer was reported to us by Shorncliffe Military Hospital as having been landed dead from a hospital carrier. We had no information as to how he became a casualty.
>
> In the course of 8 months we wrote upwards of 38 letters and did a great deal of telephoning, and we were able eventually to put his family in touch with an officer who was with him in the hospital train just after being shot down; with another who occupied a stretcher next to him on the floor of a French school used as a dressing station; and a third who could give some account of his movements prior to being shot down.[7]

More often the work involved working out who the men washed up on beaches were. An officer found on a beach in Essex was identified by the laundry mark found on his shirt. Such marks proved to be a key to identifying men.[8]

The MRS remained small and over-stretched. In the last three months of 1942, the Section were successful in 29 cases, unsuccessful in 20 cases, and were still working on another sixteen. As well as this detective work the team was expected to run the enquiry room at the Air Ministry, where members of the public could come to find out more about missing relatives. [9]

As RAF casualties rose and as the Allies advanced across Europe, it was increasingly clear that more needed to be done to locate missing aircrew. In July 1945, the Air Member for Personnel Sir John Slessor wrote to Air Chief Marshal Sir Sholto Douglas commanding British Air Forces of Occupation (BAFO):

> It has become obvious that we have got to undertake this work on a very much larger scale than at present if we are to have a hope of tracing anything more than a very small percentage of our missing aircrew before all clues are obliterated and local inhabitants forget or lose interest in evidence that we know is still available ... unless we can show everything reasonably possible is being done to trace them, we shall be falling in our duty.[10]

Slessor estimated that there were some 30,000 bodies to find across Western Europe and that it would take twelve months to locate and rebury them. This was rather an underestimate: there were 41,881 such cases worldwide, 37,000 of which were in Europe. By 1951, when the units in the Missing Research and Enquiry Service (MRES) was wound up, 23,881 men had been located (a success rate of 57 per cent). It was known that roughly 9300 aircrew had been lost at sea. No information had been found about another 6745 men (16 per cent). And another 1974 personnel (5 per cent) were, in Stuart Hadaway's words: 'totally unaccounted for in the statistics, possibly bodies buried as "unknown airmen".'[11]

Eight MRES units were set up to comb North West Europe and Italy. Another section was based in Burma. Members were all volunteers, and all had previously been aircrew. Squadron leader Bill Lott remembered:

> There was [no training] so far and as I was concerned nor was any necessary. My experience as former aircrew was sufficient for the purpose: to find a designated place, question local German authorities and independent citizens about aircraft crashes or associated burials in the area, dig holes, record evidence from recovered uniform and aircraft remains and, therefore, to complete an exhumation report for onward transmission to the Air Ministry. Recovered aircrew remains were wrapped in Service Blankets and handed over to the Army Graves Service for transportation and reinternment in the nearest Allied Military Cemetery.[12]

It was not of course easy work: the trauma of dealing with human remains, the day-to-day difficulties of working in devastated areas, and the constant battle for resources, particularly staffing the Units at a time when the RAF was rapidly demobilising. Despite the grimness of the task, morale remain high as members realised the importance of their work. One member described their task as being the 'greatest detective work in the world'.[13]

In the Army, responsibility lay largely with Grave Registration Units (GRUs), part of the Royal Army Service Corps. They also had the duty of recovering the bodies of the small number of merchant and navy personnel with no known grave. Their work was made much easier during an advance, where it might be simple to locate the deceased, but much harder during the chaos of a retreat where the deceased had to be abandoned where they fell, with little chance of completing the necessary paperwork. This was particularly the case during the Fall of France in May 1940 and especially during the Malayan Campaign of late 1941 and the Fall of Singapore in February 1942.

At Dunkirk, those who returned to England commented on the dead that lay all around. One survivor wrote about the 'horrible stench of blood and mutilated flesh' that permeated the place. The GRUs only managed to identify 552 of a total number of the dead and missing of over 3500.[14] It is perhaps unsurprising that the War Office Casualty Branch entertained hopes that a few at least of those who had not returned home had managed to evade capture by the enemy.

A South African Captain Archibald Gourley, Union Defence Force received an MBE for his 'outstanding work in registering and concentrating the dead under the difficult conditions at Anzio Beachhead':

> This task [he] has carried out with energetic cheerfulness and with extraordinary success. Capt Gourley is a courageous officer who when the explosion of mines killed one and blinded another soldier of his unit at Anzio on 27 June 1944, without regard to his own safety unhesitatingly went to the assistance of both casualties and brought them out.[15]

Anzio Beach Head Cemetery 'originally lay close to a casualty clearing station. Burials were made direct from the battlefield after the landings at Anzio and later, after the Army had moved forward, many graves were brought in from the surrounding country.'[16]

Their work could be impressive, as a British sergeant, Alan Hicks, Kings Royal Rifle Corps, found when his unit arrived at Heppen in Belgium on 13 September 1944. The village had fallen to the British a few days previously:

> Behind the house we occupied at Heppen was a very modern version of this idea [of a Catholic road shrine]. It consisted of an asymmetrical concrete block with the usual window, painted in blue and white. My attention was drawn towards this, for it looked so bright and gaudy in so rural a setting. Beside it were the new graves of the Guardsmen who had been killed during the capture of the village. Amongst them a plain white cross bore the name of Lord Hartington.[17]

To an extent the Grave Registration Units depended on the work of Army units to locate and bury their dead, even in the most inhospitable of conditions. After the battle of Monte Cassino, where it was often deemed too dangerous for men to venture out of the trenches to rescue the wounded and the deceased, men drew lots to comb the battlefield looking for the dead. Selected by lot, Private Ken Smith, Essex Regiment, remembered that: 'I personally found two of our own lot. They were just lying there all those months after, among many more including Germans.'[18]

It was generally expected that this work would be led by the padre attached to the battalion, who would conduct an appropriate funeral service. One of the most assiduous was the Revd Leslie Skinner who was attached to the Sherwood Rangers. During the weeks after the Rangers landed in France on D-Day he spent much time trying to identify the bodies where identification was proving difficult. As he noted in his diary, Skinner was very aware of the distress that having a man posted as being missing would cause to their families.[19]

An officer from his battalion described the search made for their son's body in a letter to the parents of Private Basil Spendlow, Suffolk Regiment. He had disappeared returning from a patrol:

> ...after the territory on the far bank of the Maas had been cleared of the enemy our unit 'Padre' and one other officer went back over the route taken by the patrol to see if they could find any signs of a grave or graves, and they questioned all the Dutch civilians they came across in the area whether they were aware of any graves about or had seen the Germans bury anyone. They found no trace of any graves, but you must realize the patrol covered a very large area and therefore it cannot be stated definitely there are no military graves in the area.[20]

Almost as soon as the war ended the War Office established search parties to comb Germany and the formerly occupied countries of Europe to look for missing personnel and where necessary to retrieve bodies found during their work. Most of the missing had been prisoners of war who had somehow got lost during the chaotic last few weeks of the war. Similar parties were later established in South East Asia.

In Germany, the Allied Control Commission directed that the civic authorities had to co-operate with the search for the missing. There were tensions with the Russians in eastern Germany, and with the Poles who now controlled the former German territories to the east of the Oder-Neisse rivers. The Russians were suspicious that any search parties might be made up of spies looking for information about the Red Army. In the end they grudgingly allowed British parties to look for any men still on the run.

Most of the missing men were quickly located and identified. Some were former prisoners of war who had fallen out of the system. Others had been killed in action.

Their work was often frustrating. In 1945 a New Zealand Searcher Party combed Crete looking for information about New Zealanders who were known to have hidden from the Germans on the island. They were forced to conclude:

> So many escaped prisoners moved around the island and so much happened to them that it is practically impossible to trace all of them or relate all their adventures. Lack of records and passage of time are yet further bars. This list of escapes has been made as complete and accurate as possible. Enough has been written to mark these soldiers as men of hope and courage.[21]

By the middle of 1947, there were a few cases which seemingly looked unsolvable. Rifleman C Harvey, Royal Ulster Rifles, who was apparently sent to a Field Ambulance in March 1945 to be treated for wounds, but nobody was sure which unit it was. Private A J Fairbanks, Parachute Regiment, was actually born in Germany, although his parents were Polish. He disappeared after landing during Operation Varsity in March 1945. The War Office thought he might have gone to look for his family in Düsseldorf. Both Harvey and Fairbanks had almost certainly taken the opportunity to desert.

Or somewhere a mistake had been made. Craftsman J H MacGinn, REME, was reported as having been captured at Crete in May 1941. There's a note on the list that: 'He is reported to have escaped from Stalag VIIIB on 13 June 1944. In letter to wife Subject complained of non-receipt of letters – parcels – photos appeared worried. (last seen at Auschwitz 2 January 1945).' The Commonwealth War Graves Commission records that he is buried in Krakow, having died on 1 August 1944. The circumstances of his death are not known, but they may well be connected to his escape.²²

The case of Private William Turton, Yorkshire and Lancashire Regiment, is particularly tragic. Initially he was presumed drowned when HMS *Dido* was torpedoed off Crete on 29 May 1941. However, he had remained on the island where he took up with a local woman. He had eventually surrendered to the Germans to get medical attention for a wound received in a quarrel, although he desperately wanted to return to Crete to marry his girlfriend. However, Turton was unlucky as he was taken to the Gestapo HQ in Athens. At Averoff Prison, Turton explained his situation to another British prisoner, who was freed when the British took the city in October 1944.²³ On the wall on their cell was found this message: '746753 William Turton, I am to be executed tomorrow.'

By the end of August 1947, just 28 other ranks and two officers had not been located out of the two million men who had served in the Army. Inquiries were ongoing in ten cases.²⁴ After the war the Army's Grave Registration Units were responsible for locating and reburying bodies of British and Commonwealth soldiers in the appropriate military cemetery. Spendlow's body as mentioned earlier, for example, was found near a village called Bergen, and was later moved to the Mook Military Cemetery.²⁵

Few of the reports compiled by Units appear to survive. But one that does concerns sixteen bodies recovered from a mass grave by 11 GRU at San Nazario near Padua in northern Italy They were so badly decomposed and had no identification that allowed individuals to be identified. The local mayor and the cemetery custodian told investigators that the men had been fighting with the partisans when they were captured by the Germans on 27 September 1944. They were shot in the head, 'and those who did not die, had their heads smashed by clubs.' The custodian had been told by a labourer who had retrieved the bodies that they were either British or American: 'He thought that two were New Zealanders because they had slightly yellow faces.' The deceased were dressed in a mixture of military and civilian clothes. Detailed descriptions were recorded of each of the bodies. The first one uncovered was 'badly decomposed, and mixed up with clothing, wearing a khaki pullover of apparently British design and Civilian navy-blue trousers. Impossible to distinguish anything else.'[26] The sixteen bodies were taken for formal burial to the Padua War Cemetery where they now lie among the 32 men who have never been identified.

There were a few exceptions to this rule, if local people wished to maintain the graves of servicemen who had died nearby. The best-known example of this is the case of Wing Commander Guy Gibson VC DSO DFC and his navigator Squadron Leader John Warwick DFC, whose Mosquito crashed near the Dutch village of Steenbruggen. They were buried in the local Catholic cemetery where they lie today.

For both SOE and SAS, the hunt for members who had been killed by the Germans was personal. At the end of the War, Vera Atkins, a senior officer in SOE, set herself the mission to find all the female agents executed by the Nazis. In her unpublished memoir she wrote that when SOE closed in January 1946, there was only one task remaining: 'It was one that touched my heart and my conscience. I had to find out what happened to the missing, among whom were twelve women of SOE who had failed to return.'[27]

Vera Atkins spent months criss-crossing war-torn Germany uncovering what had happened to her agents. All too often, German records had been destroyed, and witnesses could not be found to confirm the fates of SOE personnel. In her memoirs Miss Atkins was 'depressed and disgusted' by the 'abject evasions which even the most high-ranking Nazi officers tried to shelve responsibility.'[28] But often the vital evidence came from junior officers and civilians who had little to lose by telling the truth.

She followed the trail of the twelve women, four of whom were murdered at Ravensbrück, three at Natzwiler near Strasbourg, one in the hospital at Bergen-Belsen a few days after Liberation, and four at Dachau. When she visited Dachau in February 1946, it looked much as it did when it had been liberated by the Americans ten months previously. She found it a 'hideous chamber of horrors.' For the four women executed at Dachau – Yolanda Beekman, Madeliene Damerment, Elaine Plewman, and Nora Inyat Khan (known to the Germans as Sonia Olschanski) – an SS guard, Christian Ott, who had escorted the four from Natzwiler to Dachau, provided a graphic description of their final moments, although he was not an eyewitness:

> The four prisoners were ordered to kneel with their heads facing a small mound of earth before they were killed by the two SS men, one after another by a shot through the back of the neck. During the shooting, the two Englishwomen held hands, and the two Frenchwomen did the same. For three of the prisoners, the first shot caused their deaths, but for the German-speaking Englishwoman, a second shot needed to be fired because she still showed signs of life after the first shot was fired.[29]

Ott reported that their bodies were carried away on a handcart and promptly burned in the crematorium.

However, there was some doubt about the actual circumstances of the women's deaths. Atkins initially concluded that they had been killed by lethal injection but eventually came to accept Ott's account. How exactly they were murdered will never be known.[30]

Uncertainty also surrounds the death of another agent, Roland Eugene Alexandre. Born in 1921 he had grown up in France but had come to England as a teenager after his father's death.

In August 1943, Roland joined SOE. His trainers reported that Alexandre was 'A good, competent, cheerful little man, full of zeal and with a good head. Would make a most competent organiser.'[31]

On 8 February 1944, Roland was parachuted into France. Unfortunately, he immediately fell into the hands of the Germans. Thereafter little is known of his fate. An eyewitness reported he and several other agents had been interrogated in Paris and then they had 'travelled for four days to Germany' and then were taken to Ravitsch in Poland, where 'they were badly treated in solitary confinement and handcuffed at night.' There's note on his file that he was 'believed killed at Grossrosen'. Gross-Rosen concentration camp lay only a few miles away. The exact date of death could not be confirmed. The chances are that Roland was murdered on arrival at Ravitsch, perhaps in July 1944.[32] Because of the secrecy of his work his fiancée Joan Sutton was only provided with brief details months after his death, after she wrote to the War Office. She concluded her letter: 'I have been very patient but really cannot stand this uncertainty any longer.'

Occasionally, the next-of-kin were supplied with detailed, if perhaps sanitised accounts of how their loved ones had died. In July 1945, the widow of one agent, Jean Georges Duboudin, received a letter from Vera Atkins, explaining the circumstances of his death at Buchenwald concentration camp. 'He did not want to report sick as he felt sure he would be able to pull through until the day of Liberation, but on 19th March he developed pleurisy and in his weakened state a violent temperature set in and he fell delirious on 21st March.' He died on the following day. She enclosed the name and address of the doctor who had nursed him in his final hours for Madam Duboudin to contact if she wished.[33]

Within the Special Air Service, Colonel Brian Franks, who commanded the second battalion, promised the families of those who had lost men after the Germans had rounded up and murdered SAS men who dropped over central France as part of Operation Loyton, during the summer of 1944, that their fate would be investigated and their murderers brought to justice. According to Damien Lewis: 'As far as Colonel Franks was concerned, the SAS owed it to all the missing to trace their whereabouts, to track down their oppressors and to see justice done.'[34] A day or two before the camp at Bergen-Belsen was formally liberated by the British, an SAS jeep entered to compound to rescue a comrade held there.[35]

There are just two memorials specifically to the missing of the Second World War, both in Britain. The largest of which is the Runnymede Memorial to the Missing of the RAF, which commemorates 20,254 airmen who have no known grave. Within an easy drive is the Brookwood 1939-1945 Memorial for 3,500 service personnel who for one reason or another are not commemorated elsewhere. They died in Norway in 1940, or in the various raids on enemy-occupied territory in Europe such as Dieppe and St Nazaire. Others were special agents who died as prisoners or while working with Allied underground movements. Generally, however the names of the missing are recorded on memorials near where they were thought to have fallen. With the worldwide nature of the war, it was not practical to build large dedicated memorials as had happened after the Great War.

Nor was there the will. After VJ-Day, the Cabinet set up a committee to look at how to commemorate the sacrifices made. Desmond Morton, an adviser to the Prime Minister Clement Attlee, wrote in October 1945: 'It is ridiculous in the present state of England and the world to waste labour and materials erecting complicated groups of stone hippopotami presided over by the Angel of the Resurrection.'[36] He thought that there was a movement across the country to build war memorials to honour the dead of the second Great War, but there is little evidence that this was the case.

Clement Attlee set up a committee to look at the need for a 'national war memorial', but its suggestions were inconclusive and rather unimaginative.[37] In the end, the Cenotaph was amended to include the dates of the Second World War. Up and down the country local memorials were also similarly amended to include the names of men from the area who had fallen.

The only national memorial in the United Kingdom, the Royal Air Force Memorial to the Missing of the War was unveiled by HM Queen Elizabeth II at Cooper's Hill overlooking the Thames Valley on 17 October 1953. In an echo of Lord Plumer at the opening of the Menin memorial twenty years previously, she concluded her speech by saying: 'For whatever and for so long as freedom flourishes on the earth, the men and women who possess it will thank them and say that they did not die in vain. This is their true and everlasting memorial.'[38] The ceremony was well attended by relatives of those whose names are inscribed in the walls around the memorial. *The Times* reported that:

> Thousands had brought with them flowers, some simply, others elaborately put together. These were the tokens of affectionate memory that could at last, after so many years of waiting lay down in some tangible spot, as close as might be possible to a name cut into the stone embrasure of one of the hundreds of slit windows piercing the walls.

Designed by the eminent architect of the period Edward Maufe, it reflects the uncertainties of the 1950s and seems to lack the confidence of Lutyens' and Bloomfield's memorials built a generation before.

Since the 1990s several new memorials to the fallen of the Second World War have been dedicated. The reasons for this may lie behind the re-evaluation of the war, from being a grim conflict best forgotten (except in the cinema) during the 1950s to an emphasis on British pluck and heroism. As British prestige and power ever decreases, there has been an emphasis on the glorious exploits of the war. The fallen of course are expected to play their part, particularly if their demise was heroic or brutal. The men of Bomber Command for example are commemorated on a memorial in London's Green Park, unveiled in October 2012 by Queen Elizabeth II. It is by far the largest such memorial in the capital.[39] Of more interest architecturally at least are the nearby Memorial Gates, which pay powerful tribute to the five million people from India, Africa and the Caribbean who served in the two world wars.[40]

Even after eighty years, the missing are still being found as the result of work conducted by the Ministry of Defence's Joint Casualty and Compassionate Centre (the 'MOD War Detectives'). In September 2024, for example, two previously unidentified soldiers, Pte Henry Moon, Green Howards and Lt Dermod Green Anderson, Glider Pilot Regiment, who had both died at Arnhem in 1944, were reburied with military honours.

12

AFTER THE WAR

> No Man Left Behind
> United States military doctrine

Although British armed forces have been action somewhere in the world almost continuously since 1945, the records show that the numbers of men who genuinely have been posted as being missing is very small. The vast majority occurred during the Korean War, where 241 officers and other ranks were given as being either Missing in Action (120); missing believed killed (66), Missing believed died as prisoner of war (29), or Missing believed to be prisoner of war (22). All in all, 1109 British service personnel were killed in action or died of wounds during the war, so those Missing in Action were roughly 17 per cent of the total. Incidentally the Korean War was the first time that British forces officially used the American term 'Missing in Action'.[1]

British casualties in subsequent conflicts have been far fewer. In part this was because the forces used were much smaller, with units rotated in and out of the battle zone over short periods of time. Since the Falklands War no service men or women has been recorded as being Missing in Action and there were very few before then. It is also now much easier to extract those killed from the battlefield, usually by air.

Since the 1960s the British government has increasingly brought bodies back home for burial in the United Kingdom. Initially, it was the choice of the family to either have the body of a loved one repatriated or for two members of the family to be allowed to attend a funeral where the body was to be buried. The South Atlantic Campaign led to the construction of a new cemetery at San Carlos in the Falkland Islands.[2] Fourteen families elected to have their sons and husbands buried there. The remaining 66 bodies were subsequently repatriated by the Ministry of Defence for burial at home. Since 2003, all service personnel who die overseas have been repatriated to the UK at the government's expense. This work is co-ordinated by MoD's Joint Casualty and Compassionate Centre. An Armed Forces Memorial dedicated to all Post-War service personnel killed during the course of their duties is located at the National Arboretum in Staffordshire.

In the campaigns of the twenty-first century great care has been taken to recover the fallen and return their bodies for reburial at home. There is a very strong feeling among frontline troops that it is their duty to retrieve the wounded and dead whatever the cost. Memorably, for four years, the bodies of personnel killed in Iraq and Afghanistan were repatriated to RAF Lyneham for transport to Oxford's John Radcliffe Hospital. As the hearses passed through the Wiltshire town of Wootton Bassett local members of the Royal British Legion formally showed their respect to the deceased as the cars passed through the town. This soon became a major event reported worldwide. Anne Bevis who organised the ceremony told The Guardian: 'People call it a parade, but it is not a parade. It's a gathering to pay tribute with a few moments of our lives – a few moments of our lives is nothing compared with what they have given.'[3] When the repatriations finished in 2011 the town received as a reward the great honour of being granted the prefix Royal.

No Man Left Behind: The Vietnam War and the Israeli Defence Force

As we have seen the Americans decided to leave the bodies of their fallen during the First World War in Europe, although it was possible for families to have their sons and fathers repatriated. This contrasts with subsequent wars, as the US developed a doctrine of 'No Man Left Behind', retrieving the bodies of the dead and reburying them at home. The policy seems to have had its origins in disputes with the Soviet Union in the early 1930s over the return of the remains of 127 doughboys who had died at Murmansk during the Russian Civil War in 1919. This established a principle, which Michael Sledge says played an important role after both the Korean and Vietnam Wars: the refusal to negotiate with supposedly politically unacceptable parties in power, the later agreement to supply aid, the subsequent return of remains, and the failure to secure a final accounting – established a pattern that has been repeated.[4]

In Vietnam the Americans lost 58,318 men Killed in Action (including non-combatant deaths, the missing and deaths in captivity) together with 2634 men who were posted as being Missing in Action. The North Vietnamese figures for the period between 1946, when the insurrection against the French began, and 1975, when the South Vietnamese government collapsed, indicate that the country lost 939,460 men whose bodies were recovered and another 207,000 whose bodies were never found.[5] A 1999 *New York Times* article by Seth Mydan suggested that there might be as many as 300,000 Vietnamese soldiers whose bodies were either not found or not identified. It cited the case of Mrs Pham Kim Hy who had spent nearly three decades looking for her son Ho Viet Dung, who was lost near Dak To. She had, the article reported

> ... devoted her life to a fruitless search for her son's remains, writing letters, distributing his portrait, talking to his fellow soldiers, studying maps and hiking into the jungle, over and over

again, to dig for his bones. She says she will know immediately when she finds him because of the fine shape of his jaw.

'I climb into every hole and feel around with my hands,' she said, describing her excavations. 'All I ever find is dirt and pebbles, so I've begun to take a little bit from each place. I thought, 'This is the soil where my son fought and died. His blood is on this soil.' So I keep it, if I may say, as the soul of my son.'[6]

Seth Mydans wrote that the Vietnamese had 'no organised programme to search for its own missing soldiers' compared with the 'well-equipped, well-run' office which helped the search for the 1500 American missing in action. General Vu Xuan Vinh from the Veterans Association told the journalist: 'Compared with the American cases, ours are a very big number ... that's just the reality of it. Just so many people died in the jungles and mountains and rivers: how can you hope to find them?'

On the American side there has been considerable speculation and subsequent investigation into reports that a significant number of missing service members were kept as prisoners after United States involvement in the war ended in 1973. In part, this arose from deep suspicion of the former enemy and the perhaps understandable preference of the next of kin of the prisoners to believe stories rather than facts. There have been several private missions to try and locate the missing men. During the 1980s, a former US Army Special Forces member, Bo Gritz, undertook a series of private trips into Southeast Asia, which were partly funded by the film stars Clint Eastwood and William Shatner, to find prisoners of war still in Laotian and Vietnamese hands.[7] The missions were heavily publicised and controversial. It is rare for secret missions to sell commemorative POW-rescue T-shirts! But Gritz and the other expeditions found no new evidence. The US National Security Council concluded that: 'Throughout his years of involvement, Mr. Gritz contributed nothing of value to the POW/MIA issue. In fact, his activities have been counter-productive.'[8]

To its credit, the United States government has steadfastly denied that prisoners were left behind or that any effort has been made to cover up their existence. Indeed, there is some frustration behind the scenes that such claims made the normalisation of diplomatic and, especially, trade relations with Vietnam and other countries in Indochina much more difficult. Several congressional investigations have looked into the issue, culminating with the largest and most thorough, the Senate Select Committee on POW/MIA Affairs of 1991-1993, which concluded:

> Some prisoners of war may not have returned at the end of the Vietnam War in 1973, although there was no credible evidence to suggest that any were still alive in captivity, that there was no 'conspiracy' to cover up for POWs, but there was serious neglect and mismanagement of the issue; that about 100 POWs expected to be returned were not, and that in spite of some dismissals of the possibility that some POWs were still alive, the committee could not make a similar firm dismissal. [9]

And yet continuing public concerns have ensured that successive American administrations have insisted that all bodies be located and returned home before relations were fully restored in Vietnam. In 1999, the American Ambassador in Hanoi, Douglas Petersen, was reported as saying that he put the search for missing Americans at the top of his list of priorities in United States-Vietnamese relations, above trade and regional stability.[10]

It probably has not helped that the Vietnamese were often reluctant to let in investigators, whom they feared might have other intentions than the exhumation of bodies. After relations improved, the Vietnamese naturally used the concern over the missing as a way to exert pressure in the United States for other concessions.

It was inevitable that the Vietnamese expressed weariness at this continued insistence by the United States. 'It's crazy for the

Americans to keep asking us to find their men,' A veteran Dr Le Cao Dai said. 'We lost several times more than the Americans did. In any war there are many people who disappear. They just disappear.' And Nguyen Khuyen, editor in chief of the English-language daily *Viet Nam News*, commented, 'The MIA issue is an overblown one on your side. You are still looking for MIA's in Korea, even Normandy. And now you want every case cleared up in Vietnam. It's nearly impossible.'[11]

Even when investigations were permitted, the results were disappointing. The British Embassy in Hanoi reported in December 1985 that a team had excavated a B-52 bomber site, 'digging a huge hole from which they extracted a very small number of bone fragments which may or not be identifiable.' The reason may be that the Vietnamese had insisted that the US team dig at this site, rather than more promising ones suggested by the Americans. However, the investigators returned home with the remains of '7 MIAs (from other sites) turned over by Vietnamese plus docs'.[12]

The issue has dragged on for many years. At the time of writing, the Defense POW/MIA Accounting Agency, which is responsible for the identification and recovery of the bodies of the American missing in action, reported that there were still 1587 military and civilian personnel missing in Indochina. Teams comb Indochina looking for remains. Several dozen bodies or so are recovered and identified each year.[13]

Just as happened after the First World War, not every grieving relative can accept that their boy will not return home. In November 1988, fifteen years after the end of the Vietnam War, Barbara Scharf Lowerison wrote letters to Mrs Thatcher and other British and Russian politicians in the vain hope of finding information about her brother Colonel Charles Scharf, USAF, whom she believed to still be a prisoner of the North Vietnamese: 'Perhaps you might consider using your influence with Mr Gorbachev and the [Russian] Ambassador for the safe return of my brother to his home in America.'[14] In fact, Scharf had been killed when his plane crashed in combat. His body was located in 1990, but it was not until 2006 that it was formally identified by the Agency. He was finally buried with full military honours in Arlington National Cemetery. The *Washington Post* noted that for Barbara Scharf Lowerison,

> ... the announcement was a slap. It meant she was losing – if she had not already lost – her fight to convince officials that her brother is alive, a prisoner of war... 'I don't know what they are burying,' she said. 'That is not my brother... No one is telling the truth in this story, That's the bottom line. No one is telling the truth.'[15]

This issue is also a factor in the relations between the Americans and North Korea. As part of the Singapore Agreement signed by the US and the Democratic People's Republic in June 2018, one of the four main points was that the North committed itself 'to recovering POW/MIA remains, including the immediate repatriation of those already identified'.[16] This was the only demand made by President Trump. As a result, a few weeks after the signing, North Korea turned over 55 boxes purported to contain the remains of American servicemen killed during the Korean War. The boxes were passed to the Defense POW/MIA Accounting Agency's laboratory in Honolulu for identification. [17]

The Israeli experience
Like the Americans the Israel Defence Force (IDF) has made special efforts to retrieve its missing. The Israeli journalist Pesach Benson suggests that: 'While governments have a duty to bring back those missing in action, the state's responsibility to "bring them back" is magnified when military service is mandatory. And that's without getting into the Jewish ethos of redeeming captives.'[18]

In 2019, the *Times of Israel* reported that Lieutenant Colonel Nir Israeli, the head of the Defence Force's missing soldiers' unit

EITAN, said: 'We want all IDF soldiers to know that when they enlist, the State of Israel will do everything it takes, if they – heaven forbid – fall captive or go missing, in order to bring them home.' In total, since the foundation of the State of Israel in 1948, 175 soldiers have been designated as 'killed-in-action but whose exact burial places are not known'. The majority – 95 – were posted missing during the 1948 War of Independence.[19]

In Israel, Yona Baumel spent two decades researching the fate of his son Zechariah who was killed in Lebanon in 1982. In the same way that a few determined parents did after the First World War, Mr Baumel did his best to keep his son's case in the public eye, travelling around the world to uncover leads to verify the persistent rumours that his son was still alive, and criticising the Israeli army for not pursuing the case.[20] Yona Baumel wrote in the *Jerusalem Post* in 2006: 'You can't imagine what it's like to wake up in the middle of the night thinking about your kidnapped son. All the time, when you're not thinking about something else, you are thinking about your son.'[21] Baumel died in 2009 without having found his son. However, in April 2019, the Russian President Vladimir Putin announced that the Russian army, in coordination with the Syrian military, had located Baumel's remains. The Israeli–Russian cooperation was part of a two-year military operation called *Bittersweet Song*, which endeavoured to locate remains of missing Israeli soldiers in Syrian territory formerly controlled by the Islamic militant group ISIL. When Baumel's grave was opened, the searchers immediately noticed that the body was dressed in an IDF uniform and tzitzit (ceremonial tassels worn by some orthodox Jews). Both the uniform and military boots bore the name Baumel. After the soldier's identity was confirmed, Benjamin Netanyahu flew to Moscow to receive the remains in a ceremony at the Russian defence ministry, where he was presented with the soldier's uniform and boots. Baumel was interred at the Mount Herzl military cemetery in Jerusalem on 4 April 2019, in the presence of Netanyahu and Israeli President Reuven Rivlin. Early in 2020, Israel released two Syrian prisoners as a 'goodwill gesture' in relation to the transfer of Baumel's remains.[22]

It is not known whether Yona Baumel met any British politicians, but the father of another Israeli MIA certainly did. In January 1994, the British Prime Minister John Major met the wife and brother of Ron Arad, an Israeli airman who had gone missing probably in Lebanon in 1986. The Prime Minister promised to write to President Assad of Syria about Arad and another Israeli soldier missing in action, Joseph Fink. In a draft letter John Major wrote: 'I know their fate has been bound up in the much larger issues now being negotiated within the framework of the peace process... But I know that any information confirming whether their sons are alive or dead would bring enormous relief to the two families who have suffered for so long not knowing the fate of their loved ones.' It is unlikely, however, that the letter was ever sent as the Foreign Office felt 'it might offend Assad rather than secure his co-operation. Our best guess is, in any case, that Iran now controls Ron Arad's fate: Syria's influence is probably marginal and indirect.'[23] Investigations by the Israelis concluded that Arad probably died in 1988. However, in 1993 the Israeli government had apparently offered a loan to Iran of $10 billion in exchange for information on Arad, whom they believed was 'kidnapped in Lebanon and handed to Iran, dead or alive. However, the Iranians declined to cooperate.[24]

As we have seen, in many countries the cases of the missing have become politicised; take, for example, the sparring between the US and Vietnam and North Korea over American missing in action. Two missing Israeli soldiers, Baumel and Arad, have been pawns in the game of Middle Eastern politics. Sometimes this can be in a good way: the Cyprus Committee on Missing Persons, for example, brings people from both the Greek and Turkish communities together in the search for the missing in order to return the remains to their families.[25]

CONCLUSION

As we have seen the missing soldier – whether there is a grave for him but no name, or a name but no body – is a phenomenon of modern warfare. The American Civil War between 1861 and 1865 was the first industrial war: the sheer scale of the casualties had never been seen before. So many men were killed who could not be identified. What was worse was that in many cases no body was ever found. The deceased literally vanished into thin air. This was repeated all too frequently during the two world wars.

In 1914 the public and the military were unprepared for the scale of casualties, which were a magnitude greater than anything that previously occurred in warfare, as least in Europe. What was, perhaps, worse, their deaths were in a war where human beings seemed subservient to machines: where the individual soldier increasingly seemed irrelevant.

Civilians at home were shocked by the loss of life on the battlefields and tried to make amends to the families of the fallen by commemorating their losses through memorials to the missing, such as Thiepval in France and the Tomb of the Unknown Warrior in Westminster Abbey. The memorials on the Western Front today give a different message than that intended: they are instead powerful reminders of the waste of war. As the academic Ross Wilson suggests: 'The "absent dead" would appear to validate the lingering perception of the conflict as a prolonged, unnecessary, and torturous event...'[1]

There wasn't the same urgency after the Second World War to commemorate the missing. The Commonwealth War Graves Commission built smaller memorials across the world, reflecting the global nature of the War. The symbolism of the Cenotaph, however, remained as relevant in 1945 as it had in 1918 and, indeed, remains so today.

Regardless of when and where bodies were found they could not always be identified. It was thus impossible to give them a proper funeral, let alone to tell their families where their dear ones lay. For many families it was almost inconceivable that it could happen to their son or husband. They wondered how could this be.

For good reasons and bad, the British authorities were unable to recover as many bodies as they could have done. Understandably it was almost impossible to do this in a thorough way on the Western Front. Even after the Second World War where more resources were devoted to battlefield clearance (and the work generally easier to do) success was inevitably partial. The continuing rediscovery of corpses of young men all the way along the Western Front and elsewhere remains a direct link to the two world wars and a poignant point of remembrance. Every year several dozen bodies of British and Commonwealth soldiers are recovered and reburied in war cemeteries with due ceremony. For the most part the bodies remain unidentified. The biggest such excavation was of 250 Australian and British troops at Fromelles in 2008. Using the latest techniques, such as DNA analysis, investigators was eventually possible to identify 144 of the bodies.[2]

The families of the missing could persuade themselves that their sons and husbands lay in the Tomb of the Unknown Warrior in Westminster Abbey or that his name inscribed high up on the Menin Gate was evidence of a sacrifice well made. But for many there cannot have been any real closure. There must always have been the hope, however remote, that your 'boy' would return home one day.

Conclusion

What lessons can be learnt from the experiences of the families of the missing over the past 160 years? First, there has to be clear and prompt communications between the authorities and individual families, and an acceptance by the military that families have a legitimate right to know what happened to their sons and daughters on the battlefield. This communication was slow to develop on both sides in the American Civil War and certainly in the British Army and War Office during the Great War. But during the Second World War greater efforts were made to recover and identify bodies and also to keep families informed of the fate of their loved ones.

There should also be support for the families where appropriate. Such counselling as was available during the American Civil War and the two world wars was left to family, friends and a few charity workers. It is clear, in particular, that much unnecessary trauma and grief was caused by the lack of support during the First World War and by the unhelpful, if well-meaning, advice offered by families and friends. It is perhaps only since the 1960s that the emotional needs of the grieving have begun to be understood and targeted support been made available, at least within Western armed forces. Inevitably this support is undoubtedly very helpful, but of course it can't entirely assuage the sense of grief and the loss.

The authorities should of course trace and identify the missing and, where necessary, decide whether to return the body to their families or to bury it in an appropriate manner. Again, the British were slow to realise this in the Great War, initially leaving much of the work to the voluntary sector. It took nine months for the British Army to finally begin to accept its responsibilities.

Unfortunately, the missing soldier, sailor or pilot and the trauma that their disappearance causes is likely to be a continuing feature of wars to come:

'Known Only Unto God'.

APPENDICES

Breakdown of numbers of war dead by Dominion and by world war[1]

Nationality	1914–18 war		1939–1945 war		Both wars	
	Identified burials	Memorials	Identified burials	Memorials	Identified burials	Memorials
Australia	38,914	23,245	28,588	12,096	67,502	35,341
Canada	45,552	19,442	37,309	8,060	82,861	27,502
India	8,260	65,649	18,223	68,806	26,483	134,455
New Zealand	11,770	6293	9044	2887	20,814	9180
South Africa	6706	3197	10,020	1888	16726	5,085
United Kingdom	480,769	407,370	244,906	138,899	725,675	546,269
TOTAL	591,971	525,196	348,090	232,636	940,191	756,832

In addition, there are 212,244 unidentified Commonwealth war burials, that is graves with the epitaph 'Known unto God'. The figures can be broken down as being 187,821 from the First World War and 24,423 from the Second World War.

This brings the total Commonwealth war burials to 1,152,305.

Appendices

The memorials

In January 1922, the Imperial War Graves Commission's Committee on Memorials to the Missing estimated that there were 213,000 men whose bodies had not been found, of which 18 per cent came from the Dominions.[2] It proposed a series of memorials to the missing along the Western Front, from the Belgian coast to the Marne:

Proposed memorials to the missing (February 1922)

Sector	Proposed location of memorial	Number to be commemorated
Operations of 1917 on the Belgian coast	Nieuport	420
For the Battle of Ypres and other operations on the salient ('Note it may be necessary to erect another memorial within this group if the number of names to be commemorated is too great in one memorial')	Menin Gate, Ypres	'Say 50,000'
Operations around Ploesteert and on the Lys	Armentières	15,000
Battles of Neuve Chapelle & Festubert and other operations in the locality	Bethune	20,000
Arras offensive (1917) and other operations in the locality	Arras	22,000
Battle of Cambrai	Cambrai	6,000
Battle of Gommecourt and subsequent fighting on the Ancre, 1916–1917	Butte de Warlencourt	5,000
Battle of the Somme, 1916	Contalmaison [Thiepval]	55,000
Picardy, 1918	Amiens	50,000
Battle of Mons and the battles of the Marne & Aisne, 1914	La Ferte-sous-Jouarre	5,000

Sector	Proposed location of memorial	Number to be commemorated
Battles of the Aisne and Marne, 1918	Soissons	5,000
For the advance to Victory 1918	St Quentin	30,000
TOTAL		213,000

Actual memorials to the missing[3]

The Commission underestimated by about a third the number of the missing they would eventually commemorate. The numbers decline slightly from year to year as new bodies are discovered, identified and their names removed from the memorials. New Zealand decided to mark its men on separate memorials, but the missing of the other dominions and India are largely commemorated together.

Actual memorials to the missing – Belgium

Name	Commemorating	Numbers
Buttes New British Cemetery (N.Z.) Memorial, Polygon Wood	New Zealanders who died in the Polygon Wood sector between September 1917 and May 1918	378
Messines Ridge (N.Z.) Memorial	New Zealanders who died in or near Messines in 1917 and 1918	828
Nieuport Memorial	For men who died during Allied operations on the Belgian coast	552
Ploegsteert Memorial	Men who died in the sector	11,349
Tyne Cot memorial	For the men who died around Ypres between August 1917 and November 1918	35,001
Ypres (Menin Gate) Memorial	For the men who died in Belgium before 16 August 1917	54,603
TOTAL		102,711

Actual memorials to the missing – France

Name	Commemorating	Numbers
Arras Flying Services Memorial	Airmen with no known grave	985
Arras memorial	Mainly losses during Battle of Arras, 1917	34,759
Beaumont-Hamel (Newfoundland) Memorial	Men of the Newfoundland Regiment as well as Newfoundlanders in the Merchant Marine and Royal Naval Reserve	809
Cambrai	Battle of Cambrai, 1917	7111
Caterpillar Valley (New Zealand) Memorial	New Zealanders killed during the Somme	1205
Cite Bonjean (New Zealand) Memorial	New Zealanders killed near Armentières	47
Grevillers (New Zealand) Memorial	New Zealanders killed during the March offensive and the March to Victory	446
La Ferte-soue-Jouarre	For men who fell at Mons, Le Cateau, the Marne and the Aisne, August-October 1914	3743
Le Touret	For men who died in the sector between October 1914 to the eve of the Battle of Loos, September 1915	13,413
Loos Memorial	For men who fell in the Battle of Loos and subsequent engagements in the area.	20,559
Marfaux (New Zealand) Memorial	For members of the New Zealander Cyclist Battalion who died during July 1918	10
Neuve-Chapelle Memorial	For Indian soldiers and labourers who have no known grave	4653
Noyelles-Sur-Mer Chinese Memorial	For the Chinese Labour Corps	39

Name	Commemorating	Numbers
Pozieres Memorial	For men who died on the Somme between March and August 1918	14,684
Soissons Memorial	For men who died in the battles of the Aisne and Marne, 1918	3912
Thiepval Memorial	For men killed during the Battle of the Somme, 1916	72,182
V C Corner Australian Cemetery and Memorial, Fromelles	For Australian missing	1171
Villers-Bretoneux Memorial	Australians killed at the Somme, Passchendaele and other battles between 1916 and 1918	10,719
Vimy Memorial	The missing of the Canadian Expeditionary Force	11,240
Vis-En-Artois Memorial	For those killed between 8 August and 11 November 1918	9,834
		211,521
TOTAL (France and Belgium)		314,322

Actual memorials to the missing: other theatres of operations

In addition, there are memorials to the missing in the other theatres of operation and elsewhere across the world. The largest of which are the memorials at Basra with 40,500 names of men who fell during the Mesopotamia campaign and Helles in Gallipoli, with 20,906 names.

Theatre of operations	Approximate number of missing[4]
Gallipoli	27,049
Egypt and Palestine	9033
Mesopotamia and Persia	44,090
East Africa	3392
Salonika	2500

Theatre of operations	Approximate number of missing[4]
India	15,247
Italy	422
Russia	219
Africa (South and West)	2784
Rest of world	1558
Sub-total	**106,294**
Lost at sea: Royal Navy	25,700
Lost at sea: Merchant Navy and civilian losses at sea	14,491
Sub-total	40,191
TOTAL	**146,485**

In total, nearly half a million men who served in the First World War and who have no known grave are commemorated on memorials erected and maintained by the Commonwealth War Graves Commission. In many cases their last resting places were destroyed in subsequent fighting.

Relative percentages pertaining to the missing

Proportion of missing and prisoners of war to the number of men killed in action (BEF France and Flanders)[5]

	Total number officers and men killed in action	Total number officers and men missing or prisoners of war	Total	Percentage of missing or prisoners of war to killed in action
1914	13,009	28,425	43,348	66
1915	48,602	26,561	77,078	34
1916	107,413	45,591	154,920	29
1917	131,761	55,711	189,389	29
1918	80,476	173,706	256,100	68

The Bedfordshire Regiment[6]

This line regiment was selected as being a typical infantry regiment. Battalions fought in all theatres of war. In particular it played a full part in the events of August to November 1914 and at Gallipoli which may explain why the figures for 1914 and 1915 are higher than might be expected.

	Killed	Missing	TOTAL	Percentage missing of total
1914	113	291	404	72
1915	360	523	883	60
1916	818	886	1626	54
1917	933	918	1851	50
1918	1060	486	1546	31
FINAL TOTAL	4102	3104	7206	43

Isle of Man Roll of Honour[7]

Originally published in 1934, the Roll of Honour lists 1489 Manxmen who died in action or of wounds or who were posted missing. The number of missing is rather low, partly because the lists names of those Killed in Action contain details of many men 'officially presumed killed' but who have no known last resting place.

	Killed	Missing	TOTAL	Percentage missing of total
1914	57	4	61	7
1915	151	11	162	7
1916	231	22	253	9
1917	343	51	394	13
1918	420	62	482	13
TOTAL	1202	150	1352	11

Rank	
Captain	1
Company Sergeant Major	2
Corporal	4
Lance Corporal	4
Lieutenant	6
Private	128
Sergeant	5
TOTAL	150

The Red Cross Wounded and Missing Enquiry Bureau work[8]

Year	Inquiries received	Reports obtained
1915 (from 10 April)	34,036	34,195
1916	58,269	102,431
1917	77,246	109,729
1918	164,485	116,251
1919 (to 7 March)	8,212	22,153
TOTAL	342.248	384,758

ENDNOTES

Preface

1. During the COVID-19 pandemic in 2020 special dispensation was given so that the ceremony continued even though the bugler played without an audience.
2. Figures from 2011 census http://lovemytown.co.uk/populations/townstable1.asp [accessed 12 April 2020]
3. Scott Bennett, *The Nameless Names: recovering the missing Anzacs* (Scribe, 2018), p2.
4. Fabian Ware, *The Immortal Heritage: an account of the Work and Policy of the Imperial War Graves Commission during twenty years 1917-1937* (Cambridge UP, 1937), p27. The Imperial War Graves Commission was renamed the Commonwealth Graves Commission in March 1960.

1 *Introduction*

1. Max Pemberton, 'Missing: what it means to mothers' *The World's News* (Sydney), 3 November 1917, p19. The article was originally published in the *Weekly Despatch*, 3 September 1917.
2. Pemberton, p19.

3. Based on searches for the phrase in *The Times* and British Newspaper Archive.
4. The phrase sounds biblical but was in fact written by Rudyard Kipling.
5. And a few also deserted.
6. Michael Sledge, *Soldier Dead: how we recover, identify, bury and honor our military Fallen* (Columbia UP, 2005), p271.
7. Minute by Major William Chettle, Head of the Records Branch 7 December 1918 IWGC WG 219 pt1.
8. The National Archives (TNA) WO 95/2841, 13 August 1915. Although Armentières was in a quiet sector it is likely that the grave was disturbed by subsequent fighting.
9. Irish National Roll of Honour. [Available at www.findmypast.co.uk].
10. TNA WO 339/801. He is commemorated at Thiepval.
11. TNA WO 339/43349. He is commemorated on the Ploegsteert memorial.
12. Alan Isaac Grint, *The Faith and Fire Within: in memory of the men of Hexham who fell in the Great War* (Erigo, 2006), pp331-2.
13. Pemberton, p19.
14. A list of all the memorials to the missing is in Appendix 1.
15. Drew Gilpin Faust, "The Dread Void of Uncertainty: naming the dead in the American Civil War' *Southern Cultures* (2005) 11:2, p8.
16. William Barwick Hodge, 'On the Mortality arising from Military Operations' *Journal of the Statistical Society of London* (April 1858) 19:3, p280.
17. Paul Fussell, *The Great War and Modern Memory* (Oxford UP, 1977), pp44-45.
18. Richard Holmes, *Tommy: the British Soldier on the Western Front* (Harper, 2005), p247.
19. A J Peacock, 'A True and Unexaggerated Report' *Gunfire* (1995) 17, p13. Entries for 11-12 April 1915.
20. A J Peacock, 'True', p13. Entry for 10 April 1915. Noriss seems to have survived this experience.
21. For more about this see Chapter 7 below.
22. Sledge, p273.

23. Robert Weldon Whalen, 'War Losses (German)' https://encyclopedia.1914-1918-online.net/article/war_losses_germany.
24. Edward Blunden, 'Introduction' in Fabian Ware, *The Immortal Heritage: an account of the Work and Policy of the Imperial War Graves Commission during twenty years 1917-1937* (Cambridge UP, 1937), pp18-19.
25. Drew Gilpin Faust, 'Dread Void', p8.
26. Thomas Laqueur, 'Empires of the Dead: How One Man's Vision Led to the Creation of WWI's War Graves by David Crane – review' *The Guardian*, 23 November 2013.
27. Ariane Maggio, 'The Memory of War: the role of the Commonwealth War Graves Commission in the Identification and Memorialisation of Missing and Unknown Soldiers from WW1' *Limina* (2017) 23:2, p33
28. *The Care of the Dead* (Eyre & Spottiswood, 1916), pp10-11. The reality of burials in the front line was often rather different.
29. Peter Hodgkinson, *Glum Heroes: hardship, fear and death* (Helion, 2016), p230.
30. TNA WO 339/43349.
31. David Crane, *Empires of the Dead: how one man's vision led to the creation of WW1's War Graves* (Collins, 2013), p41.
32. Crane, pp48-49.
33. Crane, p50.
34. For more about the campaign to return bodies, see Crane, pp138-165. In any case it would have been a huge logistical challenge to exhume the bodies, transport them across the English Channel, or much further afield, for reburial. If 40% of British families had taken up the option – the same proportion as in France where bodies could be repatriated for private burial, the remains of some 190,000 bodies would have been returned to Britain and Ireland.
35. Crane, p157.
36. Maggio, p33.
37. www.westminster-abbey.org/abbey-commemorations/commemorations/unknown-warrior [accessed 25 January 2020].

38. Jay Winter *Sites of Memory, Sites of Mourning* (Canto, 2014), p24.
39. Winter, *Sites*, p25.
40. Luc Capdevila and Danièle Voldman, *War Dead: western societies and the casualties of war* (Edinburgh University Press, 2006), pp53-54.
41. Neil Hanson, *Unknown Soldiers: The Story of the Missing of the First World War* (Doubleday, 2005), pp317-324.
42. It is still carrying out this work. Its website – www.volksbund.de – is full of appeals for financial support. For €100, for example, one can sponsor the exhumation of a soldier's body.
43. Mark Connelly and Stefan Goebel, *Ypres* (Oxford UP, 2018), pp88-89.
44. Stephen Graham. *The Challenge of the Dead* (Cassell, 1921), pp102-103.
45. Marjory S West, 'A Three days' Journey in the Devastated Areas of Belgium and France in May, 1919...' IWM K96/2625, pp14-15.
46. Graham, *Challenge*, p27. Graham was told that for additional pay the gravedigger would be happy to bury Germans as well.
47. Connelly & Goebel, p159.
48. Niall Ferguson, *The Pity of War* (Allen Lane, 1998), pp292-3.
49. Gary Sheffield, 'Haig and the British Expeditionary Force in 1917' in Peter Dennis & Jeffrey Grey, *1917: Tactics, Training and Technology* (Australian Military History Publications, 2007), p15.
50. Charles Carrington, *Soldier Returning from the Wars Returning* (Pen & Sword, 2016), pp118, 120, 276. The debate over casualties is well-summarised at https://en.wikipedia.org/wiki/Battle_of_the_Somme#Aftermath.
51. Ferguson, pp292-3.
52. What really brought the enemy to their knees during 1918 was the naval blockade which had increasingly starved Germany of vital food imports combined with the catastrophic mismanagement of the economy by the German High Command.
53. Alfred M Burrage, [Ex-Private X] *War is War* (Gollancz, 1939), p82.

54. Edmund Blunden, *Undertones of War* (Folio Books, 1989), p52.
55. Even today farmers along what was the Western Front still dig up large amounts of munitions each year.
56. Gordon Corrigan, *Mud, Blood and Poppycock* (Cassell, 2004), p128.
57. See for example, Burrage, pp78-79.
58. Corrigan, p116.
59. Frederick Manning, *The Middle Part of Fortune* (Piazza Press, 1928), p20.
60. Frank Richards, *Old Soldiers Never Die* (Faber, 1933), p152.

2 Before the First World War

1. Blunden, Introduction in Ware, *The Immortal Heritage* (Cambridge, 1937), pp19-20.
2. Crane, *Empires*, p39 suggests the higher number. William Siborne, *History of the War in France and Belgium* (vol 2, Boone, 1844) suggests 3000.
3. www.battlefields.org/learn/articles/civil-war-facts The figure may well be higher, nobody knows. [accessed 22 December 2018]
4. British War Graves Committee, *British Military Casualties in South Africa.* (NAM 1992-95-2).
5. https://en.wikipedia.org/wiki/Order_of_battle_of_the_Waterloo_Campaign. These figures are based on those given by Siborne, p502. Siborne says there were 1334 British officers and other ranks killed, 4925 wounded and 592 missing. Where Siborne got his figures from is not known.
6. *London Gazette*, 8 July 1815, p1362. In addition, 773 horses were recorded as being missing.
7. Return of officers 24 October-24 November 1815 TNA WO 25/1711. It has been impossible to find out more about this man.
8. TNA WO 25/2009, TNA WO 12/8062-3, The Waterloo Medal roll is available on Ancestry.
9. Drew Gilpin Faust, "Numbers on top of Numbers": counting the Civil War dead' *Journal of Military History* (2006) 70, p997.

10. Drew Gilpin Faust, *This Republic of Suffering: Death and the American Civil War* (Vintage Books, 2009), p103.
11. Ernest B Furguson, 'The Work of Death: How the Civil War changed forever American's relationship with mortality' *American Scholar* (2008) 77: 1, p121.
12. Faust, *Dead void*, p18.
13. Faust, *Republic*, p128.
14. Faust, *Republic*, p115. It is not known what happened to Joseph.
15. Faust, *Republic*, p116.
16. Faust, *Republic*, pp216-229.
17. Faust, *Republic*, pp212-213.
18. www.civilwarmed.org/surgeons-call/payntar. [accessed 31 October 2018]. Spelling as in the original.
19. 'Memorial of Clara Barton' to the 40th Session of Congress summarised her work. For a copy of the report see www.clarabartonbirthplace.org/search-for-missing-men-and-senate-memorial. [accessed 31 October 2018]. Remarkably, in 1997 her Office of Missing Soldiers in Washington, DC was found almost as it was when she left in 1869. It is now a museum, see www.clarabartonmuseum.org. [accessed 31 October 2018]. Miss Barton went on to found the American Red Cross Society.
20. Nevil Macready, *Annals of an Active Life* (Doran, 1925), p219.
21. Hodge, p220.
22. Chaplain's Returns include records of the war dead by the Boer War. See https://wiki.fibis.org/w/Chaplains_Returns
23. Now at TNA in series WO 12, WO 16, WO 25.
24. For example, the Duke of Wellington's despatch published in the London Gazette, 22 June 1815, contains the names of some 120 officers who were killed at Waterloo.
25. Supplement to the *London Gazette* of Saturday 1 July 1815. No 7033.
26. *London* Gazette, 5 January 1858. issue 22079. The *Times*, 6 January 1858, p12

27. Major T. J. Mitchell and Miss G. M. Smith, *Medical Services: casualties and medical statistics* (HMSO, 1931, reprinted Naval & Military Press, [2010]), p269.
28. 'Memo respecting South African Casualties' TNA WO 108/362.
29. 'Instructions for Reporting Casualties in Army in South Africa' TNA WO 108/362.
30. 'Memo respecting South African Casualties' TNA WO 108/362, p2. The charities were the Patriotic Fund, the Daily Telegraph Fund and the Imperial War Fund.
31. Lord Bathurst to Duke of Wellington, 1 September 1812. TNA WO 6/51, p120.
32. TNA WO 6/51, pp120-121.
33. Vanessa Fison, 'General Gordon Forbes of Ham Common' *Richmond History* (2019) 40, p21. Richard Gordon Forbes is commemorated by a memorial in St Andrew's Chapel, Westminster Abbey.
34. Fison, p21.
35. See the comment by Bas de Groot at https://shannonselin.com/2016/07/napoleonic-battlefield-cleanup [accessed 22 October 2018].
36. *The Times*, 20 May 1856, p5.
37. Henry Windsor, rector of Kensworth, Dunstable. *The Times*, 14 November 1872, p8. The soldier's father was John Woodcroft, an agricultural labourer (TNA WO 12/3400; RG 10/1567, f60).
38. *Burton Herald and Gazette*, 27 March 1879, p3. See also Edward M. Spiers, 'Military correspondence in the late nineteenth-century press' *Archives* (2007) 114, p31.
39. TNA Muster of 2 Battalion, 24th Foot January-February 1879 TNA WO 16/1579. Medal roll on Ancestry. His absence is further confirmed as his name does not appear in the roll of the defenders of Rorke's Drift www.rorkesdriftvc.com/battle/roll.htm [accessed 5 November 2018]. However, he does appear in a published casualty list, *Observer*, 16 March 1879, p6.

40. Spiers, p31.
41. Great Britain. War Office. *The King's regulations and orders for the army. 1912: Reprinted with amendments published in Army orders up to 1st August, 1914.* (HMSO, 1916), paras 1873-1876.
42. *King's Regulations* (1912), para 1873-1874.
43. Thomas W Laqueur, *The Work of the Dead: a cultural history of mortal remains* (Princeton UP, 2015), pp454-455.
44. The burial of the dead and related matter is well covered in Paul O'Keeffe, *Waterloo: the aftermath* (Bodley Head, 2014). There is also an excellent blog posting by Shannon Selin at https://shannonselin.com/2016/07/napoleonic-battlefield-cleanup [accessed 22 October 2018]
45. *Caledonian Mercury*, 5 October 1815, p4.
46. *Windsor and Eton Express*, 5 November 1815, p3.
47. William Howard Russell, *The British Expedition to the Crimea* (Routledge, 1877), p126.
48. Richard Ellis 'Rough Work in the Crimea' in E Milton Small, *Told from the Ranks* (Andrew Melrose, 1898), p140.
49. *Illustrated London News*, 27 March 1852, p253. Remarkably the graves are still extant and are now a South African national monument, see www.travelground.com/attractions/post-retief-barracks-in-fort-beaufort [accessed 22 December 2018].
50. Crane, pp1-2.
51. Crane, pp2-3.
52. Gavin Stamp, *The Memorial to the Missing of the Somme* (Profile, 2006), p74. See also http://napoleon-monuments.eu/Napoleon1er/1815WaterlooEvere_EN.htm [accessed 3 January 2020]
53. The volume is now online at Google Books.
54. John Colborne and Frederic Brine. *Memorials of the Brave: or resting places of our fallen heroes in the Crimea and at Scutari* (Ackerman, 1857), pxiii.
55. Colborne, pxiv. Kensal Green was one of the first private cemeteries which were built around London in the 1840s.

56. Colborne, p20.
57. *Report of the Interdepartmental Committee on British Cemeteries Abroad* (HMSO, 1889), p5. TNA WO 32/3804.
58. *Report on Crimean Cemeteries* by Brigadier-General J. M. Adye and Colonel C. J. Gordon; *Reports on British Cemeteries on the Bosporus and* Smyrna PP 1873.XL.443, p3.
59. Report on Crimean Cemeteries, p5.
60. This is discussed in a blog posting by Rachel Anchor at https://victorianstudiescentre.wordpress.com/2014/01/11/a-sore-sight-britains-crumbling-crimean-memorials-and-the-campaign-to-restore-them [accessed 27 October 2018].
61. Mitchell and Smith, p270, table 5(a).
62. First published in *Literature*, 25 November 1899. For an appreciation of the poem and its context see www.hardysociety.org/files/download/250 [accessed 24 October 2018].
63. Laqueur, *Death*, p458.
64. *Pall Mall Gazette*, 3 November 1906, p5. See also TNA WO 32/6023.
65. *Pall Mall Gazette*, 1 November 1905, p10.
66. The Guild was subsumed into the Victoria League for Empire Friendship, which in 1915 proposed to the Foreign Office that it take over responsibility for war graves in France; see TNA FO 383/106.
67. This project is described in some detail at www.samilitaryhistory.org/vol154cr.html and www.samilitaryhistory.org/vol152cr.html [accessed 31 October 2018].
68. Stamp, p76.

3 *The Missing and their Disappearance*

1. Bennett, p5.
2. Capdevila & Voldman, p24.
3. Paul Ham, *Passchendaele: Requiem for Doomed Youth* (William Heinemann Australia, 2016), pp448-449. Robert T Foley 'The Other Side of the Wire: the German Army in 1917' in Peter

Dennis & Jeffrey Grey, *1917: Tactics, Training and Technology* (Australian Military History Publications, 2007), p176. See also https://en.wikipedia.org/wiki/World_War_I_casualties#endnote_UK [accessed 24 July 2019].

4. See Antoine Prost, 'War Losses' in 1914-18 Online https://encyclopedia.1914-1918-online.net/article/war_losses [accessed 3 April 2020] and *Statistics of the Military Effort of the British Army during the Great War* (War Office,1922, reprinted Naval & Military Press, 1999).

5. Richard van Emden, *Missing: the need for closure after the Great War* (Pen & Sword, 2019), pxii.

6. https://en.wikipedia.org/wiki/World_War_I_casualties#endnote_UK

7. Army Council. *General Annual Report of the British Army 1912–1919* (HMSO, 1921) Cmd.1193, pp 62–72.

8. 236,573 men or 93% of the total number missing and prisoners.

9. The figures are summarised at https://en.wikipedia.org/wiki/World_War_I_casualties#endnote_new and Prost

10. Committee on Memorials to the Missing, 31 January 1922 CWGC/ADD 1/22/1.

11. Ware, p26.

12. Ware, p47. Laqueur, pp417-8.

13. See breakdown in Appendix 1.

14. Corrigan, p114. The missing Fowlers and Wyatts compiled from the Casualty Database at www.cwgc.org.

15. Holmes, *Tommy*, p297.

16. Holmes, *Tommy*, p298. Unfortunately, there is no CWGC record for Private Hearn.

17. Holmes. *Tommy*, p299.

18. Denis Winter, *Death's Men: Soldiers of the Great War* (Penguin, 1979), p193.

19. Pat Jalland, *Death in war and peace: a history of loss and grief in England, 1914-1970* (OUP, 2010), p66.

20. Revd Samuel Bickersteth to War Office, 8 November 1916. TNA WO 339/56254.

21. Jalland, p67. Bickersteth is buried today in Queens Cemetery, Puisieux. TNA WO 339/56254, letter 21 May 1917 to the Revd Canon Bickersteth.
22. See the table in Appendix 1.
23. Grint, p2.
24. Burrage, pp227-8.
25. Jeremy and Sue Hamilton-Miller, *The Fallen of St Mary's Parish Twickenham 1914-1918* (Borough of Twickenham Local History Society, 2017).
26. www.southoxford.org/local-history-in-south-oxford/66-men-of-grandpont-1914-18 [accessed 15 December 2019].
27. Hexham figures calculated from Grint.
28. Pemberton, p19.
29. A table showing the number of British POW year on year can be found at https://encyclopedia.1914-1918-online.net/article/prisoners_of_war_germany. [accessed 15 December 2019].
30. Ferguson, pp367-394.
31. A J Peacock, 'What was it like? The story of Dick Wills of York' *Gunfire 52*, p56.
32. Ferguson, p373.
33. Ferguson, p379.
34. A D Harvey, 'Differing Accounts: British confidential and published version of the moment of capture during the Great War' *Stand To!* (2019) 114, p2. See also Ernest Warbuton, *Behind Bosch Bars* (London, 1920) and TNA WO 339/2999.
35. Cecil Thomas, *They Also Served: the experiences of a private soldier as a prisoner of war in German camp and coal mine, 1916-1918* (Hurst & Blackett, 1939), p83.
36. Thomas, p85.
37. Pemberton, p19.
38. Ernest Blackburn papers LCUL Liddle/WW1/GS/0145.
39. Stephen O'Shea, *Back to the Front* (Robson, 1997), p21.
40. Robert Graves, *Goodbye to All That* (Cape, 1929,) p188.
41. Richards, p99.

42. Cecil Summers, *Temporary Heroes* (Bodley Head, 1917). Letter dated 24 July 1915. Online at www.vlib.us/wwi/resources/flandersletters.html [accessed 8 July 2019]
43. Lyn Macdonald, *They Called it Passchendaele* (Penguin, 1993), p241.
44. Ham, p199
45. Quoted in Jan van Bergen, *Before my Helpless Sight: suffering, dying and military medicine on the Western Front 1914-1918* (Ashgate, 2009), p458.
46. Roughly 30kg.
47. Ham, p208. Mobbs was killed on 31 July 1917 and is commemorated on the Menin Gate.
48. The poem was written in October 1918 and published in *Picture-Show* (1920). Lord Derby's Scheme was an early form of conscription.
49. Charles Carrington, *Soldier Returning from the Wars* (Pen & Sword, 2016), p127.
50. Van Bergen, p487.
51. Frederick Manning, *The Middle Part of Fortune* (Piazza Press, 1928), p20.
52. Peacock, p19. Entry for 3 May 1915.
53. Laqueur, p447. Owen's letter was written on 4 February 1917.
54. Burrage, p67.
55. Van Bergan, p468.
56. Revd E V Tanner diary 9 April 1917. IWM docs 27718. The CWGC gives Private B. S. Kendrick's death as being 1 July 1916. He is buried in Gommecourt Wood New Cemetery, Foncquevillers.
57. *Southport Gazette*, 18 December 1918. Private Ellis Dean was killed on 3 May 1917 and is commemorated on the Arras Memorial. One wonders, rather uncharitably, whether Mahon was attempting to loot the body.
58. Blunden, p96.
59. The officers' files at The National Archives (in series WO 339 and WO 374) are full of complaints about the slow return of a man's possessions.

60. Burrage, p156.
61. Blunden, pp88-89.
62. Richards, p102.
63. Hodgkinson, p190.
64. Summers. Letter dated 24 July 1915.
65. Blunden, p221.
66. John Masefield, *The Old Front Line* (Macmillan 1917), p 55. The Schwaben Redoubt was near the village of Thiepval.
67. Vera Brittain, *Testament of Youth* (Victor Gollancz, 1935), p346. Thurlow was killed on 23 April 1917 and is commemorated on the Arras Memorial.
68. Van Bergen, p486.
69. TNA AIR 1/1552/204/79/51.
70. TNA AIR 1/1552/204/79/51 officer commanding 50 Squadron RFC, 28 February.
71. Cecil Lewis, *Sagittarius Rising* (Penguin, 1977), pp147-8. Ball was shot down on 7 May 1917 and is buried in Annoeullin Communal Cemetery and German Extension.
72. TNA AIR 1/1948/204/246/29. List dated 11 March 1918. 2/Lt Hutton is commemorated on the Arras Flying Services Memorial.
73. TNA AIR 2/102 minute of 11 January 1918.
74. TNA AIR 1/1948/204/246/29. List dated 11 March 1918. Capt Campbell is buried at Pont-Du-Hem Military Cemetery, La Gorgu.

4 Grief

1. Catherine Reilly (ed), *Stars upon my Heart: women's poetry and verse of the First World War* (Virago, 1981), p58.
2. W D Wetherell, *Where Wars go to Die: the forgotten literature of World War 1* (Skyhorse, 2016), p18.
3. Jalland, p35.
4. Julie-Marie Strange, *Death, Grief and Poverty in Britain 1870-1914* (Cambridge UP, 2005), pp14-15.
5. Michael Durey, 'The Great Trust: Mrs Edith Ash's Campaign of Remembrance, 1916-1954' *History* (2011) 96:3, p266. See also

Endnotes

https://www.psycom.net/depression.central.grief.html and https://en.wikipedia.org/wiki/Kübler-Ross_model [accessed 5 January 2020].

6. Michael Durey, 'The Search for Answers on the Missing in the Great War: Lt Hugh Henshall Williamson and his parent's struggle with officialdom 1916-2001' *British Journal for Military History* (2015) 2:1, p102. Lt Hugh H C Williamson, Coldstream Guards is commemorated at Thiepval. His entry in the grave register unusually says that he 'was reported missing on 15 September 1916'.
7. Juliet Nicolson, *The Great Silence 1918-1920: living in the shadow of the Great War* (John Murray, 2009), p4.
8. Helena Tym, *Chin up, Head Down* (Firestep Press, 2012), pp11-12.
9. Virginia Nicholson, *Singled Out* (Penguin, 2008), p18.
10. Nicholson, p4.
11. *Hartlepool Northern Daily Mail*, 2 December 1915, p6. Pte Michael Ferguson, Durham Light Infantry is buried at Potijze Burial Ground Cemetery.
12. Mary Morton, *A Cinder Glows: growing up in Wishaw during the Great War* (Author, 1989), pp1-19.
13. Thirza Garwood, *Long Live Great Bardwell: the autobiography of Thirza Garwood* (Persephone Books, 2016), p19.
14. Laqueur, pp398-399. Their letters are now at the IWM Docs.2554. Pte Martin, who was killed on 27 March 1917, is commemorated on the Arras Memorial.
15. Kipling to R D Blumenfeld, 6 October 1915 in Thomas Pinney (ed), *The Letters of Rudyard Kipling, 1911-19* (Vol 4, HarperCollins, 1999), p338.
16. Jalland, p50.
17. Strange, pp270-271.
18. *The Care of the Dead*, p11, p4.
19. Jeremy Gordon-Smith, *Photographing the Fallen: A War Graves Photographer on the Western Front 1915 1919* (Pen & Sword, 2017); War Office letter 25 February 1917 to Fabian Ware

Photographs CWGC DGRE 14, See also Caroline Scott, *The Photographer of the Lost* (Simon & Shuster, 2019).
20. Durey, 'Search', p91.
21. Durey, 'Search', pp92-93.
22. Jalland, p50.
23. Ludwig J Spolyar, 'The Grieving Process in MIA Wives' in Hamilton L McCubbin et al (ed), *Family Separation and Reunion: families of prisoners of war and servicemen missing in action* (Center for Prisoner of War Studies, Naval Health Research Center, San Diego [1974]), p83.
24. Spolyar, p79.
25. Richard van Emden, *The Quick and the Dead* (Bloomsbury, 2012), p103. Private Peter Miller, Royal Sussex Regiment is commemorated at Thiepval.
26. Vera Brittain, *Testament of Youth* (Victor Gollancz, 1935), p239.
27. Brittain, p439.
28. Van Emden, *Quick*, pp108-9. Donald Overall was five years old. His father Pte Harry Overall died of wounds on 15 June 1917.
29. www.surreyinthegreatwar.org.uk/story/samuel-charles-currier. (accessed 24 June 2019). Currier is commemorated at Thiepval. Marvin was killed during the German advance in April 1918.
30. Van Emden, *Quick*, p101. TNA WO 339/63999. 2/Lt Vacher was killed on 11 November 1914 and is commemorated on the Ploegsteert memorial.
31. Van Emden, *Quick*, p101.
32. Nicholson, p15.
33. Nicolson, p5.
34. Brittain, p240.
35. Spolyar, p79.
36. Spolyar, p81. See also the service record of Sydney E O Rothe TNA WO 339/58141.
37. Nicholson, p15.
38. Jalland, pp36-37. Initially posted missing, Second Lieutenant George Cecil, Grenadier Guards was killed on 1 September 1914

and is buried at Guards Grave, Villers Cotterets Forest, France. Angus Macnaghten, *Missing: an account of the efforts made to find an officer...* (Dragon Press, 1970), chapters 5-8 are devoted to Hazel Macnaghten's search for her husband across Europe. Lt Angus Macnaghten is commemorated on the Menin Gate.

39. Macnaghten, p41.
40. See the papers in the Blackburn Papers LULC Liddle/WW1/GS/0145.
41. Jalland, pp39-42.
42. Jalland, pp43-44.
43. Jalland, pp45-46.
44. Miss Lettice Foster to Hazel Macnaghten, 13 February 1914 [sic]. Macnaghten papers IWM Docs 3969. Lieutanant Herbert Knollys Foster, Gloucestershire Regiment is commemorated on the Menin Gate.
45. Lilly Dawes to Mrs S A Blackburn, 18 March [1917] Blackburn Papers LULC Liddle/WW1/GS/0145. No Rifleman with that name seems to have been killed in September 1916, so Mrs Dawes' wish may have come true.
46. Miss L C Hodges to Cpl J T Davies, 23 January 1919. JT Davies papers IWM.
47. R C Fowler, War Office to Mr W A Hodges, 2 October 1918 TNA WO 374/3382. Hodges died on 24 March 1918 and lies in Roye New British Cemetery.
48. Phyllis Helen Hodges to Cpl J T Davies, undated letter. JT Davies papers IWM. Emphasis in original.
49. Spolyar, p78.
50. Andrea Hetherington, *British Widows of the First World War* (Pen & Sword, 2018), p18. Private Norman Booth, York and Lancaster Regiment, is commemorated at Thiepval.
51. Lieutenant Rothe is also on the Thiepval memorial.
52. Mrs Joan Harbour to Australian Red Cross Missing and Wounded Bureau, 10 October 1918. AWM www.awm.gov.au/collection/R1488145. Killed on 10 May 1918 Ernest Harbour

is buried in Crucifix Corner Cemetery, Villers-Bretonneux. Her response may partly have been the due to the fact that her brother-in-law Private Walter Harbour, East Lancashires, went missing on 13 August 1915 at Gallipoli.

53. Miss Law, Australian Red Cross to Mrs Harbour, 15 October 1918. AWM www.awm.gov.au/collection/R1488145.
54. Macnaghten, p58.
55. Enid to Mrs Macnaghten, 30 June 1931 (Macnaghten Papers IWM Docs 3696), Macnaghten, pp58-61.
56. TNA FO 1103/708. Pte Allan John Tennant, London Scottish, was killed on 24 November 1917. *Daily Mirror*, 16 April 1918, p4; *Middlesex Chronicle*, 15 June 1918, p8.
57. Mrs Tennant to Foreign Office, 24 June 1926.TNA FO 369/1915, f216.
58. Richard van Emden, *Quick*, p283. Lt Isaacs is commemorated on the Arras memorial to the missing. See also www.westernfrontassociation.com/world-war-i-articles/private-memorials-on-the-western-front/henry-rowland-isaacs.
59. Durey, 'Great Trust', p268.
60. Spolyar, p80. Kipling's search for his son John is told in Tonie and Valmai Holt, *My Boy Jack: the search for Kipling's only son* (Leo Cooper, 2001).
61. Van Emden, *Quick*, p104.
62. Capdevila and Voldman, p50.
63. Jay Winter, p94.
64. Service record of Sydney E O Rothe TNA WO 339/58141.
65. Ernest Blackburn papers LCUL WW1/GS/0145.
66. Tym, p14.
67. Annual Report 1916/7 (Soldiers and Sailors Family Association, 1918), p94.
68. Macnaghten, p16.
69. Macnaghten, pp17-19.
70. Macnaghten, p20.
71. Macnaghten, p30. Italics in original text.

72. Tym, p14.
73. Laqueur, p461.
74. The 1911 census sheets for example are littered with crossing outs and amendments.
75. Australian Red Cross Society Wounded and Missing Enquiry Bureau AWM 1DLR/0428. For more about Vera Deacon see Louise Scott-Deane, 'Tracing the missing: Vera Deakin and the Australian Red Cross Wounded and Missing Inquiry Bureau', *Melbourne Historical Journal* (2017) 45 (1): 69–88.
76. www.westernfrontassociation.com/world-war-i-articles/official-correspondence-following-a-death-in-the-great-war-private-cornelius-hayes-cheshire-regiment [accessed 18 August 2019]
77. George Chrystal, Ministry of Pensions to Sir H Creedy, War Office, 31 January 1921 and subsequent papers. TNA PIN 15/1532. Oddly the CWGC indicates that Ruel was actually killed on 21 September 1918. He is buried in Grand-Seraucourt British Cemetery.
78. James Melik, *This Beastly War, 1914-18: Wyndham Family Letters* (Endeavour Press, 2014), Letter XX, 16 February 1916.

5 Informing the Relatives

1. Quoted at www.henrywilliamson.co.uk/bibliography/a-lifes-work/the-wet-flanders-plain [accessed 6 January 2020]
2. Pemberton, p19.
3. Denis Winter, p190.
4. Alexander H Fraser et al, *Ghosts on the Somme: Filming the battle June-July 1916* (Pen & Sword, 2009), p104.
5. Michael Durey, 'Search', p93.
6. War diary for 1 Coldstream Guards, entries for 15-16 September 1916. TNA WO 95/1219. Williamson is commemorated on the Thiepval Memorial. Captain Digby survived the war.
7. Pemberton, p19.
8. Burrage, p158.
9. *Burnley News*, 8 September 1917, p10. Wells is commemorated on the Thiepval Memorial. Mercer seems to have survived the war. There

is no mention of the attempt to rescue the men in the battalion war diary, so it may have been an unofficial initiative on the part of the Corporal.
10. *The Scotsman*, 20 September 1917, p6. The citation was printed in the Supplement to the *Edinburgh Gazette*, 19 September 1917, p2007. Gibson appears to have survived the war.
11. See TNA WO 32/9315. The proposal was adopted.
12. Minutes by J R Wade, 27 April 1923, [ ] 19 October 1923. TNA WO 32/9315.
13. 'M.S.3 Cas.officers: notes relating to above during the Great War', by Lt Col William Capper, March 1921, p1. TNA WO 32/9317.
14. Capper, pp10-12.
15. War Office. *The King's regulations and orders for the army. 1912: Reprinted with amendments published in Army orders up to 1st August, 1914.* (HMSO, 1916), para 1874.
16. H G Wells, *Mr Britling Sees it Through* (Macmillan, 1917), p365.
17. Mary Morton, *A Cinder Glows: growing up in Wishaw during the Great War* (Author, 1989), p2. Morton had in fact been taken prisoner by the Germans.
18. Jalland, pp38-40.
19. H G Wells, p354.
20. H G Wells, p330.
21. Capper, p11. He estimated that 178,000 cards for individual officers were created, so very roughly two letters were sent or received by the Branch for each casualty.
22. Durey, 'Search', pp86-87.
23. Rothe was killed on 13 November 1916 and is commemorated on the Thiepval Memorial.
24. TNA WO 339/58141.
25. *Missing Officers and Men* in Henry Bellerby Papers LCUL WW1/GS/0116.
26. 'Dear Meg – a compilation based on the letters from the front written by a British soldier to his wife and family during the Great War 1914-18', p. 12. Edward Stephenson papers IWM

Docs 11830. Sgt Stephenson, Machine Gun Corps was killed on 24 March 1918 and is commemorated on the Arras Memorial. The print date on the form is November 1917, so it is possible that it was introduced then. This text is very similar to that of the *Missing Officers and Men* leaflet.

27. See for example 'The Military Column', *Lichfield Mercury*, 2 November 1917, p3.
28. Laqueur, p464.
29. Stephen Graham, *A Private in the Guards* (Macmillan, 1919), p247. Emphasis in the original.
30. The time for other ranks seems to have been seven months.
31. War Office to Mrs Stephenson,16 April 1919. Edward Stephenson papers IWM Docs 11830. Stephenson died on 24 March 1918 and is commemorated on the Arras Memorial.
32. Machine Gun Corps Record Office to Mrs Stephenson, 7 June 1919. Stephenson papers IWM.
33. The introduction of the six-month limit is discussed in TNA WO 32/5950.
34. See TNA PIN 15/1530-1531.
35. H G Wells, p375-376.
36. Capper, p13.
37. Isabella St John, *A Journey in War-Time* (Bodley Head, 1919), pp10-14.
38. St. John, pp17-18. But hearing nothing she determined to go to France to discover the truth for herself. Her son had been wounded and she managed to visit him in hospital.
39. Durer, 'Secrets', pp100-101. See also Williamson's service record TNA WO 339/18542.
40. Durer, 'Secrets', p101.
41. Anon, *To the Unknown Warrior* (Hodder & Stoughton, [(1920)]), pp8-10.
42. Pinney (ed), pp337-8. Lance Corporal H Blackburn to Bureau de Secours, Berne, 23 October 1916, Blackburn Papers LCUL Liddle WW1/GS/0245.

43. *Middlesex Chronicle*, 15 June 1918.
44. van Bergen, p409.
45. *War Office Weekly Casualty List 16 October 1917*, p3. Available on Findmypast.
46. Harley Granville Barker, *With the Red Cross in France* (Hodder & Stoughton, 1916), p85.
47. Joanna Bourke, *Dismembering the Male: Mend's Bodies, Britain and the Great War* (Reaktion, 1999), p228. Unusually, Gale's service record survives which clearly gives his date of death. His private papers at the IWM (Docs 10985) include a letter from the CWGC apologising 'that his death was not commemorated for over sixty years because of some oversight.'
48. *Territorial Services Gazette,* 3 February 1919, p4. Card and registry entry for Ernest Russell, Rifle Brigade www.grande-guerre.icrc.org.
49. St John, p7. Her son Lieutenant Frederick Oliver St John, Royal Scots, survived the war.
50. Ham, p382.
51. Mrs Marion Hemming to Revd E V Tanner, 9 May 1918. Emphasis in the original. E V Tanner Papers, IWM Docs 27718. Lt Hemming is commemorated on the Ploegsteert memorial.
52. Typescript 'The History of the Chaplains Department in the World War', p28. E C Crosse papers IWM Docs 4772
53. Burrage, pp159-160.
54. Graham, *Private*, p247.
55. Henry Bellerby Papers LCUL WW1/GS/0116. Henry Bellerby was killed on 21 March 1918 and is commemorated on the Pozières memorial. Fortunately, Miss Lord's 'young man' appears to have returned safely and they married in the spring of 1919.
56. Tanner papers IWM Docs 27718. Letter from Mrs Hemming, 9 May 1918. Lt Frank Hemming died on 13 April 1918 and is commemorated on the Ploegsteert Memorial.
57. Circular letter A/59, 5 October 1917. Emphasis in the original. TNA AIR 1/1552/204/79/51

58. [unidentified] Lt Col 23rd Royal Fusiliers to Mr Bird, 13 April 1918. H D Bird Papers IWM Docs.1004.
59. Note in the H D Bird Papers IWM Docs.1004.

6 *The Search for the Missing*

1. The poem was written supposedly about Jack Cornwall, VC and first published in *Destroyers at Jutland* (1916) but many critics believe that it is really for his son John.
2. Macnaghten, pp5-7.
3. *Birmingham Mail*, 24 January 1917, p3.
4. Macnaghten, p29, p38.
5. Pinney, p337. John Kipling's body was found and subsequently reburied in the late 1990s, see Tony and Valmai Holt, *My Boy Jack?: the search for Kipling's only son* (Leo Cooper, 1998).
6. *The Red Cross*, April 1915, p82.
7. Alfred Viscount Northcliffe, *Lord Northcliffe's War Book* (New York, George Doran, 1917), p238.
8. Jay Winter *Sites of Memory, Sites of Mourning* (Canto, 2014), p36.
9. Joint War Committee of the British War Red Cross and Order of St John Minute Book 2 (RCA) J16 May 1916, pp99-100.
10. *The Times*, 14 April 1915, p4.
11. *Report by the Joint War Committee and the Joint War Finance Committee of the British Red Cross Society and the Order of St John of Jerusalem in England on voluntary aid rendered to the sick and wounded at home and abroad and to British prisoners of war, 1914-19* (HMSO, 1921), p531.
12. *Report by the Joint War Committee*, p360.
13. *Report by the Joint War Committee*, p531.
14. Details can be found in Table 4 in the Appendix.
15. Eric F Schneider, 'The British Red Cross Wounded and Missing Enquiry Bureau: a case of truth telling in the Great War' *War in History* (1997) 4:3, p299.
16. *Report of Joint War Committee*, pp 531-532.
17. *Report of Joint War Committee*, p532.

18. An example of the poster circulated to camps can be found in the Bellerby papers (LCUL Liddle/WW1/GS/0116).
19. *Report by the Joint War Committee*, p575. This work seems largely to have been for officers.
20. *The Times*, 15 April 1919, p9.
21. Ian Malcolm, *War Pictures behind the Lines* (Smith, Elder, 1915), pp 42-43. One feels that perhaps the patients often had other things on their minds than the whereabouts of missing comrades.
22. Malcolm, p44.
23. Schneider, p299.
24. *The Times*, 15 April 1919, p9.
25. Schneider, p297.
26. Harley Granville Barker, *With the Red Cross in France* (Hodder & Stoughton, 1916), p63.
27. Durey, 'Secrets', pp92-93.
28. Interviews with Private Gibson and Lance Corporal Mackay, 21 January 1915. Service record of Lt Angus Macnaghten, TNA WO 339/15594.
29. Granville Barker, p64.
30. Australian Red Cross Society Wounded and Missing Enquiry Bureau files, 1914-18 War, Australian War Memorial 1DRL/0428. Online at www.roll-of-honour.com/Buckinghamshire/FennyStratfordBletchley.html.
31. Durey, 'Secrets', p93.
32. Durey, 'Secrets', p99.
33. Schneider, p300.
34. *Report of the Joint War Committee*, p533.
35. Schneider, p308.
36. Winter, p36.
37. *The Times*, 15 April 1919, p9.
38. 'Specimen Army and War Office Death Forms' IWM Docs 9051.
39. *The Red Cross*, June 1916, p54.
40. Granville Baker, p76.
41. *Report by the Joint War Committee*, p533

42. Caroline Moorehead, *Dunant's Dream: War, Switzerland and the history of the Red Cross* (London, 1996), p182.
43. Moorehead, p184.
44. *The Times*, 28 May 1918, p3.
45. In *The Red Headed League*, a Conan Doyle short story, the plot revolves around a newspaper advertisement which offered highly paid work to red-headed male applicants.
46. *Belfast Weekly News*, 3 December 1914, p8; Macnaghten, p21, p24.
47. *Dundee Courier*, 26 October 1915, p1. Craig was killed during the Battle of Loos on 24 September 1915 and appears on the Loos memorial.
48. *Dundee Courier*, 27 October 1915, p1. Mclean was killed on 2 September 1915 and also appears on the Loos memorial.
49. *Territorial Service Gazette*, January 1916, p45.
50. *Territorial Service Gazette*, 4 January 1919, p4. Pte Champion was killed on 14 May 1917 and is commemorated on the Arras Memorial.
51. Jean–Yves La Naour, *The Living Unknown Soldier: a story of grievance and the Great War* (Heinemann, 2005) p56.
52. *Territorial Services Gazette*, 11 January 1919, p11. Pte Ronald Charles Phelps died on 9 April 1918 and is commemorated on the Ploesteert Memorial.
53. Hetherington, p17. Private George Oxley Allard, London Regiment is commemorated on the Menin Gate.
54. Pte Hainzinger was killed on 30 November 1917 and is commemorated on the Cambrai Memorial.
55. *The Times*, 12 October 1915, p9.
56. TNA FO 383/205 file 26359. Gennings was killed on 13 August 1916 and his grave can be found at the London Cemetery, Longueval.
57. Macnaghten, p23.
58. Letter Kipling to Walter Hines Page, 5 October 1915. Pinney, pp336-7. Kipling also wrote to the US Ambassador in The Hague, whom he had met in 1913, Pinney, pp340-1.

59. Communications relating to British prisoners made through the US Ambassador and the Netherlands government, 25 April 1919 TNA FO 383/547 f352.
60. 'Missing Officers and Men' leaflet in Bellerby Papers LCLU Liddle/WW1/GS/016. The leaflet is dated February 1917.
61. And, indeed, also after the Armistice: Mrs Tennant used one in the mid-1920s.
62. Jalland, pp39-40.
63. TNA WO 339/25552, Otto Lange to ICRC, 23 November 1916. Power was killed on 9 May 1915 and is commemorated on the Menin Gate.
64. Macnaghten, p24. See examples of correspondence in the Macnaghten Papers.
65. *Territorial Service Gazette*, 26 April 1919.
66. *Territorial Services Gazette*, 4 January 1919, p4. See also Hastilow's entry on the ICRC website He was captured during the Passchendaele offensive.
67. https://blog.nationalarchives.gov.uk/american-journalist-first-world-war-prisoners-war-libel-case [accessed 28 August 2019].
68. Macnaghten, p25.
69. *The Times*, 17 March 1916, p6. *Nottingham Journal*, 15 June 1915, p3.
70. *Illustrated Police News*, 4 November 1915, *Chelsea News*, 5 November 1915. See also Hetherington, p98.
71. Hetherington, p98. Pte George Ruffell, RAMC was killed on 23 March 1918 and is commemorated on the Arras Memorial.
72. *Territorial Service Gazette*, 25 July 1919.

7 The Imperial War Graves Commission

1. Quoted in Lord Ashcroft, 'The Pompeii of the First World War' *Mail on Sunday* 5 October 2019.
2. Minutes of evidence taken before the Select Committee on Public Accounts, 5 April 1927 answers 2100, 2103. Unfortunately, we know little of this correspondence because with the exception of

a small sample the files of enquiry letters have long since been destroyed.
3. Select Committee, answer 2100.
4. Quoted in a minute by Fabian Ware to Adjutant General, 27 April 1916 CWGC 1/1/1/34/1.
5. Ross Wilson, 'The burial of the dead: the British Army on the Western Front' *War & Society* (2012) 31:1, pp36-38.
6. The whole process, including post-war developments, is well covered at www.longlongtrail.co.uk/burial-clearance-and-burial [accessed 26 January 2020].
7. Fabian Ware to Captain G O Cornock Taylor, GHQ [29 June 1917] CWGC 1/1/1/34/1.
8. van Bergen, p471.
9. Charles Carrington, *Soldier Returning from the Wars Returning* (Pen & Sword, 2016), p128.
10. Max Arthur, *Forgotten Voices of the Great War* (Ebury, 2003), p105.
11. Burrage, p67.
12. Undated memorandum [1918] CWGC 1/1/1/34/1. John Starling & Oliver Lee, *No Labour No Battle: military labour during the First World War* (Spellmount, 2009), pp158-159.
13. T A Lowe, *The Western Battlefields: a guide to the British Line* (Gale & Polden, 1920), p61. A few memorials survive, see www.westernfrontassociation.com/world-war-i-articles/private-memorials-on-the-western-front/ [accessed 8 April 2020].
14. Marjory S West, 'A Three days' Journey in the Devastated Areas of Belgium and France in May, 1919...', p7. IWM K96/2625
15. Starling & Lee, p160.
16. West, p17.
17. Peter Hodgkinson, 'Identifying the Dead of Tyne Cot' *Stand To!* (2019) 114, p4.
18. Bennett, pp185-186.
19. Marianne Van Velze, *Missing in Action* (Allen & Unwin, 2018), pp154-155.

20. Bennett, pp203-204.
21. *The Times*, 10 November 1921, p14.
22. *The Times*, 12 November 1921, p6.
23. *Illustrated London News*, 19 November 1921, p18.
24. Ware, p37.
25. *Daily Express*, 23 July 1927, p2.
26. Jeremy Gordon-Smith, *Photographing the Fallen: A War Graves Photographer on the Western Front 1915 1919* (Pen & Sword, 2017), p153.
27. Wyndham Childs, *Episodes and Reflections* (Cassell, 1930), pp117-8.
28. Hodgkinson, 'Identifying', pp5-7.
29. *Western Times*, 27 January 1920, p5. He lies there still.
30. Hodgkinson, 'Identifying', pp7-8.
31. Ashcroft. Appeals for possible relatives occasionally appear on the CWGC website.
32. Starling & Lee, p159.
33. Bennett, p206.
34. Stamp, p99.
35. Rudyard Kipling, *The Graves of the Fallen* (HMSO, 1919), p12. Sir Frederic Kenyon was chief architectural adviser to the Commission.
36. Crane, p175; Ware, p26.
37. Holt, pi.
38. IWGC Commissioners meeting 15 April 1919 verbatim minutes. CWGC 2/2/1/10.
39. See discussions in the minutes of the Memorials to the Missing Committee, 24 January 1921-31 January 1922 CWGC ADD 1/22/1. A system of tablets was however adopted by the American Battlefield Monuments Commission to commemorate their missing.
40. Ware, p32.
41. O'Shea, p33.
42. Stamp, p9.
43. They are listed in Appendix One.

44. Stamp, pp106-111. The New Zealand Government chose to commemorate their missing men near where they fell.
45. Crane, p194.
46. Dominiek Dendooven, *Menin Gate & Last Post* (de Calpros, 2003), p70.
47. Dendooven, p70.
48. Quoted in John Stephens, '"The Ghosts of Menin Gate": Art, Architecture and Commemoration', *Journal of Contemporary History* (2009) 44:1, p14.
49. Report of the National Battlefields Memorial Committee (War Office, 1921), p3.
50. Stamp, p103; Dendooven, p61.
51. Geoff Dyer, *The Missing of the Somme* (Phoenix, 1994), p86.
52. Dendooven, p76. In 1927 Lord Plumer was Governor of Palestine. He had commanded the British Second Army in the Salient during the war,
53. Unfortunately, the broadcast no longer survives, but press accounts indicate that reception was very good, with only a short break in transmission when King Albert was speaking.
54. *Taunton Chronicle*, 27 July 1927, p1. *Aberdeen Press and Journal*, 25 July 1927, p7.
55. *Taunton Chronicle*, 27 July 1927, p1. Lance Corporal Louis Raemers, AIF, posted missing in action 13 October 1917 – from Norwood, South London; there is no record for a Gwynne Hardy, the journalist may have meant Guardsman Richard Hardy who was killed in November 1914.
56. *Sheffield Daily Telegraph*, 25 July 1927, p5. No record could be found for Amelia Powell's son.
57. *Berliner Tageszeitung*, 16 September 1928. The article is also reproduced in full in Dendooven, pp71-72.
58. Siegfried Sassoon, 'On Passing the New Menin Gate'. The poem was first published in Sassoon's collection *The Heart's Journey* (1928).
59. R H Mottram, *Through the Menin Gate* (Chatto & Windus, 1932), p2.

60. David Watkin, 'Cities of Silence: the cemeteries and memorials of the Great War' *Country Life* 10 November 1977, p1400.
61. O'Shea, pp94-95.
62. Dyer, pp125-126. He also makes the point that it is strangely unphotographable: 'No photograph can convey its scale, its balance, its overwhelming effect on the senses.'
63. Jay Winter Sites, p105.
64. Stamp, pp-3-4.
65. *Manchester Guardian*, 2 August 1932, p10.

8 Memorialising the Missing

1. www.iwm.org.uk/memorials/item/memorial/39291 [accessed 15 September 2019]
2. Hetherington, p167.
3. www.westminster-abbey.org/abbey-commemorations/commemorations/unknown-warrior [accessed 3 November 2019]
4. Stephen Cooper, *Private Cooper's War* (Author, 2014), p11, p59. Arthur Cooper is commemorated on the Memorial to the Missing at Tyne Cot.
5. Heatherington, p171. Reginald's body was later found and now lies in Heath Cemetery, Harbonnières.
6. Eric Homberger, 'The Story of the Cenotaph', *Times Literary Supplement*, 12 November 1976, p1429.
7. Homberger, p1429.
8. How the design evolved is discussed in Allan Greenberg, 'Lutyens' Cenotaph' *Journal of the Society of Architectural Historians* (1989) 48:1.
9. Homberger, p1429, Greenberg, p7.
10. Greenberg, p20.
11. Stamp, p42. Visitors are always surprised how small the Cenotaph is, yet despite its size how imposing.
12. *Illustrated London News*, 26 July 1919, p117.
13. Greenberg, pp14-15.
14. Greenberg, p11.

15. *The Times*, 21 July 1919, p8. Letter from 'RIP'.
16. 'The Temporary Cenotaph in Whitehall' Memorandum submitted by the First Commissioner of Works' Cabinet Memorandum CT 7784, 23 July 1919. TNA CAB 24/84/84.
17. Quoted in Greenberg, p10. Lutyens did not charge a fee for his work.
18. Stamp, p45.
19. www.westminster-abbey.org/media/11886/unknown-warrior-service-paper.pdf [accessed 4 November 2019]
20. Stamp, p45.
21. *The Times*, 12 November 1919, p15.
22. *Daily Mail*, 12 November 1920, p8.
23. *The Times*, 12 November 1920, Supplement, piv.
24. *Manchester Guardian* 12 November 1920, p9.
25. *Manchester Guardian*, 13 November 1920, p9.
26. The French had a similar idea and several other people in Britain claimed they had thought of it as well.
27. Andrew Richards, *The Flag: the story of Revd David Railton and the Tomb of the Unknown Warrior* (Casemate, 2017) p165.
28. Nicolson, pp266 -267.
29. Memorial Services (November 11th) Committee, 19 October 1920. TNA WORK 20/1/3, f55.
30. *Daily Herald*, 12 November 1920, p4.
31. *Women's Dreadnought*, 20 November 1920, p4.
32. Memorial (1920) Committee, f57, 67. This included lady members of the Royal Court.
33. Minute to Sir Lionel Earle, Office of Works, from Lt Col L Storr (secretary to the Committee), 26 October 1920. Minutes of Memorial (1920) Committee, 2 November 1920. TNA WORK 20/1/3, ff 116, 224.
34. *Daily Herald*, 6 November 1920, p5. Some 15,000 relatives applied. Minute by Ernest Bright, 12 November 1920. TNA WORK 20/1/3, ff361-362
35. Memorial (1920) Committee, note by Secretary, 28 October 1920. TNA WORK 20/1/3, f140.

36. Undated minute. TNA WORK 20/1/3, f216.
37. *Daily Graphic*, 12 November 1920, p3. Her husband was probably Sergeant Thomas Hamblett, who was killed on 31 August 1918 and lies in the H A C Cemetery at Ecoust-St. Mein. His widow Theresa lived in Hounslow. Under the criteria laid down Mrs Hamblett was not entitled to a ticket.
38. Memorial (1919) Committee, f59. Accounts differ as to whether the selection was made from four or six bodies.
39. Roger T Stearns, 'The Unknown Warrior', *Oxford Dictionary of National Biography*. See also comments in Adrian Gregory, *The Silence of Memory: Armistice Day 1919-1946* (Berg, 1994), p46, note 74. *Daily Graphic*, 13 November 1920.
40. *The Times*, 11 November 1920.
41. Nicolson, p270.
42. Gibbs, [p10].
43. *Daily Mail*, 12 November 1920, pp7-8. Mrs Macbeth's sons were Lt Stanley Macbeth, 1/18 London Regiment and 2/Lt Harold Macbeth, 17 London Regiment. Both men died on 15 September 1916 and lie almost next to each other at Caterpillar Valley Cemetery. Stanley's body, however was never identified, but is 'believed to lie in the cemetery'.
44. Anon, p14.
45. James McMillan, *The Way it Was 1914-1934* (William Kimber, 1979), p108.
46. Gregory, pp27-28.
47. *Workers' Dreadnought*, 20 November 1920, p4.
48. Gregory, pp26-27.
49. Burrage, p222.
50. Michael Gavaghan, *The Story of the Unknown Warrior* (M&L Publications, 1995), p70.
51. Greenberg, p11. Hanson, p309.
52. *Daily Graphic*, 12 November 1920, p3.
53. Gregory, p3. However, it was thought that motion picture cameras would demean the ceremony.

54. *The Times*, 12 November 1920, p25.
55. *Daily Graphic*, 12 November 1920, p1.
56. *Daily Graphic*, 12 November 1920, p3.
57. *Daily Express*, 12 November 1920, p7.
58. Hanson, pp409-410.
59. Quoted in Hanson, p410.
60. And rather neglected it seemed during the author's visit in March 2020.
61. www.iwm.org.uk/memorials/item/memorial/7444 [accessed 15 September 2019]. The memorial is actually for Frederick Courtenay Jones, who is commemorated on the Cambrai memorial.
62. Gregory, p253. See also Jay Winter, pp 97-98.
63. Homberger, p1429.
64. *The Times*, 12 November 1923, p14.
65. *The Times*, 12 November 1928, p9.
66. *Radio Times*, 9 November 1928, p374.
67. *The Times*, 13 November 1933, p12, p17.
68. *The Times*, 12 November 1938, p12, p17. Kristallnacht – the mass destruction of Jewish property across Germany – had taken place on 9-10 November.
69. Quoted in Gregory, pp165-166.
70. Gregory, p222.
71. Gregory, p222. Emphasis in the original.
72. Gregory, p109.
73. And one that now charges admission and markets itself as a tourist attraction, which must make it difficult for a mourner to visit the Tomb in the way it was intended.

9 Chasing Ghosts

1. Juliet Nicolson, *The Great Silence 1918-1920: living in the shadow of the Great War* (John Murray, 2009), p4.
2. Jay Winter, pp49-50. Her sentiments were echoed by many veterans aggrieved that governments preferred to build memorials to the dead rather than help the living.

3. Tonie and Valmai Holt, p169.
4. Stephen Cooper, p58. The disc of course is his identity disc, which suggests he wasn't wearing it when he was killed.
5. *The Times*, 10 November 1923, p14; See also www.kiplingsociety.co.uk/poems_londonstone.htm [accessed 20 December 2019]
6. Bennett, p258. *Adelaide News*, 10 July 1929.
7. Elizabeth Day, 'Testament of Youth: Vera Brittain's classic 80 Years On' *The Guardian*, 24 March 2013
8. Holt, p181, p189.
9. Brittain, p655.
10. https://en.wikipedia.org/wiki/Enoch_Arden and www.gutenberg.org/ebooks/1358 [Accessed 22 January 2020].
11. *Middlesbrough Daily Gazette*, 11 November 1915, p2.
12. Morton, p14.
13. Morton, p17.
14. Wells, *Mr Britling*, p402.
15. Their stories are told in Ben Macintyre, *A Foreign Field: a true story of love and betrayal in the Great War* (HarperCollins, 2001).
16. Richard Van Emden, *Prisoners of the Kaiser: the last POWs of the Great War* (Pen & Sword, 2000), p174.
17. *Birmingham Mail*, 14 October 1918, p4.
18. A J Peacock, 'Just a Kriegsgefangenen' *Gunfire* (56), p13. There are cards for him in the ICRC archives but the camp register in which Brammer's name might appear is missing.
19. For more about the return home of British POWs see Simon Fowler, 'Nix Mear Gefangener': the return of British prisoners of war after the Armistice' *Stand To!* (2018) 113
20. *Manchester Guardian*, 4 January 1919, p4. Holding, a former policeman, seems to have been captured during the March offensive.
21. Cecil Thomas, pp301-302.
22. TNA FO 383/498 f 183. Mrs May Elliott, 24 December 1918. Lord Lucan's committee was the Government Committee on the Mistreatment by the Enemy of British Prisoners of War.

23. John T Penrose to Lord Cave, 3 January 1919. BL Add MS 62470, f7r. Emphasis in original.
24. TNA FO 383/498 ff184-6. Mrs [Gertrude] Coleridge to [War Office] 29 December 1918. Emphasis in original. 2/Lt Luke Coleridge, Coldstream Guards was killed on 22 December 1914 and his name appears on the Le Touret memorial.
25. TNA FO 383/375 Memorandum on the Missing prepared by Lord Lucan, Dame Adelaide Livingstone and Mr B R T Grindle.
26. Report by the Sub-Committee on the Missing, 20 February 1919., BL Cave Papers (Add Ms 62470 f115). A copy can also be found in TNA FO 383/499, ff269-309.
27. *The Times*, 4 January 1919, p6; *Manchester Guardian*, 4 January 1919, p7.
28. Dame Adelaide Livingstone to Lord Cave, 4 January 1919 BL Cave Papers (Add Ms 62470 f12r).
29. *Daily Express*, 28 December 1918. Cutting in FO 383/498 f177.
30. Telegram for Dutch Chargé D'Affaires, Berlin to Foreign Office, 30 January 1919 BL Cave Papers (Add Ms 62470 f48). See also comments made by General Sir H E Belfield at the meeting of the Inter-departmental Committee on Prisoners, 16 January 1919. TNA FCO 383/536 ff66-76.
31. R C Fowler, War Office Casualties Branch, minutes of Inter-departmental Committee on Prisoners, 29 January 1919. Remark by Lord Cave, chairman of the Committee recorded in the minutes. TNA FO 383/536 f82.
32. Durey, 'Search', p95. *The Times*, 15 February 1919, p5.
33. Durey, 'Search', pp95-96.
34. Durey, 'Secret', p97
35. Cypher telegram to Lord Kilmarnock in Berlin from Army Council 16 January 1920 TNA WO 32/5377.
36. Cave Papers, f28.
37. Cave papers, f124.
38. *The Times*, 24 July 1919, p12.
39. *Aberdeen Press & Journal*, 9 December 1919, p5.

40. *Dundee Courier*, 29 November 1919, p5. See also Durey, 'Secrets', p96.
41. *The Times*, 4 March 1924, p7.
42. David Hastings, *Odyssey of the Unknown Anzac* (Monash UP, 2018), p125.
43. TNA PIN 26/558, 14137, 1405.
44. Portsmouth Evening News, 7 April 1920, p5. Major A D Stirling DSO was the Deputy Assistant Adjutant General and head of War Office branch AM(2)b.
45. *Sunday Post*, 10 October 1926, p4. Pte Jimmie Paul was killed on 29 May 1918 and is commemorated at Tyne Cot.
46. *Sunderland Daily Echo*, 13 October 1926, p7.
47. *Lancashire Evening Post*, 30 October 1926, p3. L/Cpl Sunderland is commemorated at Thiepval.
48. *The Times*, 16 December 1926, p8.
49. *Yorkshire Post*, 13 December 1926, p9.
50. *Hull Daily Mail*, 7 January 1927, p5. *Hartlepool Northern Daily Mail*, 7 January 1927, p3..
51. *Hartlepool Northern Daily Mail*, 7 January 1927, p3. *Leeds* Mercury, 31 December 1926, p1. Pte W H Newlove, East Yorkshires is buried at Euston Road Cemetery. He died on 13 November 1916.
52. *Leeds Mercury*, 8 January 1927, p5. Pte George Horn, West Yorkshires is commemorated on the Arras Memorial. He died on 11 April 1917.
53. *Leeds Mercury*, 11 January 1927, p1. The sub-heading was 'Yorkshire people deceived'.
54. Macnaghten, p62. van Emden, *The Quick*, p298.
55. John Goulding to Hazel Macnaghten, 28 October 1931. Macnaghten Papers IWM Docs 3696.
56. *The Times*, 12 October 1932, p13.
57. La Naour, p101. See also https://en.wikipedia.org/wiki/Bruneri-Canella_case. There are similarities to the Tichborne Claimant which entranced England in the 1870s. https://en.wikipedia.org/wiki/Tichborne_case

58. *Daily Herald,* 29 September 1933, p11.
59. His story is told in Jean-Yves La Naour, *The Living Unknown Soldier: a story of grievance and the Great War* (Heinemann, 2005). See also the entry in Wikipedia and Graham Stewart, 'Back from the dead, but not to a better life' *The Times,* 8 December 2007 and Adam Nicolson, 'A living ghost from the trenches whose plight confused a nation riven by grief' *Daily Telegraph,* 16 January 2005.
60. Hastings, p72.
61. Hastings, pp90-91. *Truth,* 25 March 1928, p24.
62. Hastings, pp127-8
63. Hastings, pp128-129. *Truth,* 1 April 1928, p14.
64. Quoted in Adrian Gregory, *The Last Great War* (Cambridge UP, 2008), p255. The campaign to repatriate bodies to Britain is well described in van Emden, *The Quick,* pp275-281.
65. Durey, 'Search', pp102-103.
66. H M Morton, *Evening Standard,* 26 May 1920.
67. Graham. *Challenge,* p24.
68. Mrs E N Wheeler, 'Journey to France – September 1919', p4. Transcript of a talk to Kingsland Women's Institute during the Second World War. IWM LBY K. 94 / 1964. Her husband, Pte John Frederick Wheeler still lies at Pond Farm.
69. Durey, 'Search', p103.
70. *The Times,* 2 September 1920, p13; Jeremy Gordon-Smith, *Photographing the Fallen: A War Graves Photographer on the Western Front 1915 1919* (Pen & Sword, 2017), p173. Forceville was one of three 'experimental' or pilot cemeteries completed by the Commission.

10 *Recording the Missing of the Second World War*

1. https://en.wikipedia.org/wiki/World_War_II_casualties (accessed 24 September 2024). This includes a breakdown country by country.
2. Dan Stone, *Fate Unknown: tracing the missing after World II and the Holocaust* (Oxford UP, 2023).

3. Minutes of Tracing Personnel Missing or Otherwise Unaccounted For meeting held on 8 June 1945, item 2 TNA FO 961/1211. One wonders about the psychological effect on Russian families whose soldier sons and fathers failed to return home in 1945.
4. Vernon Bartlett, 'Behind the Iron Curtain' *The Listener*, 22 September 1949.
5. CWGC, *Annual Report 2015-2016* (CWGC, 2017), p35. This figure also includes 67,100 civilian casualties, two-thirds of whom were killed during the Blitz. See also the figures presented to Parliament on 3 August 1961, https://api.parliament.uk/historic-hansard/written-answers/1961/aug/03/allied-casualties-in-second-world-war#column_317wa.
6. https://en.wikipedia.org/wiki/Personnel_numbers_in_the_Royal_Air_Force https://en.wikipedia.org/wiki/Recruitment_in_the_British_Army#Second_World_War (both accessed 26 September 2024)
7. HL Deb 03 August 1961 vol 234 columns 316-7. Available at https://api.parliament.uk/historic-hansard/written-answers/1961/aug/03/allied-casualties-in-second-world-war#column_317war (accessed 12 June 2025)
8. David French, *Raising Churchill's Army: The British Army and the War Against Germany 1919-1945* (Oxford University Press, 2000), pp113-115, 154-155.
9. As the name suggests aircrew were the men who flew the aircraft. Understandably losses in groundcrew, the men and women who maintained the aircraft and supported their crews, were considerably fewer.
10. https://en.wikipedia.org/wiki/RAF_Bomber_Command#Casualties
11. www.cwgc.org/find/find-cemeteries-and-memorials/109600/runnymede-memorial [accessed 18 January 2020]. The losses suffered by Bomber Command are also discussed in Jalland and on the International Bomber Command Centre website https://internationalbcc.co.uk.
12. https://en.wikipedia.org/wiki/Royal_Navy_during_World_War_Two https://en.wikipedia.org/wiki/Royal_Navy_during_World_War_I#Aftermath [both accessed 17 October 2024).

13. The discrepancy in the numbers is explained by the fact that seamen from the dominions and colonies who have no known grave are commemorated in their home countries.
14. Apart from two dozen or so SOE female agents who were caught and murdered by the Gestapo, those recorded as being missing in action were men, which is why the male case is used throughout.
15. A list is given in Appendix 1.
16. See TNA WO 32/6315, 6317.
17. Kemble to Barnwell, 6 December 1941 TNA WO 361/130. The file contains some speculation about the fates of the 3000 missing men.
18. The unusually detailed interrogation report can be found in TNA WO 208/3348/1.
19. Sunday Post, 16 July 1944, p3. It is not known what happened to Beattie after the war.
20. A full history of the War Office branch can be found in TNA WO 162/205. Case papers can be found in series WO 361 at Kew. No equivalent histories appear to survive for the Admiralty and Air Ministry. The history of the POW Branch is in TNA WO 162/204. An MI9 Historical Report can be found in TNA WO 208/3243 and online at www.arcre.com/archive/mi9/mi9history. See also Helen Fry, *MI9: A History of the Secret Service for Escape and Evasion in World War Two* (Yale University Press, 2020)
21. Spendlow Papers, IWM (Docs 303) Letter 14 August 1945, the original letter was sent on 5 April. Letter dates 8 August 1947. Pte Spendlow's entry in the Commonwealth War Graves Commission database suggests he had originally been buried elsewhere and was reburied at Mook, but no original date of burial is given.
22. A discussion of casualty lists in the war can be found in TNA WO 162/204, pp33-37. They are available online through Findmypast,
23. TNA WO 162/204, p3. Telegram in GH Martin Papers IWM. The crew who were members of 7 Squadron RAF, were shot down over Simmern near Koblenz on a bombing sortie to Rüsselsheim. The Squadron Record Book notes that 'Missing. Nothing heard aircraft after take-off' (TNA AIR 27/101/16 25 August 1944). The bomb

aimer F/Lt Raymond Benjamin Ede DFC was killed, the fate of the pilot T H Strong is not known.

24. TNA WO 162/204, Appendix A. An example of the unofficial lists for the men who died building the 'Burma Railway' is in TNA WO 361/2235
25. Private David Lesser, King's Own Cornwall Light Infantry was killed on 7 May 1943 and lies in Massicault War Cemetery near Tunis.
26. GH Martin Papers, IWM Docs 6076. Subsequent paragraphs based on text in Jalland.
27. Jalland, p148.
28. Jalland, p151.
29. Jalland, p146.
30. Final report of War Office Casualty Branch (Cas L) TNA WO 162/205, p33. Section G 'Relations with the public.'
31. TNA WO 162/204, p13.
32. TNA WO 162/204, p62
33. Jalland, p144.
34. Spendlow Papers, letter dated 9 July 1945.
35. Spendlow Papers. Letter dated 30 May 1945. Cray was Lt James William Cray, Royal Fusiliers.
36. Jalland, p148.
37. TNA WO 162/204, p13.
38. Final report TNA WO 162/205. Section B 'Relations with Record Offices' The Commando unit X Troop contained a wide range of Germans, Frenchmen, Belgians and other nationalities, see Leah Garrett, *X Troop: The Secret Jewish Commanders who helped defeat the Nazis* (Vintage, 2022).
39. Carlton Jackson, *Allied Secret: the sinking HMT Rohna* (University of Oklahoma Press, 2002), p144. See also two TNA ADM 199/2146 and WO 361/474. There were similar problems in releasing details of the loss another US Troop Carrier, this time the *Leopoldville* torpedoed off Cherbourg in December 1944.
40. TNA ADM 358/3045

41. https://en.wikipedia.org/wiki/HMS_Barham_(04)#Sinking (accessed 8 November 2024).
42. WO 162/204, pp13-14.
43. Revd GH Martin papers IWM Telegram 12 January 1945. Sweet was a mid-upper gunner. The target was a hydroelectric power station near Gelsenkirchen in the Ruhr. See the Squadron Record Book TNA AIR 27/101/20. The crew appears to have survived.
44. Final report TNA WO 162/205, pp50-51.
45. For more see https://msmtrust.org.uk/about. Some of the extraordinary escapes made by POWs are retold in Damien Lewis, *SAS Great Escapes Three* (Quercus, 2024).
46. The experience of the ordinary Singaporean during the War is brilliantly told at the Old Ford Factory in Singapore and in galleries at the National Museum of Singapore.
47. This section is based on Shane Cowlishaw 'Prisoners Secret War Dossier' *Stuff* 12 August 2011. https://www.stuff.co.nz/national/5433037/Prisoners-secret-war-dossier#:~:text=Bureau%20of%20records%20and%20enquiry,memory%2C%20was%20put%20in%20charge. (accessed 29 December 2024) and Melissa van der Klugt, 'The captain, the trunk and the secret Singapore papers' *The Times*, 30 July 2011, p85. Nelson's papers are at the Imperial War Museum (Docs 18738)
48. Which can now be found in TNA WO 361/2116. The section is based on Ken Hewitt, 'Killed in Action – Singapore – February 1942' *The Green Tiger* (Spring 2019), pp23-24. https://royalleicestershireregiment.org.uk/archive/journals/green-tiger-2015-spring-present/green-tiger-spring-2019/1404746-the-green-tiger-2019-spring-page-23?q=missing
49. Julian Maclaren-Ross, *Collected Memoirs* (Black Spring Press, 2004), pp269, 272-273
50. *The Green Tiger*, November 1946, p148 https://royalleicestershireregiment.org.uk/archive/journals/green-tiger-1940-1949/1946/235216-greentiger-1946-035jpg?q=missing (accessed 20 October 2024).

51. Kerry Noble, 'Blouse and Bell Bottoms!' available at www.bbc.co.uk/history/ww2peopleswar/stories/83/a2310283.shtml (accessed 20 October 2024).

11 The Search for the Missing of the Second World War

1. Sarah Helm. *A Life in Secrets: the story of Vera Atkins and the lost agents of SOE* (Abacus, 2006), pxxii.
2. Stuart Hadaway, *Missing Believed Killed: casualty policy and the Missing Research and Enquiry Service* (Pen & Sword, 2012), p6.
3. Copy of letter in TNA AIR 20/9050). It has not been possible to identify Sgt Tabuner in the CWGC casualty records.
4. Hadaway, pp6-7.
5. Lucy Noakes, *Dying for the Nation: death, bereavement and grief in Second World War Britain* (Manchester University Press, 2020), p162.
6. Hadaway, p35. TNA AIR 2/6330, minute 17 November 1941.
7. TNA AIR 2/6330, minute 31 October 1941.
8. Hadaway, pp37-38.
9. TNA AIR 2/6330, minute 3 January 1943.
10. TNA AIR 20/9050, 10 August 1945. Hadaway, p46.
11. Hadaway, p154.
12. Hadaway, p56.
13. Hadaway, pxii.
14. Quoted Noakes, pp134, 164-65.
15. TNA WO 373/74/570. The man killed was probably Corporal Ronald Millard, 102 Field Company, Union Defence Force, who is buried at the Beach Head War Cemetery, Anzio.
16. https://www.cwgc.org/visit-us/find-cemeteries-memorials/cemetery-details/70511/beach-head-war-cemetery-anzio. The contains 2,316 Commonwealth burials, 295 of them unidentified.
17. Tristram Hunt Substack 'My Dad's War' https://substack.com/@tristramhicks (accessed 13 September 2024). Lord Hartington, the eldest son of the Duke of Devonshire was killed on 9 September

1944. He was a Major in the Coldstream Guards and now lies in the Leopoldsburg war cemetery.
18. Quoted in Noakes, pp167-168.
19. Noakes, pp168-169.
20. Spendlow Papers Letter from Captain A J C Wyatt, 30 May 1945, p5.
21. Appendix 'Escapes' in M B McGlynn, *Crete* (Historical Publications Branch, 1953). Online at https://ndhadeliver.natlib.govt.nz/webarchive/20201108000000/https://nzetc.victoria.ac.nz/tm/scholarly/tei-WH2Cret-b7-11.html
22. The above paragraphs are largely based on lists and correspondence in TNA WO 361/735. MacGinn was originally buried in a village near Opole and his body was moved to Krakow in August 1948.
23. TNA WO 361/737 Sjt J Dryden was his fellow prisoner who submitted the report. Turton's name appears on the Athens Memorial to the Missing.
24. Based on table in TNA WO 361/762.
25. Details from his entry on the CWGC website.
26. The report is in TNA WO 361/737. No war diary for the Unit survives.
27. Helm Papers IWM (Docs 17889) 'Vera's acc war crimes' p1.
28. Helm Papers 'Vera Acc' p2.
29. Helm Papers Report dated 25 June 1945. P5. Helm, pp316-329. Elaine Plewman was 'the German-speaking English woman'.
30. See Helm, pp326-328.
31. For more information see his personal file TNA HS 9/21/4.
32. See also this account by Martin Sugarman about another SOE Agent Marcus Bloom, which provides another an insight to the final days of Alexandre.
33. Helm Papers. Letter Atkins to Madame Duboudin, 27 July 1945. See also his SOE file TNA HS 9/452/3.
34. Damien Lewis, *The Nazi Hunters: the ultra-secret SAS unit and the quest for Hitler's War Criminals* (Quercus, 2015), pxv. See also the report about the murder in 1944 of SAS Parachutists in TNA WO 218/222.

35. Joanne Reilly, *Belsen: the liberation of a camp* (Routledge, 1998), p135. See also Ben Shepherd, *After the Daybreak: the liberation of Belsen 1945* (Cape, 2002), p217, note 5.
36. Desmond Morton to T L Rowan, 8 October 1945. TNA PREM 8/920.
37. See Attlee's memorandum on a 'National War Memorial' presented to the Cabinet, 20 December 1947 CP (47) 339. A copy is in TNA PREM 8/920.
38. Draft of speech TNA AIR 19/604.
39. For more about the memorial, see Keith Lowe, *Prisoners of History* (Collins, 2020), pp49-60.
40. www.royalparks.org.uk/visit/parks/green-park (accessed 8 February 2025).

12 After the War

1. TNA WO 208/2999. Figures were compiled in July 1953. In 2018 The Guardian suggested that there were '336 Britons still listed as missing in action and for whom there is no known grave.' www.theguardian.com/world/2018/dec/26/war-detectives-get-new-lead-on-british-dead-from-korean-war-thanks-to-trump [accessed 13 January 2020]
2. www.cwgc.org/visit-us/find-cemeteries-memorials/cemetery-details/5001895/san-carlos-military-cemetery (accessed 26 June 2025)
3. Audrey Gillan, "How Wootton Bassett became the town that cried' Guardian, 25 February 2010.
4. Sledge, pp275-276.
5. https://en.wikipedia.org/wiki/Vietnam_War_casualties [accessed 20 January 2020].
6. Seth Mydans, 'Forgotten in Vietnam', *New York Times*, 19 April 1999
7. For the British view of such activities in 1988, see TNA FCO 15/5401.
8. https://en.wikipedia.org/wiki/Vietnam_War_POW/MIA_issue. See also www.theguardian.com/film/2017/feb/13/erase-and-forget-documentary-bo-gritz.
9. Sledge, pp274-65.
10. Mydans.

11. Mydans.
12. Telegram 13 December 1985, British Embassy Hanoi to Foreign and Commonwealth Office TNA FCO 15/4423.
13. www.dpaa.mil/Our-Missing/Past-Conflicts [accessed 18 January 2020].
14. Barbara S Lowerison to Margaret Thatcher, 16 November 1988. TNA FCO 15/5509.
15. Theresa Vargas, 'Separate Truths: When Remains of a Vietnam-Era Pilot Were Identified, One Woman Found Closure, Another Kept Up the Fight,' *Washington Post*, 27 November 2006.
16. www.whitehouse.gov/briefings-statements/joint-statement-president-donald-j-trump-united-states-america-chairman-kim-jong-un-democratic-peoples-republic-korea-singapore-summit [accessed 27 March 2020]
17. 'North Korea hands over the remains of US soldiers killed in Korean War' *The Guardian*, 27 July 2018.
18. Pesach Benson 'Who are Israel's Missing Soldiers?', https://honestreporting.com/who-are-israels-missing-soldiers. [accessed 20 January 2020].
19. Judah Ari Gross, 'Inside the 37-year search for IDF soldier Zachary Baumel' *Times of Israel*, 4 April 2019. See also EITAN's website www.eitan.aka.idf.il/894-en/eitan.aspx
20. https://en.wikipedia.org/wiki/Zechariah_Baumel
21. Allison Kaplan Sommer, 'The Missing Soldier's father felt betrayed by Israel. He died before the body could be found', *Haaretz*, 3 April 2019.
22. https://en.wikipedia.org/wiki/Zechariah_Baumel [accessed 20 January 2020].
23. Undated draft of letter from Prime Minister; letter from C R V Stagg, FCO to Robert Lyne, 10 Downing Street, 4 February 1994. TNA PREM 19/4912.
24. Ronen Bergman, 'Israel offered billions for Arad', *Ynetnews* 22 December 2005; https://en.wikipedia.org/wiki/Disappearance_of_Ron_Arad#cite_note-6 [both accessed 20 January 2020].

25. www.cmp-cyprus.org [accessed 28 April 2025].

Conclusion
1. Wilson, 'The burial', p24.
2. Maggio, pp37-38.

Appendices
1. *Annual Report of the Commonwealth War Graves Commission 2015-16* (CWGC, 2015), p35
2. Committee on Memorials to the Missing, 31 January 1922 CWGC/ADD 1/22/1
3. Figures based on data from CWGC website [accessed 21 July 2019].
4. The figures are based on those given in the cemetery descriptions on the CWGC website. Often the figures given here are only approximate.
5. *Major T J Mitchell and Miss G M Smith, Medical Services: casualties and medical statistics (HMSO, 1931, reprinted Naval & Military Press, [2010])*, p12.
6. http://bedsarchives.bedford.gov.uk/CommunityArchives/Roll-of-Honour/Roll-of-Honour-1914-to-1918.aspx
7. https://search.findmypast.co.uk/search-world-Records/isle-of-man-roll-of-honour-ww1 and www.isle-of-man.com/manxnotebook/exans/roh_1918.htm
8. 'The Work of the Wounded and Missing Department' *The Red Cross*, March 1919, p56. 'Reported missing' *Observer* 6 April 1919, p7.

BIBLIOGRAPHY

Archives

Most service records relating to individual soldiers have unfortunately long since been destroyed, although records for officers are at The National Archives at Kew.

Australian War Memorial (AWM)
Australian Red Cross Society Wounded and Missing Enquiry Bureau 3226 Francis John Vasey (1DRL/0428)

British Library (BL)
Cave Papers (Add MS 62470)
Territorial Service Gazette

British Red Cross Archives (BRCA)
Joint War Committee of the British War Red Cross and Order of St John Minute Book No 2

Commonwealth War Graves Commission (CWGC)
Annual reports
Imperial War Graves Commissioners minutes

Memorials to the Missing Committee (ADD 1/22/1)
Minute by Major William Chettle, Head of the Records Branch 7 December 1918 (WG 219 pt1)
Narrative letters and reports DGRE 1 (CWGC 1/1/1/34/1)
Photographs DGRE 14 (CWGC 1/1/1/34/14)

Imperial War Museum (IWM)
H. D. Bird Papers Docs.1004
E. C. Crosse papers Docs 4772
J. T. Davies, VC papers Docs 17153
A. C. R. S. Macnaghten Docs 3696
Edward Stephenson Docs 11830
Special War Office and Army Death Forms Docs 9051
E. V. Tanner Docs 27718
Marjory S. West, 'A Three days' Journey in the Devastated Areas of Belgium and France in May, 1919...' K96/2625
S Helm papers Docs 17889
G H Martin Papers Docs 6076
D Nelson Papers Docs 18738
Spendlow Papers Docs 303

Liddell Collection, Brotherton Library, University of Leeds (LCUL)
Henry Bellerby papers WW1/GS/0116
Ernest Blackburn papers WW1/GS/0145
Robert Renwick papers WW1/WF/REC/02/R7

National Army Museum (NAM)
British War Graves Committee, *British Military Casualties in South Africa* NAM 1992-95-2

The National Archives (UK) (TNA)
Air Ministry: Air Historical Branch: Papers (Series I) AIR 1
Air Ministry, British Air Forces of Occupation, Germany and Allied Commission for Austria (British Element), Air Division: Papers AIR 55

Air Ministry: P4 (Cas) Files relating to casualties suffered during air operations and aircraft accidents 1939-1945 AIR 81

Cabinet Minutes and Memorandum (WW1) CAB 23, CAB 24 (WW2) CAB 65, CAB 66

Foreign and Commonwealth Office: South East Asia Registered Files FCO 15

Foreign Office: Prisoner of War Department FO 383

Ministry of Pensions: War Pensions Registered Files PIN 15

War Office Registered Files WO 32

War Office War Diaries WO 95

War Office Miscellaneous Unregistered Papers First World War WO 161

War Office Officers' Service Records WO 339, WO 374

War Office: Department of the Permanent Under Secretary of State: Casualties (L) Branch: Enquiries into Missing Personnel, 1939-45 War WO 361

War Office: Japanese Registers of Allied Prisoners of War and Civilian Internees held in Camps in Singapore, Second World War WO 367

War Office: Army Casualty Lists, 1939-45 War WO 417

Office of Works: London: statutes and memorials registered files WORK 20

Books

Key sources

Scott Bennett, *The Nameless Names: recovering the missing Anzacs* (Scribe, 2018)

Jan van Bergen, *Before my Helpless Sight: suffering, dying and military medicine on the Western Front 1914-1918* (Ashgate, 2009)

Luc Capdevila and Danièle Voldman, *War Dead: western societies and the casualties of war* (Edinburgh University Press, 2006)

David Crane, *Empires of the Dead: how one man's vision led to the creation of WW1's War Graves* (Collins, 2013)

Dominiek Dendooven, *Menin Gate & Last Post* (de Calpros, 2003)

Geoff Dyer, *The Missing of the Somme* (Phoenix, 1994)

Drew Gilpin Faust, *This Republic of Suffering: Death and the American Civil War* (Vintage Books, 2009)

Michael Gavaghan, *The Story of the Unknown Warrior 11 November 1920* (M & L Publications, 1995)

Stuart Hadaway, *Missing Believed Killed: Casualty Policy and the Missing Research and Enquiry Service 1939-1952* (Pen & Sword, 2012)

Neil Hanson, *Unknown Soldiers: The Story of the Missing of the First World War* (Doubleday, 2005)

David Hastings, *Odyssey of the Unknown Anzac* (Monash UP, 2018)

Sarah Helm. *A Life in Secrets: the story of Vera Atkins and the lost agents of SOE* (Abacus, 2006)

Andrea Hetherington, *British Widows of the First World War* (Pen & Sword, 2018)

Peter Hodgkinson, *Glum Heroes: hardship, fear and death* (Helion, 2016)

Tony and Valmai Holt, *My Boy Jack? The search for Kipling's only son* (Leo Cooper, 1998)

Pat Jalland, *Death in war and peace: a history of loss and grief in England, 1914-1970* (Oxford UP, 2010)

Jean-Yves La Naour, *The Living Unknown Soldier: a story of grievance and the Great War* (Heinemann, 2005)

Thomas W. Laqueur, *The Work of the Dead: a cultural history of mortal remains* (Princeton UP, 2015)

Hamilton L. McCubbin et al (ed), *Family Separation and Reunion: families of prisoners of war and servicemen missing in action* (Center for Prisoner of War Studies, Naval Health Research Center, San Diego [1974])

Angus Macnaghten, *Missing: An Account of the Efforts Made to Find an Officer of the Black Watch Reported "Missing" on 29th October, 1914, During the First Battle of Ypres* (Dragon Press, 1970)

David Nelson, *The story of Changi, Singapore. The story of the UK Bureau of Record and Enquiry set up in Changi* (West Perth, WA: Changi Publication, 1974)

Lucy Noakes, *Dying for the Nation: death, bereavement and grief in Second World War Britain* (Manchester University Press, 2020)

Andrew Richards, *The Flag: the story of Revd David Railton and the Tomb of the Unknown Warrior* (Casemate, 2017)

Michael Sledge, *Soldier Dead: how we recover, identify, bury and honor our military Fallen* (Columbia UP, 2005)

Gavin Stamp, *The Memorial to the Missing of the Somme* (Profile, 2006)

Richard van Emden, *Missing: the need for closure after the Great War* (Pen & Sword, 2019)

Richard Van Emden, *Prisoners of the Kaiser: the last POWs of the Great War* (Pen & Sword, 2000)

Richard van Emden, *The Quick and the Dead: fallen soldiers and their families* (Bloomsbury, 2012)

Marianne Van Velze, *Missing in Action* (Allen & Unwin, 2018)

Fabian Ware, *The Immortal Heritage: an account of the Work and Policy of the Imperial War Graves Commission during twenty years 1917-1937* (Cambridge UP, 1937)

Jay Winter *Sites of Memory, Sites of Mourning* (Canto, 2014)

Secondary sources

Max Arthur, *Forgotten Voices of the Great War* (Ebury, 2003)

Harley Granville Barker, *With the Red Cross in France* (Hodder & Stoughton, 1916)

Edmund Blunden, *Undertones of War* (Folio Books, 1989)

Joanna Bourke, *Dismembering the Male: Men's Bodies, Britain and the Great War* (Reaktion, 1999)

Vera Brittain, *Testament of Youth* (Victor Gollancz, 1935)

Alfred M Burrage, [Ex-Private X] *War is War* (Gollancz, 1930)

Charles Carrington, *Soldier Returning from the Wars Returning* (Pen & Sword, 2016)

Wyndham Childs, *Episodes and Reflections* (Cassell, 1930)

Laura Clouting, *A Century of Remembrance* (IWM Books, 2018)

John Colborne and Frederic Brine. *Memorials of the Brave: or resting places of our fallen heroes in the Crimea and at Scutari* (Ackerman, 1857)

Mark Connelly and Stefan Goebel, *Ypres* (Oxford UP, 2018)

Tim Cook, *The Fight for History: 75 Years of Forgetting, Remembering and Remaking Canada's Second World War* (Penguin Random House, 2020)

Stephen Cooper, *Private Cooper's War* (Author, 2014)

Gordon Corrigan, *Mud, Blood and Poppycock* (Cassell, 2004)

Niall Ferguson, *The Pity of War* (Allen Lane, 1998)

Alexander H Fraser et al, *Ghosts on the Somme: Filming the battle June-July 1916* (Pen & Sword, 2009)

Paul Fussell, *The Great War and Modern Memory* (Oxford UP, 1977)

Thirza Garwood, *Long Live Great Bardwell: the autobiography of Thirza Garwood* (Persephone Books, 2016)

Jeremy Gordon-Smith, *Photographing the Fallen: A War Graves Photographer on the Western Front 1915 1919* (Pen & Sword, 2017)

Adrian Gregory, *The Silence of Memory: Armistice Day 1919-1946* (Berg, 1994)

Stephen Graham, *A Private in the Guards* (Macmillan, 1919)

Stephen Graham. *The Challenge of the Dead* (Cassell, 1921)

Robert Graves, *Goodbye to All That* (Cape, 1929)

Alan Isaac Grint, *The Faith and Fire Within: in memory of the men of Hexham who fell in the Great War* (Erigo, 2006)

Paul Ham, *Passchendaele: Requiem for Doomed Youth* (William Heinemann Australia, 2016)

Jeremy and Sue Hamilton-Miller, *The Fallen of St Mary's Parish Twickenham 1914-1918* (Borough of Twickenham Local History Society, 2017)

Richard Holmes, *Tommy: The British Soldier on the Western Front* (Harper, 2005)

Tonie and Valmai Holt, *My Boy Jack: the search for Kipling's only son* (Leo Cooper, 2001)

Cecil Lewis, *Sagittarius Rising* (Penguin, 1977)

Damien Lewis, *The Nazi Hunters* (Quercus, 2015)

T. A. Lowe, *The Western Battlefields: a guide to the British Line* (Gale & Polden, 1920)

Lyn Macdonald, *They Called it Passchendaele* (Penguin, 1993)

Ben Macintyre, *A Foreign Field: a true story of love and betrayal in the Great War* (HarperCollins, 2001)

Nevil Macready, *Annals of an Active Life* (Doran, 1925)

James McMillan, *The Way it Was 1914-1934* (William Kimber, 1979)

Ian Malcolm, *War Pictures behind the Lines* (Smith, Elder, 1915)

Frederick Manning, *The Middle Part of Fortune* (Piazza Press, 1928)
John Masefield, *The Battle of the Somme* (William Heinemann, 1919)
John Masefield, *The Old Front Line* (Macmillan 1917)
James Melik, *This Beastly War, 1914-18: Wyndham Family Letters* (Endeavour Press, 2014)
Caroline Moorehead, *Dunant's Dream: War, Switzerland and the history of the Red Cross* (London, 1996)
Mary Morton, *A Cinder Glows: growing up in Wishaw during the Great War* (Author, 1989)
George Mosse, *Fallen Soldiers: Reshaping the memory of the world wars* (Oxford University Press, 1990)
R H Mottram, *Through the Menin Gate* (Chatto & Windus, 1932)
Virginia Nicholson, *Singled Out* (Penguin, 2008)
Juliet Nicolson, *The Great Silence 1918-1920: Living in the shadow of the Great War* (John Murray, 2009)
Alfred Viscount Northcliffe, *Lord Northcliffe's War Book* (New York, George Doran, 1917)
Paul O'Keeffe, *Waterloo: the aftermath* (Bodley Head, 2014)
Thomas Pinney (ed), *The Letters of Rudyard Kipling, 1911-19* (Vol 4, HarperCollins, 1999)
Frank Richards, *Old Soldiers Never Die* (Faber, 1933)
William Howard Russell, *The British Expedition to the Crimea* (Routledge, 1877)
Isabella St John, *A Journey in War-Time* (Bodley Head, 1919)
Stephen O'Shea, *Back to the Front* (Robson, 1997)
William Siborne, *History of the War in France and Belgium* (Vol 2, Boone, 1844)
E. Milton Small, *Told from the Ranks* (Andrew Melrose, 1898)
John Starling & Oliver Lee, *No Labour No Battle: Military labour during the First World War* (Spellmount, 2009)
Julie-Marie Strange, *Death, Grief and Poverty in Britain 1870-1914* (Cambridge UP, 2005)
Cecil Summers, *Temporary Heroes* (Bodley Head, 1917)

Julie Summers, *Remembering: A history of the Commonwealth War Graves Commission* (Merrell, 2007)

Cecil Thomas, *They Also Served: The experiences of a private soldier as a prisoner of war in German camp and coal mine, 1916-1918* (Hurst & Blackett, 1939)

Helena Tym, *Chin up, Head Down* (Firestep Press, 2012)

Richard Van Emden, *Prisoners of the Kaiser: the last POWs of the Great War* (Pen & Sword, 2000)

Hester Vaizey, *Surviving Hitler's War: Family life in Germany, 1939-48* (Palgrave Macmillan, 2010)

W. D. Wetherell, *Where Wars go to Die: The forgotten literature of World War 1* (Skyhorse, 2016)

Henry Williamson, *The Wet Flanders Plain* (Faber, 1929)

Denis Winter, Death's Men: Soldiers of the Great War (Penguin, 1979)

Helen Fry, *MI9: A History of the Secret Service for Escape and Evasion in World War Two* (Yale University Press, 2020)

Keith Lowe, *Prisoners of History: What monuments tell us about our history and ourselves* (Collins, 2020)

Julian Maclaren-Ross, *Collected Memoirs* (Black Spring Press, 2004)

Dan Stone, *Fate Unknown: tracing the missing after World II and the Holocaust* (Oxford University Press, 2023)

Oxford Dictionary of National Biography
Sir Fabian Ware
The Unknown Warrior

Fiction and poetry
Zbigniew Herbert, 'Mr. Cogito On the Need for Precision' in *Report from The Besieged City and Other Poems* (Oxford Poets, 1987)

Anna Gordon Keown, 'Reported Missing' in Catherine Reilly (ed), *Stars upon my Heart: Women's poetry and verse of the First World War* (Virago, 1981)

Rudyard Kipling, 'London Stone' in *Inclusive Verse* (1927)

Rudyard Kipling, 'My Boy Jack' in *Destroyers at Jutland* (1916)

W. F. Morris, *Pagan* (Geoffrey Bles, 1931. Reprinted Casemate, 2016)

Siegfried Sassoon. 'On Passing the New Menin Gate' in *The Heart's Journey* (William Heinemann, 1928)

Siegfried Sassoon, 'Memorial Tablet (Great War) in *Picture-Show* (E P Dutton, 1920).

Caroline Scott, *The Photographer of the Lost* (Simon & Shuster, 2019)

Alfred Tennyson, 'Enoch Arden' in *The Poetical Works of Alfred Tennyson Volume 5* (Tauchnitz, 1866) www.gutenberg.org/cache/epub/1358/pg1358-images.html

H. G. Wells, *Mr Britling Sees it Through* (Macmillan, 1917. Reprinted Casemate, 2016)

Pamphlets

Annual Report 1916/7 (Soldiers and Sailors Family Association, 1918)

The Care of the Dead (Eyre & Spottiswood, 1916)

Anon, *To My Unknown Warrior* (Hodder & Stoughton, 1920)

Philip Gibbs, *The Unknown Warrior* (R G McLean, [1920])

Rudyard Kipling, *The Graves of the Fallen* (HMSO, 1919)

Official publications

Army Council, *General Annual Report of the British Army 1912–1919* (HMSO, 1921) Cmd.1193

Correspondence between His Majesty's Government and the United States Ambassador respecting the Treatment of Prisoners of War and Interred Civilians in the United Kingdom and Germany respectively (HMSO, 1915) Cd 7817

Major T. J. Mitchell and Miss G. M. Smith, *Medical Services: Casualties and medical statistics* (HMSO, 1931, reprinted Naval & Military Press, [2010])

Report on Crimean Cemeteries by Brigadier-General J. M. Adye and Colonel C. J. Gordon; Reports on British Cemeteries on the Bosporus and Smyrna Parliamentary Papers (PP) 1873.XL.443

Report by the Joint War Committee and the Joint War Finance Committee of the British Red Cross Society and the Order of St John of Jerusalem in England on voluntary aid rendered to the sick and wounded at home and abroad and to British prisoners of war, 1914-19 (HMSO, 1921)

Report of the Interdepartmental Committee on British Cemeteries Abroad (HMSO, 1889)

Report of the National Battlefields Memorial Committee (War Office, 1921)

Statistics of the Military Effort of the British Army during the Great War (War Office, 1922, reprinted Naval & Military Press, 1999)

War Office. *The King's regulations and orders for the army. 1912: Reprinted with amendments published in Army orders up to 1st August, 1914.* (HMSO, 1916)

Articles

Lord Ashcroft, 'The Pompeii of the First World War', *Mail on Sunday* 5 October 2019.

Ronen Bergman, 'Israel offered billions for Arad', *Ynetnews* 22 December 2005

Michael Durey, 'The Great Trust: Mrs. Edith Ash's Campaign of Remembrance, 1916-1954', *History* (2011) 96:3

Michael Durey, 'The Search for Answers on the Missing in the Great War: Lt Hugh Henshall Williamson and his parent's struggle with officialdom 1916-2001', *British Journal for Military History* (2015) 2:1

Drew Gilpin Faust, 'The Dread Void of Uncertainty: Naming the Dead in the American Civil War', *Southern Cultures* (2005) 11:2

Drew Gilpin Faust, '"Numbers on top of Numbers": Counting the Civil War dead', *Journal of Military History* (2006) 70

Vanessa Fison, 'General Gordon Forbes of Ham Common', *Richmond History* (2019) 40

Robert T Foley 'The Other Side of the Wire: The German Army in 1917' in Peter Dennis and Jeffrey Grey, *1917: Tactics, Training and Technology* (Australian Military History Publications, 2007)

Simon Fowler, '"Nix Mear Gefangener": The return of British prisoners of war after the Armistice', *Stand To!* (2018) 113

Ernest B. Furguson, 'The Work of Death: How the Civil War changed forever American's relationship with mortality', *American Scholar* (2008) 77:1

Malcolm Gaskill, 'Plot 6. Row C. Grave 15: Death of an Airman', *London Review of Books* (8 November 2018), pp11-16.

Allan Greenberg, 'Lutyen's Cenotaph', *Journal of the Society of Architectural Historians* (1989) 48:1

Judah Ari Gross, 'Inside the 37-year search for IDF soldier Zachary Baumel', *Times of Israel*, 4 April 2019

A. D. Harvey, 'Differing Accounts: British confidential and published version of the moment of capture during the Great War', *Stand To!* (2019) 114

William Barwick Hodge, 'On the Mortality arising from Military Operations', *Journal of the Statistical Society of London* (July 1857, April 1858) 19:3

Peter Hodgkinson, 'Clearing the Dead', *Birmingham University Centre of First World War Studies* (2007) 3:1 www.vlib.us/wwi/resources/clearingthedead.html

Peter Hodgkinson, 'Identifying the Dead of Tyne Cot', *Stand To!* (2019) 114

Eric Homberger, 'The Story of the Cenotaph', *Times Literary Supplement*, 12 November 1976, p1429

Thomas Laqueur, 'Empires of the Dead: How One Man's Vision Led to the Creation of WWI's War Graves by David Crane – review', *The Guardian*, 23 November 2013

Ariane Maggio, 'The Memory of War: the role of the Commonwealth War Graves Commission in the Identification and Memorialisation of Missing and Unknown Soldiers from WW1', *Limina* (2017) 23:2

Seth Mydans, 'Forgotten in Vietnam', *New York Times*, 19 April 1999

A. J. Peacock, 'A True and Unexaggerated Report', *Gunfire* (1994) 17

_____ 'Just a Kriegsgefangenen', *Gunfire* 56

_____ 'What was it like? The story of Dick Wills of York', *Gunfire* 52

Max Pemberton, 'Missing: what it means to mothers', *The World's News* (Sydney), 3 November 1917

Eric F Schneider, 'The British Red Cross Wounded and Missing Enquiry Bureau: a case of truth telling in the Great War', *War in History* (1997) 4:3

Louise Scott-Deane, 'Tracing the missing: Vera Deakin and the Australian Red Cross Wounded and Missing Inquiry Bureau', *Melbourne Historical Journal* (2017) 45: 69–88

Gary Sheffield, 'Haig and the British Expeditionary Force in 1917', in Peter Dennis & Jeffrey Grey, *1917: Tactics, Training and Technology* (Australian Military History Publications, 2007)

Allison Kaplan Sommer, 'The Missing Soldier's father felt betrayed by Israel. He died before the body could be found', *Haaretz*, 3 April 2019

Edward M Spiers, 'Military correspondence in the late nineteenth-century press', *Archives* (2007) 114

Ludwig J Spolyar, 'The Grieving Process in MIA Wives', in Hamilton L McCubbin et al (ed), *Family Separation and Reunion: Families of prisoners of war and servicemen missing in action* (Center for Prisoner of War Studies, Naval Health Research Center, San Diego [1974])

John Stephens, '"The Ghosts of Menin Gate": art, architecture and commemoration', *Journal of Contemporary History* (2009) 44:1

David Tattersall, 'Raiders Lost – Now Found: the Tyneside Scottish at Armentières – February 1917', *Stand to!* (2017) 109

Theresa Vargas, 'Separate Truths: When Remains of a Vietnam-Era Pilot Were Identified, One Woman Found Closure, Another Kept up the Fight', *Washington Post*, 27 November 2006

David Watkin, 'Cities of Silence: the cemeteries and memorials of the Great War', *Country Life* 10 November 1977, pp1399-1400

Ross Wilson, 'The burial of the dead: the British Army on the Western Front' *War & Society* (2012) 31:1

Newspapers and Journals

Daily Express; *Illustrated London News*; *Manchester Guardian*; *New York Times*; *The Observer*; *Radio Times*; *The Red Cross*; *Territorial Service Gazette*; *The Times*

Film and TV

Activities of the [US] Graves Registration Service 1919-1920 https://www.youtube.com/watch?v=zVgua3PlEQQ

All My Life's Buried Here: The story of George Butterworth (Stewart Hajdukiewicz, 2019, GB)

'An Imperial Hero' (Gaumont Graphic, November 1920) www.youtube.com/watch?v=giJlKBKzy-8

Long Lost Families: Unknown Soldiers (ITV Tx 21 October 2019)

'The Missing' Wind and Sky Productions (Australia) https://www.youtube.com/watch?v=YwVDDXN6Lpk&feature=youtube

'The prisoners came back' (British Pathé, 19 October 1955). www.britishpathe.com/video/the-prisoners-come-back/query/returned+German+prisoners+of+war

Websites

(Specific webpages given in text)

Ancestry www.ancestry.co.uk

Australian War Memorial www.awm.gov.au

British Newspaper Archive www.britishnewspaperarchive.co.uk

Commonwealth War Graves Commission www.cwgc.org.uk

Findmypast www.findmypast.co.uk

Imperial War Museum www.iwm/org.uk

International Encyclopedia of the First World War/1914-1918 Online https://encyclopedia.1914-1918-online.net/home/

Internet Archive www.archive.org

Liddell Collection explore.library.leeds.ac.uk/special-collections-explore

London Gazette www.thegazette.co.uk

National Army Museum www.nam.ac.uk

The National Archives www.nationalarchives.gov.uk

Trove http://trove.nla.gov.au

Western Front Association www.westernfrontassociation.com

Wikipedia en.wikipedia.org